How Students Can Join the
Fight for Gun Safety

ENOUGH
IS
ENOUGH

MICHELLE ROEHM McCANN

FOREWORD BY SHANNON WATTS
FOUNDER OF MOMS DEMAND ACTION FOR GUN SENSE IN AMERICA

SIMON PULSE

New York   London   Toronto   Sydney   New Delhi

BEYOND WORDS
Hillsboro, Oregon

PULSE

An imprint of Simon & Schuster
Children's Publishing Division
1230 Avenue of the Americas
New York, NY 10020

BEYOND WORDS

8427 N.E. Cornell Road, Suite 500
Hillsboro, Oregon 97124-9808
503-531-8700 / 503-531-8773 fax
www.beyondword.com

This Beyond Words/Simon Pulse edition October 2019
Text copyright © 2019 by Michelle R. McCann
Cover copyright © 2019 by Beyond Words/Simon & Schuster, Inc.
Cover illustration copyright © 2019 by iStock.com
Bullhorn and target illustration by Katherine Hill
Interior illustrations copyright © 2019 by Beyond Words

For information about special discounts for bulk purchases, please contact
Simon & Schuster Special Sales at 1-866-506-1949 or business@simonandschuster.com.

The Simon & Schuster Speakers Bureau can bring authors to your live event. For more
information or to book an event contact the Simon & Schuster Speakers Bureau at
1-866-248-3049 or visit our website at www.simonspeakers.com.

Managing Editor: Lindsay S. Easterbrooks-Brown
Copyeditor: Kristin Thiel
Proofreader: Gretchen Stelter
Illustrator: Katherine Hill
Design: Sara E. Blum
The text of this book was set in Bembo

Manufactured in the United States of America

10 9 8 7 6 5 4 3 2

Library of Congress Cataloging-in-Publication Data

Names: McCann, Michelle Roehm, 1968- author.
Title: Enough is enough : how students can join the fight for gun safety /
    Michelle Roehm McCann ; foreword by Shannon Watts, founder of Moms
    Demand Action.
Description: New York : Simon Pulse, [2019] | Includes bibliographical references.
Identifiers: LCCN 2019009560 (print) | LCCN 2019011830 (ebook) |
    ISBN 9781534442306 (ebook) | ISBN 9781582707013 (paperback) |
    ISBN 9781582707006 (hardcover)
Subjects: LCSH: Gun control—United States. | School shootings—United
    States—Prevention. | Students—Political activity—United States. |
    Protest movements—United States.
Classification: LCC HV7436 (ebook) | LCC HV7436 .M347 2019 (print) | DDC
    363.330973—dc23

LC record available at https://lccn.loc.gov/2019009560

CONTENTS

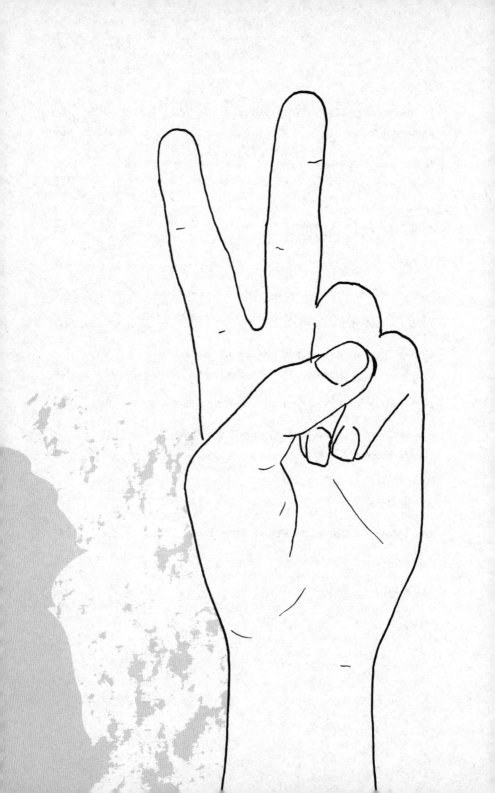

FOREWORD

SHANNON WATTS, MOMS DEMAND ACTION FOR GUN SENSE IN AMERICA

I never expected to become an activist. That seemed like a calling for important people or someone with a special degree. But all that changed in 2012, after a man with a semiautomatic rifle killed twenty children and six educators inside an elementary school in Newtown, Connecticut. I had no choice but to act.

It was kind of by accident. I was so angry about what happened inside the Sandy Hook school that I created a Facebook page calling on other American moms to get off the sidelines and start fighting for laws that would make it harder for dangerous people to get guns. Suddenly, thousands of mothers— and others—were joining me online and offline in social media campaigns, at rallies and marches, and in state capitols and at the Capitol in Washington, DC. Before I knew it, I'd created Moms Demand Action for Gun Sense in America, now one of the largest grassroots movements in the nation.

But it wasn't easy. Activism is hard work. Every day, Moms Demand Action volunteers spend much of their free time educating lawmakers and fellow Americans about how to stop gun violence. We go up against powerful, well-funded lobbyists who don't want us to pass stronger gun laws. We help elect political candidates who make gun violence prevention a top priority. We put pressure on companies to make sure their policies protect customers. And we teach Americans about responsible gun storage.

It's because of all this hard work by Moms Demand Action volunteers that we've made so much progress since 2012, including strengthening gun laws in dozens of states. And we've helped stop thousands of bad bills that would have weakened our nation's gun laws. We've also helped elect more than a thousand "gun sense candidates"[*] and we've helped change gun policies at dozens of major corporations.

As a full-time volunteer, I've devoted my life to helping prevent the gun violence that kills one hundred Americans every single day. As the mom of five kids, I'm passionate about gun violence prevention because I want to protect my children—and all children—from senseless and preventable gun violence. Gun homicides and suicides are at crisis levels, yet gun lobbyists have worked for decades to prevent many lawmakers from acting to make it stop.

Despite the progress of Moms Demand Action, this work will take many years to fix. Gun violence prevention activism is like a relay marathon—and we've already begun the process of handing over the baton to you, the younger generation.

Teens in America—especially in cities—have been working on the issue of gun violence prevention for decades, but because many of them live in marginalized communities, their voices rarely made

---

[*] 2018 candidates who ran for US Senate, House, governor, and other offices, who pledged to vote on the side of gun safety once elected.

it into the national news. It took school shootings in mostly white, wealthy communities—from Sandy Hook to Parkland to Santa Fe—to get influencers' attention. Now that this issue is in the spotlight, it's more important than ever for young people to get involved in gun safety and turn the nation's attention into action and change.

The tide is turning in America on the issue of gun safety. As I write this, polling shows the public supports gun laws and policies that are proven to keep guns out of the hands of people who shouldn't have them, and this is starting to show in Congress and many statehouses for the first time in decades.

So, how can you get involved in gun violence prevention? The good news is that there are lots of options. You could start your own online movement on social media. Start a Students Demand Action chapter in your school or community if one doesn't already exist. If it does, join it! You can join Students Demand Action by texting STUDENTS to 64433.

And be sure to bookmark this page, because I know that after you read the powerful and inspirational stories in this book, you'll be moved to act. After all, the biggest obstacle to bringing about change is apathy—by picking up and reading this book, you've already taken the first step toward being an activist.

INTRODUCTION

Why did I write this book? I am not an expert on the gun issue, and I'm not a leader of the gun safety movement. I normally write books about inspiring women in history. And fairies. But I was compelled to write *Enough Is Enough* because I am a mom with two teenage kids. I have watched them grow up in scary times, in a country that gets more dangerous by the day. Like millions of other parents, I worry about my kids' safety, and I'm incredibly frustrated by the lack of action in Washington, DC.

Are my worries mere media-stoked paranoia? I wish. There have been at least five mass shootings near us within my kids' lifetimes—two high schools, one community college, an underage nightclub, and the mall where we shop. Last year, their high school had three active shooter false alarms: students thought there was a shooter coming to the school, parents got a text warning of a threat, and kids were frantically texting their parents asking what they should do ("Should I run away from the building or stay inside?"). One of these terrifying lockdowns happened while we were hosting a foreign exchange student from Austria—she got quite the education about America that day! The terror and helplessness that we parents felt during those hours is indescribable. I cannot even imagine if one of them had turned into an actual shooting.

And I cannot believe this is the world we live in now. It makes me angry.

For years, I dealt with my anger by volunteering for Moms Demand Action. It was the only thing that made me feel better: action. I watched our Oregon chapter grow from a small group of passionate parents into a serious political force that helped pass several important gun laws in our state. But progress is slow, and change often feels small and inadequate.

I thought about what I personally could do to make a bigger impact and realized, "Hey, I write books for kids! If kids get involved, they can actually *solve* this thing." So, I started writing. Then, in 2018, Parkland happened, and I witnessed the power of student activism. The Parkland survivors and other young activists I interviewed inspired me. They are incredibly brave and are working hard to make change—and you can help.

I'm sure you've heard some of these comments about America's gun problems:

"THE NRA iS TOO STRONG."

"WE CAN'T FIGHT THE SECOND AMENDMENT."

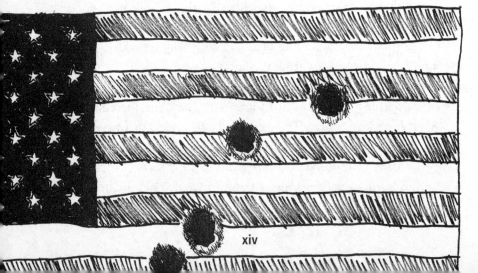

"AMERICANS LOVE THEIR GUNS TOO MUCH."

"THERE'S NOTHING WE CAN DO."

"WE SEND OUR THOUGHTS AND PRAYERS TO THE VICTIMS' FAMILIES."

These words make us feel more depressed, scared, and overwhelmed. But are they true? Is there really nothing we can do to fix America's gun problem? To paraphrase the words of student activist Emma Gonzalez, that hopelessness is BS.

This is the same way people talked during the civil rights movement of the 1960s. Black people couldn't ride at the front of the bus and couldn't eat at the same restaurants or drink from the same fountains as whites. In many places, they couldn't vote or go to the same schools as whites. They were being beaten and murdered just for requesting equal rights. Many people at the time said, "It can't be changed. Americans are too racist. It will never happen." But black students and white students—young people like you—took to the streets. They marched. They boycotted. They got arrested. And they changed America.

I believe we can do it again. All it takes is the will and the work.

Changing gun laws and protecting ourselves from gun violence is definitely possible. Don't let anyone convince you otherwise. But it's going to take the dedication of the group most affected by the problem. A group willing to stand up for the change they want. That group is YOU!

You, students and other young people, are the ones who will make the change happen.

You will make your schools and our country safe again.

HOW WILL YOU DO iT?

GOOD QUESTION.

First, you need to educate yourself about the issue. If you're going to argue with politicians, other adults, and your peers about why we need gun safety in this country, you will have to understand the issue pretty deeply. You will need to know the obstacles and how to overcome them.

Second, you need to know what to *do* with your anger and your passion. This book will give you some ways to take action today, tomorrow, and for the long term.

This book will give you the background you need to know about the gun issue, and it will show you how you can begin taking action. It will also introduce you to some incredible role models, young people just like you who are getting sh#% done.

The time for sitting on the sidelines and waiting for grown-ups to fix the problem is *over*. You can't wait around for it to happen. It's time to get involved and make change happen for yourselves. Listen to the words of Emma Gonzalez, Parkland massacre survivor and badass activist:

> The people in the government who were voted into power are lying to us. And us kids seem to be the only ones who notice and call BS. Politicians who sit in their gilded

House and Senate seats funded by the NRA telling us nothing could have been done to prevent this, we call BS. They say tougher guns laws do not decrease gun violence. We call BS. They say a good guy with a gun stops a bad guy with a gun. We call BS. They say guns are just tools like knives and are as dangerous as cars. We call BS. They say no laws could have prevented the hundreds of senseless tragedies that have occurred. We call BS. That us kids don't know what we're talking about, that we're too young to understand how the government works. We call BS.[1]

NOW IS THE TIME TO
STOP THE BS.

I hope this book will inspire you to become a gun safety activist. To fight for the world you want to live in and a future without gun violence.

You have a voice. You have power. It's time to use them.

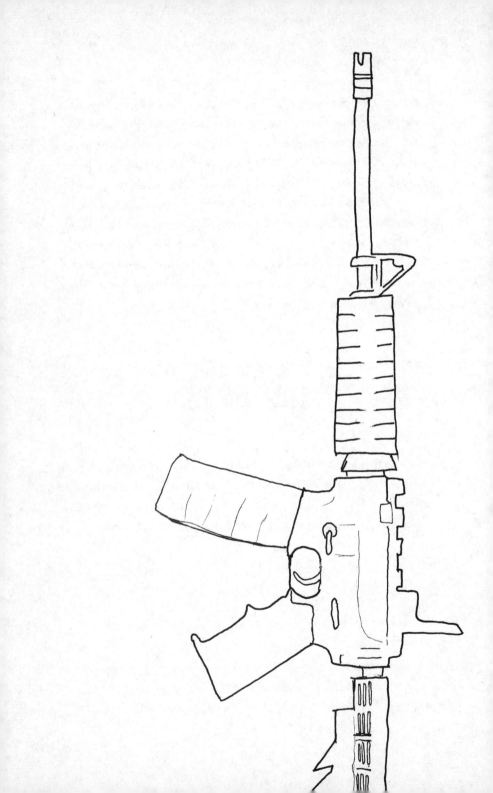

A NOTE TO GUN OWNERS

We are not enemies. It is not gun owners versus gun controllers, although the gun lobby would like us to think that way.

My grandpa, who I loved very much, was an avid hunter. My husband and his family grew up hunting, and those are some of his fondest childhood memories. I am not against hunting or owning guns, and I am not against gun owners. Not at all. If you or your parents own guns and you keep them locked up safely, we are in agreement. If you think other gun owners should follow the same safety rules you follow, we are in agreement.

If you think that dangerous criminals, people with severe mental illness, domestic abusers, and people on federal no-fly lists should not be able to buy guns, we are in agreement. If you believe our country has too much gun violence and needs to change, we are in agreement.

Believe it or not, gun owners and gun sense advocates agree on a ton of stuff. More than 90 percent of households with and without guns want background checks for *all* gun buyers. And a majority on both sides want background checks for private and gun show sales, mandatory waiting periods, and bans on bump stocks and high-capacity magazines. In fact, 81 percent of households without guns and 56 percent of households with guns agree that Congress needs to do more to reduce gun violence.[1]

With so much agreement, what's the hold up?

The National Rifle Association (NRA), a powerful political lob-bying group, does not speak for all gun owners. And even most NRA members agree with the majority of gun sense laws being proposed. You should know that people arguing for gun safety do not want to take guns away from responsible gun owners. We do not want to stop families from hunting together, or stop people from protecting their homes or enjoying target practice.

WE DO NOT WANT TO TAKE YOUR GUNS AWAY.

We want commonsense gun laws. Effective background checks. Guns locked up safely and responsibly in homes. More gun safety training.

We want schools to be safer. We want movie theaters, malls, and concerts to be safer. We want our country to be a safer place than it is now.

We are not so different, you and I. We need to stop letting the gun lobby put us on opposite sides of this issue—there are no opposite sides. It's time to unite and work together. It's time to unite and demand that our politicians strengthen gun laws to make our country and our kids safe again.

Moms Demand Action includes thousands of gun owners who are working for commonsense gun solutions. Find out what you can do at momsdemandaction.org and at responsibleownership.org.

PART 1

THE PROBLEMS

Police brutality, firearm homicide, firearm
suicide, domestic abuse with guns in the house,
mass shootings = gun violence. Dispute that
and you're part of the problem.

—MARCEL MCCLINTON, STUDENT ACTIVIST, FOUNDER
OF ORANGE GENERATION

CHAPTER 1

AMERICA'S GUN VIOLENCE EPIDEMIC: THE BIG PICTURE IN BIG PICTURES

**COLUMBINE ... VIRGINIA TECH ... SANDY HOOK ... AURORA ...
SAN BERNADINO ... ORLANDO ... LAS VEGAS ... PARKLAND ...**

We all recognize these names. We know what this list means. It's a very short list of some of the deadliest mass shootings in recent US history. The sad part is that this list stretches back further than you would think. America's first mass shooting happened in 1949 when a man strolled around his Camden, New Jersey, neighborhood gunning down thirteen of his neighbors. The sadder part is that, without our action, this list will continue to stretch out into the future, as more mass shootings are added to it.

How bad is gun violence in America today? Take a look at the big picture . . .

IT'S BAD

100 AMERICANS ARE KILLED BY GUNS **EVERY DAY** IN AMERICA.[1]

15,593 AMERICANS WERE KILLED BY GUNS IN ONE YEAR (2017).[2]

$229 BILLION! THAT'S THE COST OF GUN VIOLENCE IN THE US EACH YEAR.[3]

MORE AMERICANS HAVE BEEN KILLED BY GUN VIOLENCE SINCE 1968 THAN IN ALL US WARS COMBINED!

US WAR DEATHS SINCE THE REVOLUTIONARY WAR: **1.2 MILLION**

US GUN VIOLENCE DEATHS SINCE 1968: **1.5 MILLION**[4]

DEATHS FROM WARS VS.
DEATHS FROM FIREARMS, 1968–2017

FIREARM-RELATED DEATHS 1968–2017 1.5 MILLION

DEATHS IN WARS 1775–2017 1.2 MILLION

REVOLUTIONARY WAR	1775–1783	4,435
WAR OF 1812	1812–1815	2,260
AMERICAN INDIAN WARS	AROUND 1817–1898	1,000
MEXICAN WAR	1846–1848	13,283
CIVIL WAR	1861–1865	498,332
SPANISH-AMERICAN WAR	1989–1902	2,446
WORLD WAR I	1917–1918	116,516
WORLD WAR II	1941–1945	405,399
KOREAN WAR	1950–1953	54,246
VIETNAM WAR	1964–1975	90,220
DESERT SHIELD/ DESERT STORM	1990–1991	1,948
GLOBAL WAR ON TERROR	2001–2017	6,949

Source: "National Center for Health Statistics," Centers for Disease Control and Prevention, section "Mortality: All Firearm Deaths," last modified May 3, 2017, https://www.cdc.gov/nchs/fastats/injury.htm; war casualties come from Department of Veterans Affairs, accessed March 12, 2019, https://www.va.gov/opa/publications /factsheets/fs_americas_wars.pdf, and iCasualties.org, accessed February 10, 2019, http://icasualties.org.

SCHOOL AND MASS SHOOTINGS ARE GETTING WORSE

THERE HAVE BEEN MORE MASS SHOOTINGS AT US SCHOOLS IN THE LAST EIGHTEEN YEARS THAN IN THE ENTIRE TWENTIETH CENTURY (1900–1999).[5]

INCREASE OF AMERICANS KILLED IN MASS SCHOOL SHOOTINGS

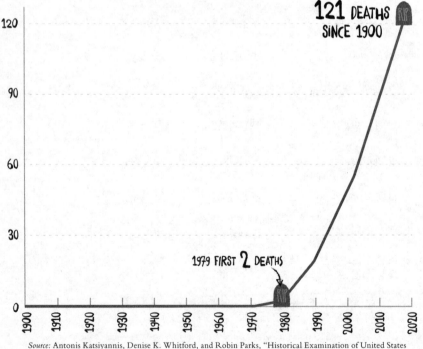

Source: Antonis Katsiyannis, Denise K. Whitford, and Robin Parks, "Historical Examination of United States Intentional Mass School Shootings in the 20th and 21st Centuries," *Journal of Child and Family Studies*, April 19, 2018, https://mijn.bsl.nl/historical-examination-of-united-states-intentional-mass-school-/15708240.

AMERICA HAS A MASS SHOOTING
9 OUT OF 10 DAYS, ON AVERAGE.[6]

AFTER THE MASSACRE OF CHILDREN AT SANDY HOOK ELEMENTARY SCHOOL IN 2012, POLITICIANS SAID "NEVER AGAIN." BUT THERE HAVE BEEN 1,977 MASS SHOOTINGS IN AMERICA IN THE 2,272 DAYS SINCE THEN.[7] THAT NUMBER KEEPS GOING UP EVERY WEEK. YOU CAN CHECK THE CURRENT GUN DEATH AND INJURY TOLL AT THE GUN VIOLENCE ARCHIVE (GUNVIOLENCEARCHIVE.ORG).

WHAT IS A MASS SHOOTING?

When you read *mass shooting* in the media, it usually means a shooting where four or more people are injured or killed, not including the shooter. Mass shootings don't include all the other shootings with fewer than four people.[8]

7

AMERICA IS DROWNING IN A SEA OF GUNS

THERE ARE **393 MILLION GUNS** IN AMERICA. THAT'S MORE THAN ONE GUN PER MAN, WOMAN, AND CHILD.[9]

3% OF GUN OWNERS OWN MORE THAN 50% OF THOSE GUNS.[10]

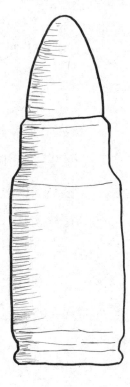

NEVER FORGET

All these mass shootings can numb us. We forget that each gun death statistic was a unique individual with friends, family, and a story. Teen journalists across America are helping us remember through sinceparkland.org, a website they've created where they are sharing stories about the American kids who have been killed by gun violence.

THE CONCENTRATION OF GUN OWNERSHIP IN AMERICA

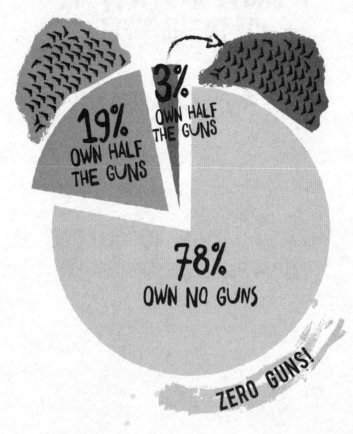

19% OWN HALF THE GUNS

3% OWN HALF THE GUNS

78% OWN NO GUNS

ZERO GUNS!

Source: Deborah Azrael, Lisa Hepburn, David Hemenway, and Matthew Miller, "The Stock and Flow of US Firearms: Results from the 2015 National Firearms Survey," *Russell Sage Foundation Journal of the Social Sciences,* February 12, 2019, https://www.jstor.org/stable/pdf/10.7758/rsf.2017.3.5.02.pdf. Original study conducted in 2015.

YOUNG PEOPLE (YOU) GET HIT THE HARDEST

1,297 AMERICAN CHILDREN ARE KILLED BY GUNS EACH YEAR. 5,790 MORE ARE INJURED.[11]

GUN VIOLENCE IS THE #2 KILLER OF YOUNG PEOPLE, NOW KILLING MORE KIDS THAN CAR ACCIDENTS.[12]

THE LGBTQ+ COMMUNITY HAS PLENTY TO FEAR FROM GUNS

10% OF LGBTQ+ STUDENTS WERE THREATENED OR INJURED WITH A WEAPON AT SCHOOL IN 2015.[19]

GUN VIOLENCE WAS THE **#1 CAUSE OF DEATH FOR LGBTQ+ VICTIMS** OF HATE CRIMES, RESPONSIBLE FOR 52% OF MURDERS IN 2016.[20]

NEARLY 25% OF LGBTQ+ YOUTH **ATTEMPTED SUICIDE** AT LEAST ONCE IN THE PRIOR YEAR, COMPARED TO 6% OF HETEROSEXUAL YOUTH. **ACCESS TO GUNS MAKES SUICIDE MORE LETHAL** FOR AT-RISK LBGTQ+ YOUTH.[21]

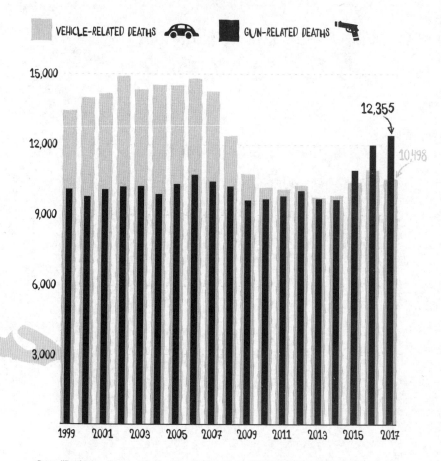

GUN VIOLENCE OVERTAKES CAR ACCIDENTS AS LEADING CAUSE OF DEATH FOR AMERICANS AGES 15–29

Source: "Fatal Injury Reports, National, Regional and State, 1981–2017," *Centers for Disease Control and Prevention*, last accessed February 9, 2019, https://webappa.cdc.gov/sasweb/ncipc/mortrate.html.

150,000+ STUDENTS HAVE EXPERIENCED
A SHOOTING AT THEIR SCHOOL SINCE 1997[13]

57% OF TEENS **LIVE IN FEAR** THAT THERE
WILL BE A SHOOTING AT THEIR SCHOOL.[14]

YOUNG PEOPLE (AGES 15-29) ARE HURT BY
GUN VIOLENCE MORE THAN ANY OTHER AGE GROUP.
31% OF ALL GUN DEATHS AND NEARLY 50% OF
GUN HOMICIDES **ARE YOUNG PEOPLE.**[15]

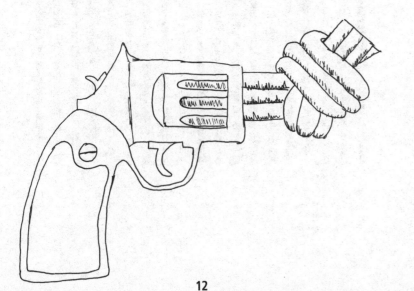

IT'S WORSE FOR PEOPLE OF C

YOUNG HISPANICS (AGES 15-19) AR
4 TIMES MORE LIKELY THAN YOU
WHITES TO BE MURDERED BY GUNS

YOUNG BLACK AMERICANS (AGES 15-1
18 TIMES MORE LIKELY THAN YOUN
AMERICANS TO BE **MURDERED BY**

POLICE SHOOTINGS KILL **9 TIMES**
YOUNG BLACK AMERICAN MEN (AGES
THAN YOUNG WHITE AMERICAN N

GUNS ARE DEADLY FOR WOMEN

6,313 WOMEN WERE MURDERED IN DOMESTIC VIOLENCE INVOLVING A GUN FROM 2004 TO 2015.[22]

AMERICAN WOMEN ARE 16 TIMES MORE LIKELY TO BE KILLED WITH A GUN THAN ARE WOMEN IN OTHER HIGH-INCOME COUNTRIES.[23]

IN HOUSEHOLDS EXPERIENCING DOMESTIC VIOLENCE, WOMEN ARE 5 TIMES LIKELIER TO BE MURDERED IF THERE IS A GUN IN THE HOUSE THAN IF THERE IS NOT.[24]

SOME STATES ARE DEADLIER THAN OTHERS

STATES WITH WEAKER GUN LAWS HAVE MORE GUN DEATHS. STATES WITH STRICTER GUN LAWS HAVE FEWER GUN DEATHS. PERIOD.[25]

GUN DEATHS ARE HIGHER IN STATES WITH WEAK GUN LAWS

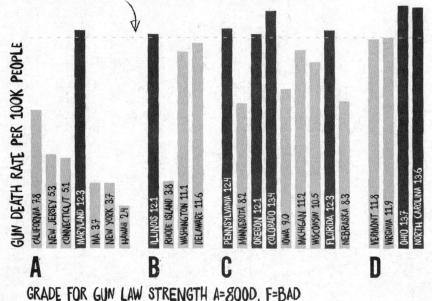

2018 NATIONAL AVERAGE GUN DEATH RATE: 11.9

GUN DEATH RATE PER 100K PEOPLE

A
- CALIFORNIA 7.8
- NEW JERSEY 5.3
- CONNECTICUT 5.1
- MARYLAND 12.3
- MA 3.7
- NEW YORK 3.7
- HAWAII 2.4

B
- ILLINOIS 12.1
- RHODE ISLAND 3.8
- WASHINGTON 11.1
- DELAWARE 11.6

C
- PENNSYLVANIA 12.4
- MINNESOTA 8.2
- OREGON 12.1
- COLORADO 13.4
- IOWA 9.0
- MICHIGAN 11.2
- WISCONSIN 10.5
- FLORIDA 12.3
- NEBRASKA 8.3

D
- VERMONT 11.8
- VIRGINIA 11.9
- OHIO 13.7
- NORTH CAROLINA 13.6

GRADE FOR GUN LAW STRENGTH A=GOOD, F=BAD

WHO MAKES THE GRADE?

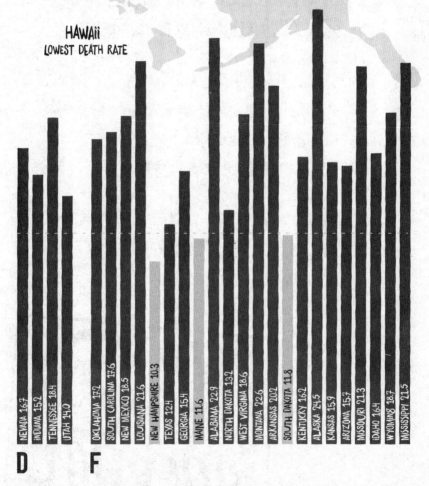

ALASKA
HIGHEST DEATH RATE

HAWAII
LOWEST DEATH RATE

NEVADA 16.7
INDIANA 15.2
TENNESSEE 18.4
UTAH 14.0

D

OKLAHOMA 17.2
SOUTH CAROLINA 17.6
NEW MEXICO 18.5
LOUISIANA 21.6
NEW HAMPSHIRE 10.3
TEXAS 12.4
GEORGIA 15.4
MAINE 11.6
ALABAMA 22.9
NORTH DAKOTA 13.2
WEST VIRGINIA 18.6
MONTANA 22.6
ARKANSAS 20.2
SOUTH DAKOTA 11.8
KENTUCKY 16.2
ALASKA 24.5
KANSAS 15.9
ARIZONA 15.7
MISSOURI 21.3
IDAHO 16.4
WYOMING 18.7
MISSISSIPPI 21.5

F

Source: "2018 Annual Gun Law Scorecard," Giffords Law Center to Prevent Gun Violence, accessed February 9, 2019, https://lawcenter.giffords.org/scorecard/

AMERICA IS THE GUN-CRAZIEST COUNTRY IN THE WORLD

AMERICA HAS THE **MOST GUN VIOLENCE** OF ANY **DEVELOPED COUNTRY** IN THE WORLD.

6 TIMES HIGHER THAN CANADA
7 TIMES HIGHER THAN SWEDEN
16 TIMES HIGHER THAN GERMANY
21 TIMES HIGHER THAN AUSTRALIA

EVEN AMONG THE MOST VIOLENT COUNTRIES ON THE PLANET, **AMERICA RANKS #2** FOR MOST GUN DEATHS.[26]

TOP 20 COUNTRIES FOR TOTAL FIREARM DEATHS IN 2016

TOTAL DEATHS

#	Country	Total Deaths
1	BRAZIL	43,200
2	UNITED STATES	37,200
3	INDIA	26,500
4	MEXICO	15,400
5	COLOMBIA	13,300
6	VENEZUELA	12,800
7	PHILIPPINES	8,020
8	GUATEMALA	5,090
9	RUSSIAN FEDERATION	4,380
10	AFGHANISTAN	4,050
11	THAILAND	3,830
12	SOUTH AFRICA	3,740
13	ETHIOPIA	3,270
14	IRAQ	3,240
15	ARGENTINA	3,120
16	CHINA	2,910
17	PAKISTAN	2,780
18	EL SALVADOR	2,500
19	TURKEY	2,430
20	FRANCE	2,330

Source: GBD 2016 Injury Collaborators, "Global Mortality from Firearms, 1990–2016," *Journal of American Medical Association*, August 28, 2018, http://www.healthdata.org/research-article/global-mortality-firearms-1990%E2%88%922016.

THE US HAD THE **SECOND-HIGHEST GUN SUICIDE RATE** IN THE WORLD IN 2016. ONLY GREENLAND HAD MORE SUICIDES PER CAPITA.[27]

AMERICA HAS LESS THAN 5% OF THE WORLD'S POPULATION BUT HAS **31% OF THE WORLD'S MASS SHOOTINGS.**[28]

91% OF CHILDREN KILLED BY GUNS IN HIGH-INCOME COUNTRIES ARE AMERICAN.[29]

AMERICA HAS LESS THAN 5% OF THE WORLD'S POPULATION BUT **OWNS 45% OF THE WORLD'S GUNS.**[30]

YEMEN HAS THE SECOND-HIGHEST GUN OWNERSHIP IN THE WORLD. IT IS A WAR-TORN, DEVELOPING COUNTRY, YET AMERICA HAS MORE THAN TWICE AS MANY GUNS PER CAPITA.[31]

THERE'S HOPE!

OVER 90% OF AMERICANS SUPPORT EXPANDING BACKGROUND CHECKS, INCLUDING MOST GUN OWNERS.[32]

2/3 OF AMERICANS UNDER AGE 30 WANT TO STRENGTHEN OUR GUN LAWS.[33]

MORE THAN 2 MILLION AMERICANS JOINED THE 2018 MARCH FOR OUR LIVES PROTESTS, DEMANDING GUN LAW REFORM.[34]

A Final Word

Although America's gun problem looks enormous, there are lots of good solutions on the table and smart people working to change things. Progress is already being made. The next chapters will give you deeper information about each of these gun problems, the proposed solutions, and how *you* can help.

STUDENTS TAKING A STAND

HUNTER YUILLE, AGE 19, GUN VIOLENCE SURVIVOR AND PUBLIC SPEAKER[1]

"Thank you all for being here. It means a lot to me." Hunter speaks quietly into the microphone, his eyes scanning the hundreds of supporters who have come to this somber event. It is silent for a long moment, until a friend in the front row yells, "Go, Hunter!" The crowd laughs with relief, and Hunter flashes a grin and continues.

"Five years ago, my mother was shot and killed in a mass shooting . . . "

It happened on December 11, 2012. Hunter Yuille was 13 years old and just home from school. He opened the fridge and groaned. No milk.

"That's a big thing for me," he says. "I love milk. I can drink milk all day long." He was planning to make a quesadilla, but it wouldn't be as good without a glass of milk. So, he called his mom, Cindy.

"Hey, we're outta milk," he complained.

"I'm on my way home now," she told him. "I just have to stop at the mall; then I'll pick up some milk."

Hunter remembers the last words he said to her: "See you when you get home. I love you."

Hunter ate his quesadilla (without milk, which was a bummer), then went to gymnastics practice. Afterward, his dad picked him up, which was weird because his dad *never* picked him up from gymnastics. It was always his mom. But Cindy wasn't home yet. Nobody was worried—it was December, and the malls were packed with holiday shoppers. They figured Cindy's errands took longer than expected. Hunter tried calling her but got no answer.

Hunter and his dad ate dinner. Then, because of the season, they turned on *A Christmas Story*. Near the end of the movie, the doorbell rang. Hunter was sure it was his mom—maybe she'd lost her house keys.

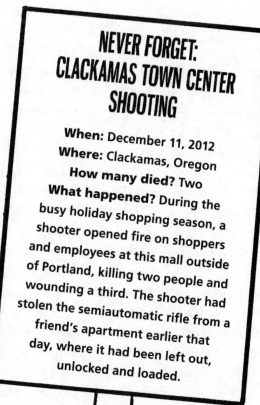

NEVER FORGET: CLACKAMAS TOWN CENTER SHOOTING

When: December 11, 2012
Where: Clackamas, Oregon
How many died? Two
What happened? During the busy holiday shopping season, a shooter opened fire on shoppers and employees at this mall outside of Portland, killing two people and wounding a third. The shooter had stolen the semiautomatic rifle from a friend's apartment earlier that day, where it had been left out, unlocked and loaded.

But it wasn't Cindy. It was a police officer. And a therapist. Hunter's dad told him to stay in the house while he stepped outside. "I knew something was wrong. I could feel it," said Hunter.

His dad came back in with tears in his eyes. "It was the first time I'd ever seen my dad cry," Hunter remembers. His dad told him that his mom wouldn't be coming home. She had been shot. There had been a shooting at Clackamas Town Center—a young man opened fire in the food court. Two people had been shot and killed—Hunter's mom was one of them.

When Hunter heard the news, he froze. He didn't believe what he was hearing. "No, she's not dead," he said to himself. "She's on her way home. She's caught in traffic. This is not happening." He didn't cry. He didn't feel anything at all.

Hunter went a couple months like that, expecting his mom to come home, expecting life to go back to normal. Hunter's life didn't go back to normal, however. In fact, it got worse. "I'm a 19-year-old addict in recovery trying to figure out how I'm supposed to grow up," he says now.

Cindy Yuille, who Hunter calls Mom, was his adoptive dad's wife—so, stepmom might be a more accurate term, technically. But for Hunter, Cindy was just Mom—the most stable, loving person in his life. She was a hospice nurse and the best parent he'd ever had. "Cindy was an amazing mom. She took me in, always treated me like her own. She cooked dinner, helped me clean my room, helped me do my homework. She was one hell of a person."

After Cindy was shot and killed, Hunter's life spun out of control. Less than a year later, 14-year-old Hunter was chain-smoking cigarettes, drinking beer, and smoking pot regularly. "It seemed like what every other teenager was doing. But my drug use progressed a lot quicker than other kids."

Before long, Hunter found his way to more dangerous drugs and got addicted. He tried to get himself clean, but without Cindy's support, it was all too much, and he found himself homeless, living on the streets. The summer after his junior year, Hunter dropped out of school. He thought about killing himself.

Today, Hunter is doing a lot better. "Drugs and alcohol didn't get me anywhere. They got me homeless, on the streets. I had to make a change." He got himself into a treatment program and into "sober housing." He's been clean and sober for nine months and plans to go back and finish high school soon. "My mom put that in my head: 'You need to go to school.'"

Hunter has also started speaking out, telling his story to help educate and inspire. A few months after getting clean, he went to the five-year remembrance of the Clackamas Town Center shooting. He wasn't planning to speak, but when he heard others speaking, he thought, "Why not? I've got something to say too." His words moved the crowd—the applause was loud and long. "It felt good. It felt really good. I was really nervous, but I made it through."

In July 2018, he won a Giffords Courage Fellowship and flew to Washington, DC, where he joined twenty-eight other young people from across the country. They gathered to discuss the gun violence crisis and brainstorm solutions. Hunter was honored. "I never thought I would have this kind of opportunity. I think that we actually have a chance to change something."[2]

Considering what he's lost to gun violence, he is surprisingly open-minded about possible solutions. "Before the shooting, I loved guns. Lots of people I know have guns, and I think that's fine. We shouldn't take guns away from law-abiding citizens. We should focus on taking guns away from convicted felons. There's a huge black market for guns," he says. "And we should focus more on gun control. Background checks. Making sure gun owners are not mentally ill. Making sure people who have the guns lock them up."

Hunter is working on forgiving his mom's killer. "I can't hate him anymore. You have to learn to forgive—you can't hold on to stuff like that."

Hunter's advice for young activists:

"LET YOUR VOICE BE HEARD."

◎ ◎ ◎

Learn more about what Hunter is working on and get involved at momsdemandaction.org.

CHAPTER 2

GUN VIOLENCE AND STUDENTS: WHY IT MATTERS TO YOU!

Hunter Yuille's life was torn apart by gun violence. But some of you might still be thinking: *There has never been a shooting at my school. What are the odds it will happen to me? Why should I care?*

It's true that the chances of you or someone you know getting shot at school or in a mass shooting are low. But will you be impacted by gun violence? Will your life be changed because of America's gun policies? The odds of *that* happening are much higher. Think about it . . . Hasn't gun violence *already* impacted your life?

Lockdown Drills Are the New Norm

Most of you know what lockdown drills are—similar to a fire drill, but instead of heading outside, you hide in a closet or behind a locked classroom door with the lights off, remaining absolutely still and silent until it's over. The idea is that an active shooter won't notice you and will pass by, leaving you and your classmates alive.

Lockdown drills were unheard of just a few decades ago. That's because school shootings were incredibly rare. Not anymore. Since the massacre at Columbine High School in 1999, these drills have become all too common in US schools. That includes drills with kindergarteners and even preschoolers!

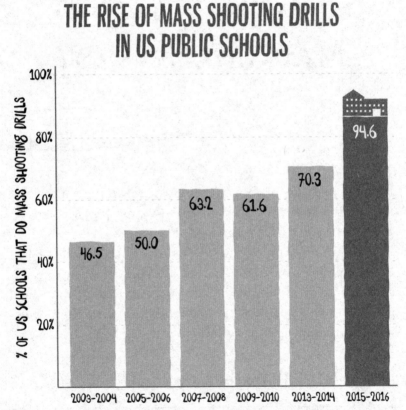

THE RISE OF MASS SHOOTING DRILLS IN US PUBLIC SCHOOLS

Source: "After Parkland, a Push for More School Shooting Drills," Vox, accessed March 25, 2019, https://www.vox.com/policy-and-politics/2018/2/16/17016382/school-shooting-drills-training; "Fast Facts: Violence Prevention," National Center for Education Statistics, accessed February 10, 2019, https://nces.ed.gov/fastfacts/display.asp?id=54.

TODAY, 9 OUT OF 10 PUBLIC SCHOOLS CONDUCT MASS SHOOTING DRILLS.[1]

There is no standard way to run these drills, so some schools make them very realistic, simulating gunshot sounds and using smoke and fake blood. These drills can be incredibly disturbing, even for adults.

In 2013, a teacher in Halfway, Oregon, sued her school district after a goggle-wearing, gun-toting attacker burst into her classroom, pointed a gun in her face, and shouted, "You're dead!"—then pulled the trigger. The gun was full of blanks, but she didn't know that.

NEVER FORGET: COLUMBINE

When: April 20, 1999
Where: Columbine, Colorado
How many died? Thirteen
What happened? Two students shot and killed twelve fellow students and one teacher and injured twenty-one more. At the time, it was the deadliest school shooting ever in the United States.

She and her class of elementary school kids had no idea they were part of a drill. The teacher, who had worked at the school for more than thirty years, was diagnosed with post-traumatic stress disorder (PTSD) after this incident and had to leave her job. Another teacher at the school was so terrified during the drill she wet her pants.[2]

Imagine how the kids felt.

These drills can be so scary yet may not help keep students and adults safe. At Marjory Stoneman Douglas High School in Parkland, Florida, the lockdown drills they'd been doing for years made no difference at all during a shooting there in 2018. The gunman, a former student, knew exactly how the drills worked and set off the fire alarm just before the end of the day. All classrooms except for two flooded the hallways, where he opened fire.

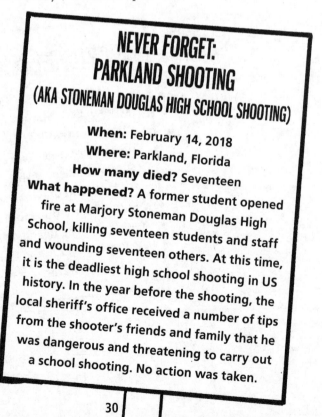

NEVER FORGET: PARKLAND SHOOTING
(AKA STONEMAN DOUGLAS HIGH SCHOOL SHOOTING)

When: February 14, 2018
Where: Parkland, Florida
How many died? Seventeen
What happened? A former student opened fire at Marjory Stoneman Douglas High School, killing seventeen students and staff and wounding seventeen others. At this time, it is the deadliest high school shooting in US history. In the year before the shooting, the local sheriff's office received a number of tips from the shooter's friends and family that he was dangerous and threatening to carry out a school shooting. No action was taken.

Instead of preparing for a school shooting in ways that are both traumatizing and ineffective, wouldn't it be better to work to make our country a place where drills aren't necessary? Back in the 1950s, students did "duck and cover" drills at school, crouching under desks to prepare for a nuclear bomb. Those scary and ineffective drills don't happen anymore because activists fought for decades to reduce the number of nuclear weapons around the world, lowering the threat of nuclear war.

DID YOU KNOW THAT AMERICA IS THE ONLY COUNTRY IN THE WORLD THAT HAS THESE KINDS OF DRILLS IN SCHOOLS?

European countries don't do them. Australia and New Zealand don't do them. Canada doesn't do them. Other countries don't do shooter drills because no other country has anywhere near the number of school shootings America has. In England, in the past two hundred years, they have had just one.

One.

Arming Teachers—The Worst Idea Ever

Arming teachers is a proposed "solution" to gun violence being pitched by the NRA and some politicians and school districts. In some states, it's already legal. You are in school every day. You deal with teachers every day. Does this seem like a good idea to *you*?

America's teachers think it's a terrible idea. Seventy-three percent of K–12 teachers *do not* want to be armed. The majority of teachers believe that arming them would make schools *less safe*.[3] "I think the idea of arming teachers is frankly one of the dumbest policy ideas I have heard recently," said Nate Bowling, Washington State's 2016 Teacher of the Year and a gun owner.[4]

Teachers' unions strongly oppose the idea as well. Lily Eskelsen García, president of the National Education Association, put it this way: "Bringing more guns into our schools does nothing to protect our students and educators from gun violence. Our students need more books, art and music programs, nurses and school counselors; they do not need more guns in their classrooms."[5]

These teachers know that real life is not like an action movie. Arming teachers is not going to turn them into heroes. What is more likely to happen if more teachers have guns is there will be more gun accidents in schools, like these:

- In 2014, while lab students watched, an Idaho State University chemistry professor shot himself in the foot when the concealed gun in his pants pocket accidentally went off.[6]

- That same year, a Utah elementary school teacher carrying a concealed gun accidentally shot herself in the leg while using the restroom.[7]

- In 2016, a group of elementary school students in Pennsylvania found a loaded gun in the bathroom where a teacher had forgotten it.[8]

In each scenario, it was dumb luck that no child got hurt. Imagine if this were legal, or even required, in American schools.

And let's not forget, there was an armed guard stationed at Marjory Stoneman Douglas High School during the 2018 shooting. He was outside when the massacre was happening and didn't fire a shot.

Yes, Mass Shootings Are on the Rise

Do you feel a little bit nervous when you head off to school or to the mall? When you are at a concert or a movie, is there a little voice in your head wondering how you would get out if someone opened fire? Your paranoia is not unjustified. Not only does America have more mass shootings than anywhere else in the world, but these events are on the rise.

MASS SHOOTINGS iN AMERICA HAVE TRIPLED SINCE 2011.

Data published in 2014 by researchers at the Harvard School of Public Health showed that for thirty years (1982–2011), mass shootings in America took place every 172 days on average. But starting in 2011, that rate increased to one mass shooting every sixty-four days on average.[10] If you feel like mass shootings are happening more often, that's because they are. This chart shows that deaths from mass shootings have also risen sharply in recent years.

THE RISE IN MASS SHOOTING DEATHS

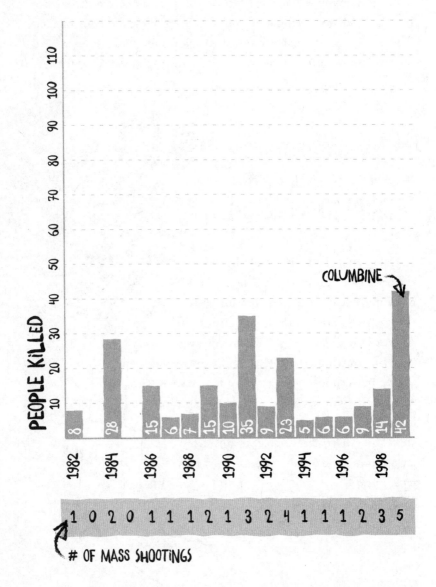

PEOPLE KILLED

COLUMBINE

8 28 15 6 7 15 10 35 9 23 5 6 6 9 14 42

1982 1984 1986 1988 1990 1992 1994 1996 1998

1 0 2 0 1 1 1 2 1 3 2 4 1 1 1 2 3 5

OF MASS SHOOTINGS

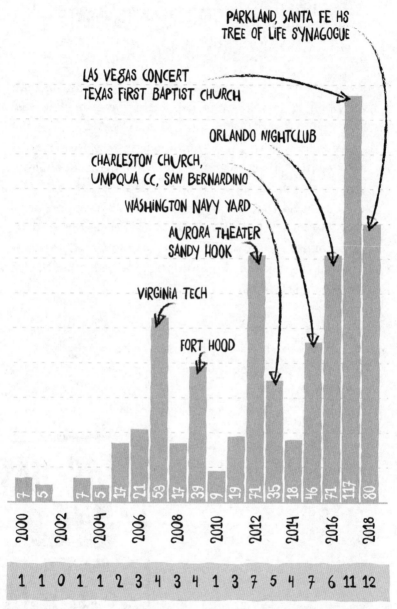

PARKLAND, SANTA FE HS
TREE OF LIFE SYNAGOGUE

LAS VEGAS CONCERT
TEXAS FIRST BAPTIST CHURCH

ORLANDO NIGHTCLUB

CHARLESTON CHURCH,
UMPQUA CC, SAN BERNARDINO

WASHINGTON NAVY YARD

AURORA THEATER
SANDY HOOK

VIRGINIA TECH

FORT HOOD

2000		2002		2004		2006		2008		2010		2012		2014		2016		2018
7	5		7	5	17	21	53	17	39	9	19	71	35	18	46	71	117	80
1	1	0	1	1	2	3	4	3	4	1	3	7	5	4	7	6	11	12

Source: Mark Follman, Gavin Aronsen, and Deanna Pan, "US Mass Shootings, 1982–2019," *Mother Jones*, last updated February 15, 2019, https://www.motherjones.com/politics/2012/12/mass-shootings-mother-jones-full-data/.

COLUMBINE SHOOTING SURVIVOR WANTS MORE GUNS IN SCHOOLS

Patrick Neville was a 16-year-old student at Columbine High School when a mass shooting happened there in 1999. Two of Neville's friends were killed in the massacre, which at the time was the deadliest school shooting in history. Neville grew up and ran for office, eventually becoming the Republican Minority Leader in Colorado's House of Representatives.

Neville believes that arming teachers would have prevented the shooting at his school. Every year since his election in 2014, he has introduced bills to arm teachers in Colorado. Coloradans have continually rejected his proposals at the ballot, but Neville stands firm in his beliefs:

> I think the current policy we have just invites these heinous acts where I actually think the criminals look for these locations, because they know they're going to be unopposed. It'll be a deterrent more than anything that folks are going to stop targeting our young kids in schools.[9]

36

Just after the Marjory Stoneman Douglas shooting in Parkland, Florida, senior Emma Gonzalez gave voice to teen frustration about being a part of that horrifying statistic:

I found out today there's a website shootingtracker. com. Nothing in the title suggests that it is exclusively tracking the USA's shootings and yet does it need to address that? Because Australia had one mass shooting in 1999 and after the massacre introduced gun safety, and it hasn't had one since. Japan has never had a mass shooting. Canada has had three and the UK had one and they both introduced gun control. And yet here we are, with websites dedicated to reporting these tragedies so that they can be formulated into statistics for your convenience.[11]

IN 2016, GUN VIOLENCE (HOMICIDES AND SUICIDES) **KILLED MORE YOUNG PEOPLE THAN CAR ACCIDENTS** FOR THE FIRST TIME EVER.

Guns Make Suicide Too Easy

Although mass shootings and school shootings are terrifying, the truth is that most gun deaths are suicides. And gun suicides impact young people more than you might expect—suicide is the second leading cause of death among young people ages 15 to 19. On average, four teenagers die by suicide every day, and that number is rising. Guns are the cause of death nearly half the time, making them the most frequent way teens kill themselves.[12]

Why is that? Because guns are so deadly.

In suicide attempts, guns succeed 82.5 percent of the time. By contrast, jumping off a bridge works 34.5 percent of the time and overdosing on drugs works only 1.5 percent of the time.[13]

Many teens who attempt suicide do so because of a temporary problem, like a breakup or issues with parents. Teen suicide is usually an impulsive act, decided on the spot. Studies show that most young survivors of a suicide attempt are glad they didn't die and don't try to kill themselves again.[14]

Guns, however, leave little room for second chances.

Does having a gun in the home increase the risk of suicide? Yes! In states where there are more guns, more people die by suicide. Studies have shown that the risk of suicide is four to ten times higher in homes with guns than in homes without. If the gun is stored loaded or unlocked, that risk is even higher. The vast majority of teens who die by suicide with a gun (more than 75 percent) do so with a gun from their own home or from the home of a relative or friend.[15]

Alarmingly, a recent study found that of the teens who live in homes with guns, roughly 40 percent of them had serious risk factors for suicide, such as recent depression or suicidal thoughts. And around 40 percent of teens who attempted suicide in the past year reported having "easy access" to the guns in their home.[16]

Would decreasing access to guns cut down on teen suicides? Yes! A 2018 study conducted by Boston University School of Public Health found that with every 10 percent increase in household gun ownership, the youth suicide rate jumped 27 percent.[17]

This chart shows the clear link between easy access to guns and increased suicides:

GUN OWNERSHIP AND FIREARM SUICIDE RATE, BY STATE

SUICIDE RATES (OVER A 5-YEAR PERIOD)

HIGHEST	LOWEST
ALASKA 14.77	MASSACHUSETTS 1.81
WYOMING 14.70	NEW JERSEY 1.9
MONTANA 14.03	NEW YORK 2.30
IDAHO 11.40	RHODE ISLAND 2.40
OKLAHOMA 10.82	HAWAII 2.47

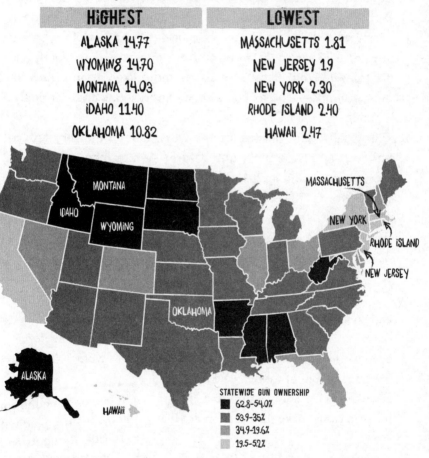

STATEWIDE GUN OWNERSHIP
- 62.8–54.0%
- 53.9–35%
- 34.9–19.6%
- 19.5–5.2%

Source: Catherine A. Okoro, David E. Nelson, James A. Mercy, Lina S. Balluz, Alex E. Crosby, Ali H. Mokdad, "Prevalence of Household Firearms and Firearm Storage Practices in the 50 States and the District of Columbia: Findings from the Behavioral Risk Factor Surveillance System, 2002," *Pediatrics* 116, no. 3 (September 2005), http://pediatrics.aappublications.org/content/116/3/e370.figures-only; "Injury Prevention & Control: Data and Statistics (WISQARS), Centers for Disease Control and Prevention, last updated January 18, 2019, from http://www.cdc.gov/injury/wisqars/index.html; "The Truth About Suicide & Guns," Brady Center to Prevent Gun Violence, accessed June 27, 2018, http://www.bradycampaign.org /sites/default/files/Brady-Guns-Suicide-Report-2016.pdf.

WHITE MEN AND GUN SUICIDES

Guns make suicide easier for everyone, not just teenagers. Of the ninety-three Americans who die from guns every day, nearly two-thirds of those are suicides.[18] And while women are more likely to *attempt* suicide, men are more likely to die from it. Why? Because men are more likely to use guns in their attempts—and as you already know, guns are extremely lethal.[19]

Ironically, gun suicides are the worst among the very group fighting hardest against gun reform—white men. In a nine-year study ending in 2016, white men were found to be more than twice as likely as black men to die by suicide with a gun.[20]

Guns Make Domestic Violence Deadlier

Did you know that gun violence is a feminist issue too? Due to our lax gun laws, America is the most dangerous country in the developed world when it comes to gun violence against women.[21] Abuse impacts millions of women every year, and just like suicide, adding guns to that equation can easily make the situation deadlier.

If you or someone you know is struggling with suicidal thoughts and needs to talk, the National Suicide Prevention Lifeline is always open: 800-273-8255.

- Women in the US are sixteen times more likely to be killed with a gun than women in other high-income countries.[22]

- Fifty American women are shot to death in an average month by their partners, and many more are injured.[23]

- Over the past twenty-five years, more intimate partner homicides have been committed with guns than with all other weapons combined.[24]

- In homes where there has already been domestic violence, women are five times more likely to be murdered if there is a gun in the house.[25]

- Millions of American women—4.5 million, to be exact—have had an intimate partner threaten them with a gun.[26]

- In 54 percent of mass shootings, shooters killed their partners or other family members.[27]

Federal gun laws ban *some* domestic abusers from buying and owning guns, but there are huge loopholes, which leave women and their families vulnerable to deadly violence.

Guns Make Accidental Shootings Too Easy

We've established that guns make it more dangerous for students in school, for teens thinking about suicide, and for women in abusive relationships. Guns also make it more dangerous for kids in their own homes. Here are just a few recent news stories:

Two Detroit grandparents were babysitting their five-year-old granddaughter when she found a loaded pistol under their pillow, shot herself in the neck, and died.[28]

A 12-year-old in North Carolina found his mother's shotgun leaning against the refrigerator. It felt too light to be loaded when he shook it, so he pointed it at his 9-year-old brother, pulled the trigger, and shot him; his brother died.[29]

A dad in Louisiana cleaned his guns one morning and then left for work. When he realized he left one gun out on the couch, he texted his girlfriend and asked her to put it away when she got home with their 3-year-old daughter. But the girlfriend let the dog out first, and in those few seconds, the toddler found the gun and shot herself; she died.[30]

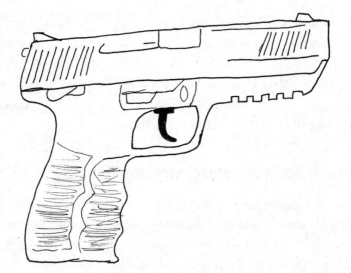

After grieving and processing her father's death for years, at age 12, Julia decided she wanted to do something. "I realized that I didn't want anyone else to feel the way I did. I didn't want any other little girl to lose her father the way I did and to feel the heartbreak that I did," she says.

Her first step was joining her local Moms Demand Action (MDA) group. Her first protest was a march in Philadelphia. "I just loved it. I loved being around like-minded people. People were so energetic and optimistic and passionate. It made me feel empowered," she says. She decided then and there that she would get more involved. For several years, she went to meetings and marches and rallies with MDA. But she had an idea bouncing around in her brain:

I'd seen a lot of complacency from my peers, which frustrated me, but I've also seen a lot of my peers who are super passionate and want to get involved, but they don't know how. My goal was to create a youth-led movement where students make the rules and speak for themselves. Where they have a platform to speak out without being talked over by adults.

Julia helped launch Students Demand Action (SDA) in 2018, just two days after the Parkland, Florida, massacre. The group, which is affiliated with Moms Demand Action and Everytown for Gun Safety, is led by and open only to students—from middle schools, high schools, and colleges. Within months of the launch, sixty-five thousand young people had joined SDA.

Their first goal was voter registration for the 2018 midterm elections. "Our big push was to get as many young people registered as possible, trying to make sure as many students who can vote will vote." They are also focused on informing young people about gun sense candidates they can support where they live and nationally.

These are horrible stories. But every one of them was preventable. From 2005 to 2014, roughly twenty thousand American children were killed or seriously injured in accidental shootings. The majority of children killed in these tragic gun accidents were 12 or younger.[31]

MORE AMERICANS OWN GUNS THAN OWN CATS![32]

America is awash in guns. A 2015 study showed that 4.6 million children live in a home where at least one gun is stored unlocked and loaded.[33]

Most parents who own guns believe their kids know better than to play with those guns. Or they believe their children don't know where they are hidden. But research tells a different story. In one study, 73 percent of children aged nine and younger said they knew where their parents' guns were stored. Thirty-six percent admitted they had handled those weapons—that included the kids whose parents reported their children didn't know the guns' locations![34]

It shouldn't be too surprising to find out that 89 percent of accidental shooting deaths by children occur in their own homes and most occur when children are playing with a loaded, unsecured gun while parents are absent. A disturbing report published by the US Secret Service found that in 65 percent of school shootings, shooters used guns they got from their own home or the home of a relative.[35] And yet in all states except Massachusetts, it is perfectly legal for adults to leave a gun unlocked and loaded, where a child can get it and accidentally shoot themselves or others, die by suicide, or go on a shooting rampage.

A Final Word

Like you, the teens of Marjory Stoneman Douglas High School in Parkland, Florida, never thought they'd be part of a mass shooting. In a cruel irony, Parkland had been declared Florida's safest city the year before the shooting. But they weren't immune to the gun violence in our country, and neither are the rest of us.

Gun violence *does* impact you. It impacts you every day. But you don't have to sit back and do nothing. There are plenty of ideas for fixing these problems. Other countries have figured out ways to keep gun violence in check. And in some US states, lawmakers are already making strides in the right direction. In part 3 of this book, you will find solutions to these problems, and in part 4 are ways to get involved and do something about it. There are lots of young people working on the problem already.

STUDENTS TAKING A STAND

JULIA SPOOR, AGE 17, GUN VIOLENCE SURVIVOR COFOUNDER OF STUDENTS DEMAND ACTION

Julia adored her father, Scott. "He was a goofy guy who just had this radiance about him," she remembers. But he got depressed and twice tried to overdose on a mixture of pills and alcohol. Then he bought a gun. "That would have been the point for someone to say, 'This guy should not possess a firearm.'"[2]

Sadly, there were no Red Flag Laws in place in Florida, where Julia and her family li[ved at the] time. Ten days before Julia's eighth birthday, her dad sho[

WHAT ARE RED FLAG LAWS?

Red Flag Laws give family members and law enf[orcement] the ability to seek an Extreme Risk Protection Ord[er,] a court order that temporarily restricts a person['s access] to guns when they pose a danger to themselves [or others.] It's a way for families to act before warning sign[s turn] into deadly violence. See chapter 10 for more [

"Moms Demand Action gives seals [of approval] to candidates who are gun sense champions. We want to make sure we have a wave of gun sense candidates elected."

Another cool SDA outreach—sending out Holiday Tool Kits to students, to help them "feel confident talking to adults about gun violence prevention and why they should vote for gun sense candidates. The kits show how to start the conversation, how to stay confident, and how to persuade your relatives," she explains.

Julia wants students to get active. Find a group in your area to join by visiting the Students Demand Action website or checking on social media. If there isn't a group in your area, start one of your own.

Julia's vote for the most effective political action students can take? Canvassing. "It's proven that face-to-face contact with voters is the most effective way to reach them," she explains. "We're encouraging students to leave their houses, go knock on doors, and have individual conversations with real people to educate them about gun violence." She knows canvassing can be scary—talking to adults you don't know is hard even for other adults—but she says it gets a lot easier over time. "I always encourage students to bring a friend, or two or three. Canvassing in a group is a lot of fun. You get to spend time together and also are doing your part changing the world at the same time." Students Demand Action and its partner groups organize lots of canvassing you can participate in.

Julia's personal gun sense focus is on Red Flag Laws. "I believe Red Flag Laws would have prevented my father's death," she says. Even though we have a long way to go to fix America's gun problem, she is feeling a lot more hopeful and optimistic these days. "Sometimes it takes a huge tragedy like the Parkland shooting to open people's eyes, wake them up, and motivate them. But I think we have that now. It might take a lot of time, so it's important that we as a movement stay optimistic and hopeful but also keep fighting. We can't get complacent."

Julia's advice to student activists:

> "YOU HAVE A VOICE. YOU CAN MAKE THIS CHANGE. WE ARE THE ONES LEADING THIS MOVEMENT. WE HAVE VOICES AND WE WILL BE HEARD."

◎ ◎ ◎

Learn more about what Julia is working on and get involved at everytown.org/studentsdemand or text STUDENTS to 64433.

If you or someone you know is struggling with suicidal thoughts and needs to talk, the National Suicide Prevention Lifeline is always open: 800-273-8255.

CHAPTER 3

GUN VIOLENCE AND MARGINALIZED COMMUNITIES: HOW IS IT DIFFERENT?

In 2017, 15-year-old black American Jordan Edwards was at a party with his brothers and some friends. Kids at the party were drinking and being loud, so eventually the police arrived to break it up. As Jordan left the party, with his brother driving while he sat in the front passenger seat, a white police officer shot three rounds into their car. The bullets hit Jordan in the back of the head, killing him instantly. Jordan and the rest of the boys in the car were unarmed and driving away from the police—there was no reason for the officer to fire on them.[1]

In 2008, 15-year-old student Larry King walked onto the basketball court at E. O. Green Junior High School and interrupted the game by asking 14-year-old Brandon McInerney to be his valentine.

Brandon was upset as teammates laughed and made fun of him. Two days later as the boys sat together in class, Brandon pulled a gun out of his backpack and shot Larry twice in the head. He died a few days later.[2]

These stories are just two of the many gun tragedies that occur in black and LGBTQ+ communities every day. All Americans are impacted by gun violence, but it affects these groups in very different ways.

Gun Violence in Black Communities

Black communities have been fighting gun violence for decades, and while their goals are the same as those of every other community— less gun violence—they have additional concerns that are particular to what is happening in black neighborhoods. They are less focused on school shootings (which are uncommon in black neighborhoods) and more concerned about the "structural violence" and police shootings that happen daily in their neighborhoods.

They are also frustrated by the lack of media attention for gun violence in black communities versus in white communities.

You might have noticed that whenever white children are killed in school shootings, the news media is all over it. But the sad truth is that guns kill ten times more black children than white children in America.[3] Worst of all, black people between the ages of 15 and 29 are eighteen times more likely to be killed by a gun than their white peers.[4] These deaths are not happening because of angry school shooters. They are happening because of drugs, crime, and other issues related to poverty and systemic racism.

YOUNG BLACK AMERICANS (AGE 15–29) MOST LIKELY TO BE VICTIMS OF GUN HOMICIDE

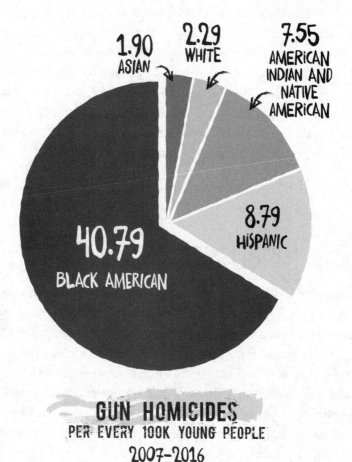

1.90 ASIAN

2.29 WHITE

7.55 AMERICAN INDIAN AND NATIVE AMERICAN

40.79 BLACK AMERICAN

8.79 HISPANIC

GUN HOMICIDES
PER EVERY 100K YOUNG PEOPLE
2007–2016

Source: "Fatal Injury Reports, National, Regional and State, 1999–2016," Centers for Disease Control and Prevention, accessed April 2018, https://webappa.cdc.gov/sasweb/ncipc/mortrate.html.

Police violence is another gun issue that impacts black communities more heavily than white communities. Increased media coverage of the many fatal shootings of unarmed black men and boys, along with the rise of the Black Lives Matter movement, have finally brought much-needed attention to this issue. According to the *Washington Post*, of the nearly 3,300 deadly shootings by police from January 2015 through April 2018, one-third were against African Americans, even though they make up just 12 percent of the US population.[6] According to the Counted, a project run by the *Guardian* newspaper to record all police killings in the US, in 2015, black males ages 15 to 34 were nine times more likely to be killed by police officers than young white men.[7]

WHAT IS STRUCTURAL VIOLENCE?

Structural violence is a way of describing social arrangements that put individuals and certain populations at risk of being harmed. These arrangements are embedded in the political and economic structure of our world. Structural violence is subtle, often invisible, and usually has no specific person who can be held responsible. Gun violence in black communities is largely a result of our government putting people in poor housing with poor educational and job opportunities, which can result in violent behavior.[5]

Although the media tends to focus on white shootings, black and white student activists are starting to work together. Bria Smith, a black student activist in Milwaukee, Wisconsin, talked about this change in the movement. She began, "In my community, it's easier to get a gun than it is to find a parking spot." She was frustrated with all the media attention on the Parkland survivors. "So many people giving media coverage to a couple students. I felt really salty." Then she met Parkland activist David Hogg at a gun violence event. She remembers, "I thought he was another white boy. [But] he asked me a question that no other person has asked me. He asked, 'What do you need? We can get it for you.' And I thought, *Whoa. Maybe I do need to speak up about that*."[8]

The Parkland kids joined with students of color for a national speaking tour aimed at registering young voters for the 2018 midterm elections. Together, they are working to create a more powerful gun safety movement. Their overall goal is the same: to make everyone safer, in *all* neighborhoods. As young activist Nza-Ari Khepra explained, "Gun violence is not just one race's issue; it's everyone's issue."[9]

SCHOOL SHOOTINGS ARE A WHITE, SUBURBAN PROBLEM

Although black communities are deeply impacted by structural violence and police shootings, it may surprise you to hear that school shootings are mostly a white, suburban problem. Of the ten deadliest school shootings in American history, nine of them took place in small towns or suburbs with fewer than seventy-five thousand residents.[10]

PARKLAND WAS VOTED SAFEST TOWN IN FLORIDA JUST BEFORE THE 2018 SHOOTING AT STONEMAN DOUGLAS HIGH SCHOOL.[11]

Experts believe small-town America has more school shootings because:

- Kids in rural or suburban communities have easier access to guns.

- There are unique frustrations to living in a small town.

- If you're a troubled teen—if you did something wrong or had something done wrong to you—everybody knows about it.[12]

Gun Violence in LGBTQ+ Communities

Gun reform priorities are also different for the LGBTQ+ community. Violence against LGBTQ+ people is on the rise. In 2017, one year into Donald Trump's presidency, the number of LGBTQ+ people killed because of their sexual orientation rose 86 percent.[13] The actual number is likely higher because the report didn't count any mass shootings, like the massacre at the Pulse nightclub.

Gun violence is the number one cause of death for LGBTQ+ victims of hate crimes, responsible for 52 percent of murders.[14]

Why the increased violence against the LGBTQ+ community after Trump's election? Many believe that the attitude at the top sets the tone for the rest of the country. Beverly Tillery, director of the National Coalition of Anti-Violence Programs, said, "[Trump's presidency] has given an opening for people to feel like they can commit acts of hate-based violence without much repercussion."[15]

Another alarming increase is the number of gun suicides in the LGBTQ+ community. In 2015, the Centers for Disease Control and Prevention conducted a national survey on teen suicide. The results they found were shocking: 40 percent of LGBTQ+ high school students were seriously considering suicide, 34.9 percent were planning to do it, and 24.9 percent had already attempted suicide in the previous year. By comparison, 14.8 percent of heterosexual teens had seriously considered suicide, 11.9 percent had planned suicide, and 6.3 percent had attempted suicide.[16]

From reading chapter 2, you know how much access to guns increases a teen's ability to successfully kill themselves. Since LGBTQ+ teens are at higher risk for suicide attempts, guns make that risk much, much deadlier. Cameron Price, a high school junior and member of Gays Against Guns Los Angeles, said, "I really want to get guns out of the hands of us and out of the hands of people who want to harm us. I am someone who has attempted suicide because of homophobia, and if I had a gun, I wouldn't be here today."[17]

The Pulse nightclub shooting spurred many in the LGBTQ+ community into action. Survivor Brandon Wolf cofounded the Dru Project, which promotes gay-straight alliances and gives scholarships to LGBTQ+ youth. An activist for LGBTQ+ rights and gun safety, Brandon has summed up the intersectionality of these two issues:

> The two movements really are uniquely intertwined, because if we create a world where everyone is safer, if we create a world where only the right people have their hands on weapons, then we create a world where LGBTQ people are safer.[18]

NEVER FORGET: PULSE NIGHTCLUB SHOOTING (AKA ORLANDO SHOOTING)

When: June 12, 2016
Where: Orlando, Florida
How many died? Forty-nine
What happened? A gunman opened fire inside Pulse, a gay nightclub. He killed forty-nine people and injured fifty more. This was the deadliest shooting attack on the LGBTQ+ community in American history.

A Final Word

The conversation about gun reform hasn't always included voices from marginalized communities. That is changing. Leaders from these groups are demanding that politicians listen. They are demanding a seat at the table where decisions are being made. Tiffany Dena Loftin, the national director of the NAACP Youth and College Division, explained their goal:

> If we want to be included and heard, we have to move past advocacy and demand shared governance. You're not just writing petitions or talking and tweeting

NEVER FORGET: PITTSBURGH SYNAGOGUE SHOOTING (AKA TREE OF LIFE SHOOTING)

When: October 27, 2018
Where: Pittsburgh, Pennsylvania
How many died? Eleven
What happened? A shooter entered Tree of Life, a Jewish synagogue, during Shabbat morning services and killed eleven people. The shooter was a white nationalist who killed his victims because they were Jewish, part of an overall rise in American hate crimes after the 2016 presidential election.

about it on social media. You are demanding as a student that you get a seat at the table and vote and decide what actions get taken.[19]

As young people work together across groups, their power grows. Loftin's advice to student activists:

"LET'S MERGE THE BLACK LIVES MATTER AND THE WOMEN'S MARCH AND THE MARCH FOR OUR LIVES AND MAKE SURE OUR AGENDAS AND **VOICES ARE HEARD.**"[20]

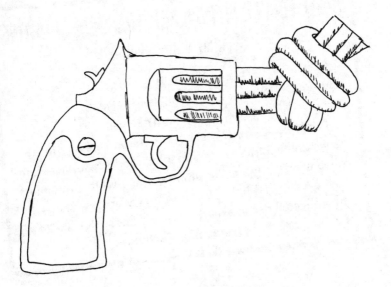

IS GUN CONTROL RACIST?

Believe it or not, the answer is *kind of*. Historically, gun control has been used against the black community. During and after slavery, many whites were terrified by the idea of armed black people who could fight back. So, they enacted gun control laws. Just after losing the Civil War, states in the South passed the Black Codes, making it illegal for free black people to own guns. To enforce the codes, posses of whites went on night raids in black communities, terrorizing families and seizing any guns they found. At first these racist vigilante groups had different names: the Black Cavalry, the Knights of the White Camellia, the Knights of the Rising Sun. But over time, the different names merged into one: the Ku Klux Klan.

In the 1960s, gun control was used to disarm black protest groups like the Black Panthers. After his house was bombed and he received countless death threats, Martin Luther King Jr. was denied a permit to carry a concealed firearm. He was shot and killed in 1968.

Does this mean we shouldn't work for gun violence prevention? Of course not. It means we should be aware of the concerns of all Americans, not just affluent, white Americans. Some of the concerns are different, but we want the same thing: a safer country for everyone.[21]

STUDENTS TAKING A STAND

BRANDON WOLF, AGE 29, GUN VIOLENCE SURVIVOR AND FOUNDER OF THE DRU PROJECT

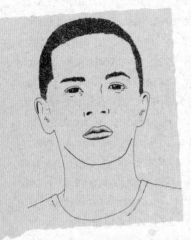

Brandon Wolf went to Orlando's Pulse dance club one night in June hoping to end the awkwardness with his ex-boyfriend Eric. He brought Drew and Juan, his two best friends, to be his buffer. And it did help—after they danced and had drinks together, Drew gathered Brandon and the others together in a group hug and announced, "You know what we never say enough? That we love each other. So I'm going to say it . . . I love you guys."[1]

A few minutes later, Brandon was crouched in the bathroom with Eric, under a urinal, hiding from a shooter out on the dance floor. His best friends, Drew and Juan, were dead. Forty-nine people were murdered that night at the Pulse nightclub, and fifty-three more were wounded. It was the deadliest mass shooting in US history—until the Las Vegas shooting the next year. It was also the deadliest attack ever on the LGBTQ+ community.[2]

Brandon was devastated by the shooting and by the death of his friends. As much as he wanted to curl up and hide after the tragedy, he knew he couldn't. His friends deserved better. If he stayed silent, no one would know what amazing people they were. Nothing would change. Nothing would get better. "We have to do something . . . say something," he told other survivors. "I knew then that if I didn't, nobody would."[3] Just two days after the shooting, Brandon did his first television interview—on CNN. It was horrible. To this day, he can't watch it because he can see the "pure anguish and agony"[4] on his face.

But Brandon has kept going—he keeps speaking out for gun reform and LGBTQ+ rights. Publicly and passionately.

He and Drew's mother, Christine Leinonen, created the Dru Project, in honor of Drew, who Brandon describes as "the best. He found it easy [to be] best friends with everybody."[5] Drew was an activist himself. He started the first gay-straight alliance in his high school, for which he won the Anne Frank Humanitarian Award. The Dru Project honors Drew's spirit by helping kids start gay-straight alliances in their schools, creating curriculum for LGBTQ+ education, and raising money for college scholarships for LGBTQ+ students. The organization's mission is to "empower LGBTQ+ youth and set them up to be the successful leaders we desperately need in this country."[6]

In its first two years, the Dru Project awarded more than $30,000 in college scholarships and $5,000 in mini-grants for gay-straight alliances and published one of the most comprehensive gay-straight alliance curriculums in the country.[7] The school curriculum is Brandon's "pride and joy," covering LGBTQ+ history, coming out, pride, and health and wellness. The curriculum is sprinkled with Drew's actual words.[8]

Brandon is just as passionate about gun reform. "I personally am not anti-gun," he explains. "I think our Second Amendment is uniquely American, and I understand people's passion around it. What I will say is the laws in this country don't work."[9] He is doing everything he can to change those laws, traveling the country speaking to media and at rallies, talking with leaders and lawmakers.

What's ahead for a charismatic leader like Brandon? Running for political office isn't out of the question, maybe in Florida, which has been plagued by mass shootings in recent years.[10]

That night at the Pulse nightclub changed Brandon forever, in tragic but also powerful ways:

> In a personal sense, I will never be the same person that I was . . . before Pulse. It was a loss of blissful joy. But it's also given me new purpose. Part of what happens after a traumatic event is you wonder why you're still here. I was really complacent before Pulse happened. I was that millennial that was more worried about avocado toast than who was running for president. What I hope for everyone is that my experience, my getting fired up about things, can . . . inspire and energize others.[11]

Brandon gave an angry, passionate speech at the first March for Our Lives, in Washington, DC. It was full of advice for Washington lawmakers:

"AFTER FIRST GRADERS WERE GUNNED DOWN AT SANDY HOOK, WHAT DID YOU DO?

NOT A DAMN THING.

AFTER 49 PEOPLE—INCLUDING MY TWO BROTHERS—WERE MURDERED AT PULSE, WHAT DID YOU DO?

NOT A DAMN THING.

[AFTER PARKLAND] WHAT DID YOU DO?

NOT A DAMN THING.

WELL, MEMBERS OF THE LEGISLATURE, I'M PROUD TO ANNOUNCE I TOOK YOUR ADVICE.

I HAVE BEEN PRAYING. I'VE BEEN PRAYING FOR YOU.

BECAUSE WE WILL VOTE YOU OUT.

NEVER FORGET: SANDY HOOK ELEMENTARY SCHOOL SHOOTING
(AKA NEWTOWN SHOOTING)

When: December 14, 2012
Where: Newtown, Connecticut
How many died? Twenty-six
What happened? A 20-year-old shooter killed his mother and then drove to his former elementary school where he shot and killed twenty children between 6 and 7 years old, as well as six adult staff members. At the time, it was the deadliest mass shooting at a high school or grade school in US history. Police later discovered the shooter had severe untreated mental illness, and his mother, a gun enthusiast, had left all the guns in a safe he had the keys to.

YOU CAN EITHER FIX THIS NIGHTMARE OR WRITE YOUR CONCESSION SPEECHES."[12]

Listen to Brandon's inspiring "Not a Damn Thing" speech in full here: pinknews.co.uk/2018/02/22/orlando-massacre-survivor -tears-into-republican-politicians-at-parkland-protest/.

Learn more about what Brandon is working on at thedruproject.org

TROLL ATTACKS

Because of his activism, Brandon has to deal with insults and death threats from gun rights supporters. Sadly, that is true for every young activist profiled in this book, even the kids. It comes with the territory. Getting death threats from angry gun owners is pretty scary, but Brandon and other activists don't let it stop them. "People were sending me death threats and profanity-laced insults—none of it bothered me. Because it doesn't even come close to what [Pulse] felt like. So people are asking, 'Are you dealing with it okay?' And I'm thinking, 'Yeah, of course I'm okay. I'm alive.' So call me anything you want to."[13]

CHAPTER 4

GUN MYTHS VS. GUN FACTS: SPEAK THE TRUTH WHEN ARGUING FOR CHANGE

One of the biggest problems facing gun reform is all the misinformation out there. Because the gun lobby and gun manufacturers want to keep selling guns and making money, it is in their best interest to spread false, unverified information. The NRA also manipulated Congress into cutting off federal funding for any research into gun violence (see chapter 8).

In the absence of legitimate scientific studies, there is misinformation.

To fully understand the gun issue, it is critical to separate fact from fiction. Here are some common arguments you hear from gun rights activists, along with the facts supported by research.

MYTH: More guns means less crime.

FACT: If guns really made us safer, the United States would be the safest country in the world. But our gun homicide rate is twenty-five times higher than the rate in other developed countries. America is 46 percent of the population of developed countries, but it makes up 80 percent of gun deaths.[1]

MYTH: They're going to take all our guns away!

FACT: After every mass shooting, there is a rush on gun stores to stock up before the government crackdown. The truth is that no president, nor any member of Congress, has ever proposed confiscating guns. Even if they wanted to, it wouldn't be easy. Private gun owners in America have way more guns than the police and military combined—seventy-one times more![2]

NUMBER OF GUNS OWNED BY US CITIZENS VS. POLICE AND MILITARY

GUNS OWNED BY LAW ENFORCEMENT AND MILITARY COMBINED (5.5 MILLION)

GUNS OWNED BY CIVILIANS (393 MILLION)

Source: "Small Arms Survey Reveals: More than One Billion Firearms in the World," Small Arms Survey, accessed June 2018, http://www.smallarmssurvey.org/fileadmin/docs/Weapons_and_Markets/Tools /Firearms_holdings/SAS-Press-release-global-firearms-holdings.pdf; Stephen Gutowski, "Report: Nearly 400 Million Civilian-Owned Guns in America," *Washington Free Beacon*, June 21, 2018, https://freebeacon .com/culture/report-nearly-400-million-civilian-owned-guns-america/.

MYTH: Guns don't kill people; people kill people.

FACT: This is another myth that gets trotted out after every mass shooting. What they mean is that even if we restrict guns, it won't help because bad people will still kill people. But they are wrong. Restricting and regulating guns *does* bring gun deaths down. States with more gun owners have more gun deaths (homicides and suicides). An analysis of thirty years of data showed that for every 1 percent increase in a state's gun ownership rate, the gun murder rate goes up by 1 percent as well. On the flip side, states with tighter gun restrictions have lower gun death rates. The numbers don't lie.[3]

MYTH: Good guys with guns will stop bad guys with guns.

FACT: Gun rights supporters claim, "Give more guns to the law-abiding citizens they can stop mass shooters!" What the NRA doesn't want you to notice is that there have been "good guys" carrying guns at many mass shootings. During the Marjory Stoneman Douglas High School massacre, there was an armed guard standing just outside the building who did not go inside and try to stop the shooter.[4]

It is true that sometimes armed civilians have intervened and stopped a handful of mass shootings over the past thirty years. One researcher found ten cases total out of hundreds of mass shootings in America.[5] But for the most part, armed people do what most unarmed people do during a mass shooting—they try to escape.[6]

WHAT ABOUT JAPAN?

Another element to consider in the video game myth is Japan. Video games are way more popular in Japan than in America. According to this myth, Japan should have more gun violence, right? Wrong. Japan has almost no gun violence. No mass shootings at all. Not one. How can that be? It's because Japan has very few guns and very tight gun restrictions (it is illegal to own, carry, buy, or sell handguns and rifles). Look at the numbers: 49 percent of American adults play video games; 60 percent of Japanese adults play video games. Yet in 2014, Japan had just six gun homicides, compared to eleven thousand in the US.[9]

MYTH: Violent video games are to blame.

FACT: After the Parkland shooting, President Trump blamed violent video games, not guns: "I'm hearing more and more people say the level of violence in video games is really shaping young people's thoughts."[7] The truth is that the Supreme Court shot that idea down in the 2011 landmark case *Brown v. Entertainment Merchants Association*: "Psychological studies purporting to show a connection between exposure to violent video games and harmful effects on children do not prove that such exposure causes minors to act aggressively."[8] Super-conservative Justice Antonin Scalia even wrote the majority opinion! Although the Supreme Court doesn't think video games are to blame, the NRA continues trying to distract us with this scapegoat.

MYTH: We don't need more gun laws—we should enforce the ones we have.

FACT: Our current laws are so weak and riddled with loopholes that it's ridiculously easy for people to buy guns illegally. It's too easy for people with violent backgrounds or severe mental illness to buy guns legally. Here are a few examples of why current gun laws aren't doing the trick:

- More than 75 percent of the guns used in mass shootings were obtained legally.

- 40 percent of gun sales are by private sellers and require no background checks at all.

- 40 percent of prisoners who used guns to commit crimes got them from private sellers.

- 62 percent of online gun sellers were willing to sell to buyers who said they couldn't pass a background check.[10]

MYTH: Having a gun in your home makes you safer.

FACT: Nope. Having a gun in your home makes you much less safe, actually. Homes with guns have a higher risk for gun murder, suicide, and accidental death. For every one self-defense shooting in the home, there are seven assaults or murders, eleven suicide attempts, and four accidental shootings. A study in the *American Journal of Public Health* found that in 43 percent of homes that have both guns and kids, there is at least one unlocked gun.[11]

IN ONE EXPERIMENT, ONE-THIRD OF 8-TO-12-YEAR-OLD BOYS WHO FOUND A HANDGUN **PULLED THE TRIGGER.**[12]

NEVER FORGET:
TEXAS FIRST BAPTIST SHOOTING
(AKA SUTHERLAND SPRINGS CHURCH SHOOTING)

When: November 5, 2017
Where: Sutherland Springs, Texas
How many died? Twenty-six
What happened? The shooter entered this First Baptist church during the crowded Sunday service and proceeded to shoot and kill twenty-six people. The shooter was shot and wounded outside the church by a local resident and NRA instructor. He died later by a self-inflicted gunshot. The shooter should have been banned from buying his weapons due to a domestic violence conviction, but it hadn't been entered into the FBI database.

MYTH: Carrying a gun makes you safer.

FACT: Again, nope. A study found that in an attack, you are 4.5 times more likely to be shot if you are carrying a gun. You are also 4.2 times more likely to be killed if you have a gun on you than if you don't.[13]

MYTH: Guns make women safer.

FACT: The NRA and gun manufacturers would certainly like women to believe this, so they can sell more pink cammo assault rifles and Glocks in purple and light teal. But the truth is a woman is five times more likely to be killed by her abuser if that person has access to a gun. And a woman who lives in a state with high gun ownership is five times more likely to be murdered by a gun than a woman living in a state with fewer guns. Women are safer wherever there are fewer guns.[14]

MYTH: Gun laws don't work. Look at the gun problem in Chicago. (Code for: gun violence is a black, urban problem.)

FACT: Data from states that require background checks on all handgun sales show 48 percent less gun trafficking in their cities. Research shows that 60 percent of guns taken from Chicago crime scenes come from out of state, especially from states with weaker gun laws.[15]

MYTH: It's a mental health issue, not a gun issue.

FACT: The NRA continually blames mass shootings on "insane" people, even though people with mental illness commit only 5 percent of gun homicides. The fact is that people with mental illness are much less likely to commit gun violence than are people who are considered mentally healthy.[16] But the biggest problem relating to guns and people with mental health issues is suicide. People with serious mental illness have a dramatically higher risk for suicide, which is made much easier with a gun.[17]

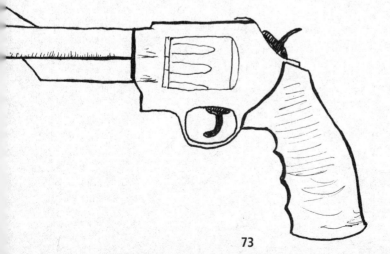

PEOPLE WITH MENTAL ILLNESS ARE USUALLY GUN VICTIMS

People with severe mental illness are eleven times more likely to be victims of gun violence than the general population, especially when it comes to interactions with the police. One study found that at least half of the people shot and killed by police each year have mental health issues.[18]

A Final Word

Don't be fooled by the myths you hear people saying. Instead, do some research and learn the facts. The truth is a powerful tool for changing hearts and minds.

Educate yourself. There's a ton of information about gun violence out there. Learn as much as you can.

Be patient. For an issue this contentious, progress is likely to be slow. Like other movements—women's rights, civil rights, LGBTQ+ rights—slow and steady wins the race. Be in it for the long haul. You may not see change immediately, but over time, your activism will make a difference.[7]

Learn more about what Nza-Ari is working on and get involved at wearorange.org.

STUDENTS TAKING A STAND

NZA-ARI KHEPRA, AGE 22, FOUNDER OF PROJECT ORANGE TREE AND WEAR ORANGE DAY

On January 29, 2013, Nza-Ari got a phone call that changed her life forever.

She and classmates at King College Prep High School in Chicago had taken final exams that day and gotten out of school early. Nza-Ari went home, but her good friend Hadiya Pendleton headed to nearby Harsh Park with a group of students to hang out on the surprisingly warm winter day. The park, which is just a mile from then-president Obama's home, looks safe with its manicured grass and little-kid play structure, but it is in the territory of a neighborhood gang, 46 Terror.

When Hadiya and her friends heard the unmistakable pop of gunshots coming from across the park, they scattered. Classmate Klyn Jones glanced back, and she saw her friend stop running. "I think I got shot," Hadiya said, clutching her chest. Klyn yelled to her, "Stop playing. We have to go." Hadiya collapsed. She had been shot twice in the back.[1]

When Nza-Ari got the phone call telling her the horrible news, she raced to the hospital. But Hadiya died before she got there. "There were no words. Only sobs," Nza-Ari says. "In the moments of her unimaginable grief, Hadiya's mom comforted me. I was shattered."[2]

Fifteen-year-old Hadiya was a black honor student and a role model for her classmates. Just a week before the shooting, she had performed as a majorette at the inauguration of Barack Obama. Nza-Ari says, "I couldn't understand how this could happen to someone who was such a force of positivity."[3]

The gun violence had been a mistake—the shooter was in a rival gang and mistook Hadiya's group for members of the 46 Terror gang.

After Hadiya's murder, Nza-Ari took her grief and transformed it into serious political action. She and her classmates at King College Prep started Project Orange Tree, a gun violence awareness group that teaches young people about the causes as well as the solutions for shootings that plague lower socioeconomic neighborhoods in America. They chose their name with care: orange because it's the color hunters wear to warn others not to shoot, plus it's bright and bold and demands to be seen, and a tree because it represents both life and shelter.[4]

In 2015, just two years after Hadiya's murder, Project Orange Tree evolved into one of the biggest gun violence campaigns in the world: Wear Orange/National Gun Violence Awareness Day on June 2. Each year hundreds of thousands of people (250,000 in 2017[5]) across the country wear orange to show their support for commonsense gun laws and to raise awareness about gun violence in all communities. The Wear Orange campaign includes a ton of celebrities, too, like Julianne Moore, Amy Schumer, Spike Lee, Sarah Silverman, J. J. Abrams, Kim Kardashian West, Lin-Manuel Miranda, Elizabeth Banks, and even Mark Hamill (light sabers are okay, apparently).[6]

All this action sprung from the grief and passion of one 15-year-old girl. Nza-Ari's advice for other student activists:

Think small to reach big goals. To change gun laws, start in your neighborhood and in your state. Small actio that you can achieve can motivate you to go for the nex goal.

Remember who you're working for. It's easy to f that behind each shooting statistic is a real person wh and was loved. Each gun death is an enormous trage impacts lives long after the headlines are gone.

Find a group that fits your passion. You can j national group or a small community group. Foc area of gun violence that you're most passionate domestic violence, suicide, accidental shootings, violence. They are all part of the same goal: en violence in America.

PART 2

HOW WE GOT HERE

A well regulated Militia, being necessary to the security of a free State, the right of the people to keep and bear Arms, shall not be infringed.

—THE SECOND AMENDMENT OF THE UNITED STATES CONSTITUTION, WRITTEN IN 1787

CHAPTER 5

GUN OWNERS: WHO ARE THEY, AND WHAT DO THEY WANT?

You know from previous chapters that America is loaded with guns (pun intended).

Americans own nearly half the world's guns but make up only 5 percent of the world's population.[1] There is more than one gun for every single person in America—man, woman, and child.

Who owns all these guns? Are they rural families who enjoy hunting together? Are they urban women worried about their safety? Are they wannabe militiamen stockpiling for a government takeover?

People on both sides of the gun debate *think* they know who America's gun owners are, but how much do we really know?

Let's look at the facts.

A Breakdown of Gun Owners in America

According to a study done in 2017 by the Pew Research Center, 30 percent of American adults own a gun. Sixty-nine percent of American adults do not own a gun, but some of those people live with someone who does own a gun (11 percent), or they could see themselves owning a gun in the future (36 percent). So really, that means 40 percent of American homes have guns in them, and 75 percent are pretty gun friendly.[2]

Here's how the stats break down:

- Men are almost twice as likely to own guns than women: 39 percent of men versus 22 percent of women own guns.

- 36 percent of gun owners are white, 24 percent are black, and 15 percent are Hispanic.

- Republicans are nearly three times more likely to own guns than Democrats: 41 percent of Republicans versus 16 percent of Democrats own guns.

- 31 percent of gun owners have a high school diploma or less, 34 percent have some college education, and 25 percent have a bachelor's degree or higher.

- People living in rural areas are more likely to own guns than people in urban areas: 46 percent rural versus 19 percent urban.[3]

Where Do Gun Owners Live?

Gun owners live everywhere, but they are most concentrated in states that have fewer people (rural) and are more conservative.

PERCENTAGES OF GUN OWNERS PER STATE

Source: Bindu Kalesan, Marcos D. Villarreal, Katherine M. Keyes, and Sandro Galea, "Gun Ownership and Social Gun Culture," *Injury Prevention* 22, no. 3 (June 29, 2015).

When you compare that map showing gun ownership to the next map showing political affiliation, you see the crossover between guns and political values is striking.

POLITICAL LEANINGS OF US STATES

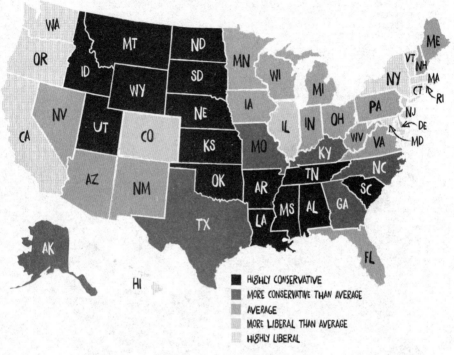

HIGHLY CONSERVATIVE
MORE CONSERVATIVE THAN AVERAGE
AVERAGE
MORE LIBERAL THAN AVERAGE
HIGHLY LIBERAL

Source: Lydia Saad, "Conservative-Leaning States Drop from 44 to 39," Gallup, February 6, 2018, https:// news.gallup.com/poll/226730/conservative-leaning-states-drop.aspx.

What Types of Guns Do People Own and Why?

The most common type of gun people own is a handgun—72 percent of gun owners have handguns. The next most popular is a rifle, owned by 62 percent of gun owners, then a shotgun, owned by 54 percent. This makes sense when you look at the reasons people give for owning guns. Most gun owners (67 percent) said protection is their top reason, which is what handguns are for. Hunting is the top reason for 38 percent, while 30 percent want guns for sport shooting, and 13 percent collect them.[4]

What About Assault Rifles?

What we call assault rifles are fast-shooting, automatic-loading, military-style rifles. The AR-15 is a specific model made by Colt, but the term is used more generically to refer to many other rifles with similar specs and capabilities. The AR-15 was the gun used in many mass shootings, including the Orlando nightclub, Sandy Hook Elementary, the Las Vegas concert, and the Parkland high school. The *Washington Post* called these guns "mass shooters' weapon of choice."[5]

**NEVER FORGET:
HARVEST MUSIC FESTIVAL SHOOTING
(AKA LAS VEGAS SHOOTING)**

When: October 1, 2017
Where: Las Vegas, Nevada
How many died? Fifty-eight
What happened? A gunman fired from the thirty-second floor of a hotel on the Las Vegas Strip down into a crowd of more than twenty thousand people gathered at a concert. He killed fifty-eight people and injured over five hundred more. As of 2018, it is the deadliest mass shooting in US history. The shooter had forty-seven guns and piles of ammunition, including bump stocks, which he used to turn his weapons into rapid-fire machine guns.

Armalite first designed the AR-15 in 1957 for the US Army. The army wanted a rifle capable of "high-velocity, full- and semi-auto fire, twenty-shot magazine, able to penetrate a standard army helmet at 500 meters."[6] The army used the gun in the 1960s, calling it the M16. The M16's semiautomatic civilian counterpart was dubbed the AR-15.[7]

While the NRA claims AR-15s are good for hunting and home defense, gun violence activists say they are even better at doing what they were designed for: shooting humans at a rapid rate. In a 2017 study of two hundred mass shootings in the US, researchers at Brigham and Women's Hospital found that if a shooter uses a semi-automatic instead of another type of gun, it doubles the chances of people being wounded or killed.[8]

With the rise of AR-15s being used in high-profile mass shootings, there has been increased pressure to ban them. Believe it or not, they were already banned from 1994 to 2004, after another series of high-profile AR-15 shootings. The 1994 Federal Assault Weapons Ban prohibited manufacturing, transferring, or possessing certain semiautomatic firearms for civilian use. When that legislation expired in 2004, Congress—under pressure from the NRA—decided not to reinstate the law. The number of assault rifles purchased legally has risen sharply ever since.

Just how popular is this deadly military-grade weapon? We don't know exact numbers because there is no national gun registry. Thanks to the Firearm Owners Protection Act of 1986, it's illegal for the government to require gun owners to register their weapons (see chapter 10). Therefore, we have no way of tracking how many Americans own AR-15s and other similar semiautomatic weapons. Researchers have attempted to estimate how many AR-15s are in the US by calculating how many were manufactured in a year and not exported out of the country. *Slate* magazine did this number-crunching in 2009 and estimated that between 1986 and 2007 there were at least 1,626,525 AR–15–style semiautomatic rifles sold in the US.[9] By generalizing to the other years when they weren't banned, the number of AR–15s in our country gets much higher.

IT IS ESTIMATED THAT THERE ARE AROUND 3.5 MILLION AR-15s IN AMERICA TODAY.[10]

A FEW WORDS ABOUT THE TERM ASSAULT WEAPON

Let's get our language straight. *Assault weapon* is not a technical definition, yet the media uses this term, which can lead to confusion (and frustration from gun owners). Here is a rundown of terms you hear in the debate about assault weapons.

assault weapon: When the Federal Assault Weapons Ban passed in 1994, the US Department of Justice defined these as "semiautomatic firearms [rifles, pistols, and shotguns] with a large magazine of ammunition that were designed and configured for rapid fire and combat use."

assault rifle: This term is sometimes used in place of *assault weapon* but really refers just to military rifles that can fire automatically and/or in burst mode.

bump stock (or bump-fire stock): A bump stock lets you use your semiautomatic rifle to bump fire—or mimic automatic firing—without breaking any laws. Each time the gun recoils, it bounces back, which causes it to automatically pull the trigger again, which causes another recoil, and so on. It turns a semiautomatic weapon into an automatic weapon, legally.

fully automatic: These are weapons that can shoot continuously with one pull of the trigger, like a machine gun. In 1986 Congress passed the Firearm Owners' Protection Act, making it illegal to manufacture new automatic weapons for civilian use. But if the automatic weapon was made before 1986, it's legal.

semiautomatic: These are weapons that reload automatically, but you have to pull the trigger each time you want to fire a bullet. Semiautomatic pistols and rifles come in all shapes and sizes, are legal for civilian use, and are extremely common in the United States. They can be turned into fully automatic weapons by adding bump stocks.[11]

Did the Assault Weapons Ban Impact Mass Shootings?

That's possible but not certain. As this chart shows, the number of people killed in mass shootings did go down in the years the ban was in effect (except for a spike in 1999, the year of the Columbine High School shooting). And the number of people killed in mass shootings did go up after the law was taken off the books in 2004.

NUMBER OF MASS SHOOTINGS IN THE US BY YEAR

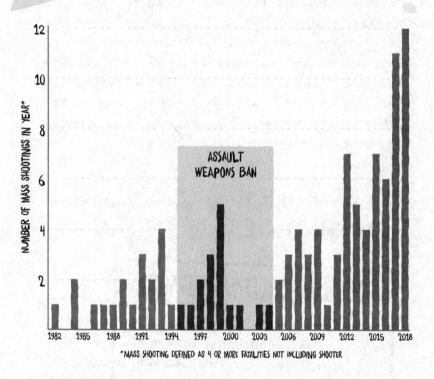

Source: Mark Follman, Gavin Aronsen, and Deanna Pan, "US Mass Shootings, 1982–2019," *Mother Jones*, last updated February 15, 2019, https://www.motherjones.com/politics/2012/12/mass-shootings-mother-jones-full-data/.

Because mass shootings are relatively uncommon, it's difficult to tell if these changes were caused by the ban. But the fact that the number of mass shootings per year has doubled since the ban expired is very interesting, to say the least.

Are White Men Stockpiling Guns?

One chilling statistic to ponder: Barack Obama was elected president in 2008, and since then, the number of guns made in America has tripled and the number of guns imported has doubled. Since 2008, guns have been flooding into the US. Yet the number of households that own guns has stayed pretty much the same.[13] That means gun manufacturers are not selling more guns to new customers—they are just selling more guns to the same customers.

It turns out a tiny percentage of people are buying most of those guns. More than half of gun owners own just one or two guns. These are the hunters and target shooters and people worried about their personal safety. But 7.7 million gun owners (or 3 percent of the US population) own between 8 and 140 guns![14]

3% OF THE US POPULATION OWNS HALF OF THE COUNTRY'S GUNS.

FEDERAL ASSAULT WEAPONS BAN

This law was passed in 1994 and banned the manufacture, transfer, or possession of certain semiautomatic weapons for civilian use. It expired in 2004 and was not reinstated by the US Congress.[12]

LINK BETWEEN GUNS AND RACISM

A study at Wisconsin's Northland College found another motivation for white men stockpiling weapons: racial fears. Many researchers have found a connection between racism and guns, including a 2013 study in England that found if a person was just a bit more racist (an increase of one point on their racism scale), their chance of owning a gun went up 50 percent. Another study in 2016 from the University of Illinois at Chicago concluded that racial resentment in some white people was fueling their opposition to gun violence prevention.[17]

Who is stockpiling all these weapons? And why?

A study conducted by the Injury Control Research Center at Harvard University found that the gun stockpiler fits a fairly narrow profile:

- White man

- Anxious about protecting himself and his family

- Insecure about job prospects and job security

- Less educated

- Less religious[15]

This last trait—being less religious—is interesting. Several studies have explored that point and found that greater religious belief means less attachment to guns. Researchers at Baylor University also found that gun stockpilers felt that "having a gun made them a better and more respected member of their communities" and that "guns are a solution to our social ills."[16] The study did not find the same results for women gun owners or gun owners of other races.

Isn't It Ironic?

The irony is that the very same white men who are buying a personal arsenal to protect themselves aren't actually using those guns to kill criminals (see chapter 4). They are, in fact, using their guns mostly to kill themselves or their families. According to the Centers for Disease Control and Prevention, white men have the highest rate of suicide by gun, especially when they are having economic troubles. White men are three times more likely to shoot themselves than black men. And having a gun in the home makes it much more likely that someone who lives in that home will be shot and/or killed by that gun.[18]

So, by allowing Americans to buy as many guns as they want and employing weak background checks, our government is not helping men defend themselves and their families. They are making it easier for them to kill themselves and their families, however.

A Final Word

While a small minority of gun owners are stockpiling weapons, the majority own guns for perfectly legitimate reasons: hunting, protection, and sport. People working for gun reform need to keep in mind the feelings of this group. Our chances of changing things are better if we can unite with gun owners on the key issues we all agree on (see chapter 9).

YOUNG HUNTER SPEAKS HER MIND

RiLEY MULBERGER, AGE 13, YOUNG HUNTER[1]

Riley Mulberger is a 13-year-old student at Wallenpaupack Area Middle School in rural Pennsylvania, where her favorite subjects are math and reading. She loves Ed Sheeran, *Stranger Things*, and chocolate lava cake. She loves playing guitar and ukulele, softball, waterskiing, and snow skiing. She loves where she lives, in the countryside of the Pocono Mountains.

Riley also loves to hunt. Her dad taught her when she was 10. Over the past three years, she has harvested two deer and one turkey. "It's pretty cool when you take home a deer or turkey that you worked hard to get," she says. "It makes me happy, and I know my dad's proud of me. When you see what you're hunting for and you're about to shoot, your adrenaline is just off the walls."

She had to take a hunter safety class before she could use a gun, which took many hours and taught her the dangers of guns and how to safely handle them. She and her father practice at a shooting range to improve their aim, and they lock their guns up when they're not using them. "We have a box where we put our guns, and then we lock it. Only my dad has the key," Riley says.

Riley doesn't want anyone to take her family's guns away or stop her from hunting. "My father and I use our guns for hunting or shooting at targets, and I feel like that's what most families in our area use them for." She believes people should be able to have guns in their homes for self-defense.

But Riley is also worried about the rise of gun violence in America: "I feel like gun violence is getting worse every year because people aren't doing enough to stop it. They're not taking the precautions that should be taken. There is a lot more the government could do to make more laws around it."

She believes in many commonsense gun regulations, like stronger background checks. She explains, "When you buy a gun, they should ask more about your background to see if you have a violent background or if you have a mental disability. With background checks, they should be 100 percent confident when they let someone buy a gun that that person won't use it to harm others in any way."

Riley supports safe storage laws (see chapter 7): "I think it's good to lock your guns up, so kids can't get ahold of them." And she believes that student activism around gun violence is a positive development for America. "It's good that students are stepping up and protesting and trying to make a difference."

Riley wants student activists to remember young hunters when they are working on new gun laws:

"WE CAN AGREE ON KNOWING THE DANGERS OF GUNS BUT ALSO THE GOOD THINGS THEY CAN BE USED FOR. MOST GUN OWNERS ARE USING GUNS FOR FUN, NOT TO HARM OTHERS."

Learn more about how gun owners can get involved in gun safety at momsdemandaction.org, responsibleownership.org, and @theorangegen.

CHAPTER 6

THE SECOND AMENDMENT: WTF IS THAT ALL ABOUT?

America has more guns than any other country in the world because we have a guarantee in our country's founding document, the Constitution, that is unique. That guarantee, laid out in the Second Amendment, is just twenty-seven words long:

> A well regulated Militia, being necessary to the security of a free State, the right of the people to keep and bear Arms, shall not be infringed.[1]

Just twenty-seven words in our Constitution that many would argue are the reason our nation is swimming in guns, our kids and schools terrorized. Some say it's not the NRA blocking change—it's the Second Amendment.

What does the Second Amendment even mean?

Why does it have so much power?

Why can't we change it or get rid of it?

Good questions.

What Did the Founding Fathers Mean by It?

Let's start with what the creators of the Constitution had in mind when they wrote it. It was just after the Revolutionary War, when the colonies fought for independence from England. Groups of armed citizen militias joined up with the undermanned Continental Army to help fight off the British Empire, a superior force. The writers of the Constitution wanted to make sure Americans could do the same again if another tyrannical force invaded.

Would the Founding Fathers consider today's private gun owners to be part of a citizen militia? Would they agree with America's unmatched lack of restrictions on guns? Probably not. During the time when the Founding Fathers wrote the Second Amendment, there actually were restrictions on where and how guns could be used. In Boston, you weren't allowed to keep a loaded gun in your home because they tended to explode and could set your house on fire. In 1824, the board of the University of Virginia banned guns on campus. Two members of that "gun control" board: James Madison, who wrote the Second Amendment, and Thomas Jefferson, who wrote the Declaration of Independence.[2]

So, it seems that the Founding Fathers were well aware that some gun safety measures were necessary to keep Americans safe.

Our Interpretation Only Recently Expanded to Include Personal Gun Use

Another interesting fact about the Second Amendment that the NRA doesn't highlight:

THE SUPREME COURT DIDN'T RULE THAT THE SECOND AMENDMENT REFERRED TO AN INDIVIDUAL'S RIGHT TO GUN OWNERSHIP UNTiL 2008.

In a 2008 Supreme Court case, *District of Columbia v. Heller*, the court narrowly voted to interpret the Second Amendment as referring to an individual's right to have a firearm in the home for personal reasons, like self-defense. Before this case, most courts considered Second Amendment protections limited to guns that would be used for military/militia purposes only. The ruling was the result of decades of political efforts by the NRA to change how we read the Second Amendment. And it worked. But even in that ruling, conservative Justice Antonin Scalia wrote that this right was not "unlimited" and that there would be no constitutional problem with banning "dangerous and unusual" firearms.[3]

What Do People Think It Means Today?

Now let's talk about how people interpret those twenty-seven words today. It's tricky. The Second Amendment is one vague piece of writing. For example, what does "a well regulated Militia" mean? The dictionary defines *militia* as "a military force that is raised from the civil population to supplement a regular army in an emergency."[4] That sounds an awful lot like the National Guard, right? Which we already have.

We should also keep in mind that when the Founding Fathers wrote the Constitution, their militias were armed with muskets, rifles, and pistols at best (pitchforks at worst). To fire a musket, the most popular weapon of the American Revolution, a soldier had to:

Open the cartridge box.

Grab a cartridge.

Bite off the end to expose the gunpowder.

Pour some gunpowder into the pan of the lock.

Close the pan.

Drop the cartridge into the barrel.

Remove the rammer.

Ram the cartridge down into the barrel.

Return the rammer.

Cock the lock.

Point the gun.

Aim.

Fire.

A speedy loader could fire maybe four shots per minute, if he was lucky. Rifles and pistols took even longer, firing just once or twice per minute.[5] Not to mention how inaccurate these guns were at hitting their targets.

By contrast, in 2018 the Las Vegas concert shooter was able to legally add a bump stock to his AR-15, turning it into a machine gun capable of firing 540 bullets per minute. In ten terrifying minutes, he was able to kill fifty-eight people and wound five hundred more.[6] It is highly unlikely that this is the kind of people's militia our Founding Fathers had in mind.

But the NRA leans more on the part of the amendment that reads, "the right of the people to keep and bear Arms shall not be infringed." "The people" is much broader than "militia." To the NRA, that means every American should have access to any kind of gun they want anytime, anywhere. No questions asked. No government regulation. Nothing.[7]

There are certainly multiple ways the Second Amendment can be interpreted. And yet the NRA interpretation is definitely the one America's lawmakers are currently following.

So, what do we do about this unclear, ambiguous, outdated amendment that has brought our country so much violence and heartbreak? There are two options to consider: throw it out or revise it.

Can We Repeal the Second Amendment?

Technically, yes. There is a way. But it's not easy. The Founding Fathers made it possible to change the Constitution, but they didn't make it easy. Changing the Constitution by deleting or repealing an amendment takes another amendment. So, if we want to repeal the Second Amendment, the Constitution says another amendment must be proposed by two-thirds of the Congress or by two-thirds of the state legislatures. The states are then in charge of approving the new amendment. Three-quarters of the states would need to vote for an amendment repealing the Second Amendment in order for it to happen.[8]

Given the gridlock in Congress and the popularity of guns in so many states, it doesn't seem likely that thirty-eight states or more would vote for it.

In the more than two hundred years that the Constitution has existed, there have been 11,699 amendment changes proposed in Congress. Only one amendment has ever been repealed. That was the Eighteenth Amendment, which banned alcohol in 1920.[9] Prohibition lasted thirteen years before Americans rose up and hollered, "Give us back our liquor, dammit!" and repealed the amendment.

It hasn't happened since.

Can We Change the Second Amendment?

Repealing the Second Amendment would be tough—but what about revising it? Revision might be an easier path. Dartmouth Professor James Heffernan recently proposed changing the Second Amendment just a teeny-weeny bit. He has advocated adding just five words:

> A well regulated Militia, being necessary to the security of a free State, the right of the people to keep and bear Arms, shall not be infringed except to ensure public safety.

Heffernan has argued that these five words would give state and federal governments an easier path to regulate guns and gun owners. They wouldn't have to battle the Second Amendment every time. These words would mean that an individual's right to bear arms doesn't trump the government's right to protect us from gun violence.[10]

This compromise would allow the NRA and pro-gun activists to keep the Second Amendment. Gun safety advocates wouldn't have to get a supermajority of Congress or the state legislatures to agree to throw it out entirely. And it could make passing gun safety legislation faster and easier.

A Final Word

Repealing or changing the Second Amendment wouldn't be easy. But is it possible? Sure it is. In 2008, we changed our interpretation of what those twenty-seven words mean, based on pressure by the NRA. That means we can change our interpretation again. Giving guns to criminals just has to become as unpopular as banning alcohol was in the 1920s. If some whiskey-smuggling bootleggers can change the Constitution, so can you!

NEVER FORGET: CHRISTCHURCH MOSQUE SHOOTINGS

When: March 15, 2019

How many died: 51

What happened? A white supremacist, using semiautomatic weapons, attacked two mosques in Christchurch, New Zealand, during popular Friday prayer ceremonies. The shooter killed 51 people in the deadliest attack in New Zealand history. Their government, however, did not respond with only thoughts and prayers. Within days they wrote new laws banning every weapon used in the shooting—semiautomatic assault rifles and high capacity magazines—which their parliament passed in a landslide vote, 119 to 1. They quickly launched a buy-back program for tens of thousands of newly illegal guns.[11]

STUDENTS TAKING A STAND

MARCEL MCCLINTON, AGE 16, GUN VIOLENCE SURVIVOR AND FOUNDER OF ORANGE GENERATION

Sixteen-year-old Marcel McClinton is a Texan who lives in a gun-owning home, but he is also a black gun violence prevention activist. "I am pro Second Amendment, anti people getting killed senselessly," he explains.[1]

Marcel grew up with guns in one of the most pro-gun states in the country. He did an internship with the Republican Party for two years. But his feelings about guns changed after he survived a mass shooting in 2016 when he was 14 years old. The gunman opened fire outside Marcel's Houston church, where Marcel was teaching Sunday school, killing one person and injuring six. For weeks after the shooting, Marcel had migraines and couldn't sleep. He had to listen to airplane noise just to calm himself down.[2]

After the shooting, he was angry. "I wasn't even mad at the shooter. I was just mad at society. But I didn't get involved in gun reform activism then. I didn't make any noise. I was just mad internally."[3]

As years passed and Marcel watched more and more shootings on the news, his anger grew. Then in 2018 there was another school shooting near him, just thirty miles from his house. In Santa Fe, Texas, a high school student killed ten kids and teachers with his father's legally purchased guns—guns that were not locked up. It got

Marcel thinking about the guns in his own home and how safety-conscious his father was. He explains, "My dad owns four guns. He locks them up. I don't know the code. He knows the code."[4]

Why weren't all gun owners like that? Why didn't the government require them to be?

Marcel started making some noise.

In 2018 he helped organize Houston's March for Our Lives, the largest student-led protest in Texas history.[5] A few months later he co-led a "die-in" in Washington, DC, where students rallied in front of the Capitol building, then lay on the ground for twelve minutes to symbolize the lives lost to gun violence and the government's failure to pass tighter gun restrictions. There were similar die-ins at state capitols all across the country. There was even a die-in in front of Trump's Mar-A-Lago Resort in Florida.[6]

After Marcel and his fellow students played dead for twelve minutes, they marched into the offices of conservative, NRA-backed Texas Republican Senator Ted Cruz and Kentucky Republican Mitch McConnell, chanting and demanding a meeting. The senators refused to meet with them, instead sending their staffers to deal with the angry teens. "They seemed scared of the fact that these students were in their conference rooms, not leaving," Marcel says. "They knew that we were demanding change and demanding discussion."[7]

What kind of change is Marcel demanding? He believes that changing gun policy is the only solution to gun violence and that making stricter gun laws can and will save lives. Along with other Houston teens, he created a gun violence prevention group called Orange Generation (OG), whose mission reads:

The OG is aimed at reducing gun violence, enacting and introducing commonsense gun legislation, and beginning a civil, constructive dialogue regarding gun reform. This includes mandatory gun lockers/trigger locks, mental health reform, and CDC research into the epidemic of gun violence. We also plan to provide rehabilitation services such as counselors and PTSD clinics for recovering survivors, as well as providing financial support to families of people injured in mass shootings. OG supports the Second Amendment and believes in Americans' right to bear arms.[8]

Marcel understands NRA members and is excited to talk to them—the OG's beef is with NRA's leaders, not its members. He knows a lot of NRA members agree with what he's proposing. "A lot of people do agree with what we're saying; it just takes a sit-down discussion," Marcel says. "It's not a political issue. It's a human one. The older generations just don't understand. They're not listening to young people. So we're going to change it."[9] Marcel's advice to young activists:

THERE'S NO EXCUSE FOR YOU TO NOT BE INVOLVED. IF YOU WON'T USE YOUR VOICE AND IF YOU WON'T VOTE, YOU'RE PART OF THE PROBLEM. PERIOD.[10]

◎ ◎ ◎

Learn more about what Marcel is working on and follow him on @MarcelMcClinton and @theorangegen.

CHAPTER 7
THE NRA:
Its Path to the
Dark Side

This battle we are engaged in—over the hearts and minds of America, over the safety and well-being of our citizens, over the light versus the dark side of the Force (be forewarned, there are some *Star Wars* references in this chapter)—this battle has a bad guy.

The National Rifle Association.

But much like Darth Vader, there is more to this villain than meets the eye. The NRA didn't start out bad. It wasn't always about increasing gun company profits and fighting for the proliferation of military-grade weapons.

Nope, the NRA began with a simple and decent mission: teach soldiers how to shoot better.

The NRA's Origin Story

The NRA was founded in 1871, just after the Civil War, by two former Union soldiers. During the war, Colonel William C. Church and General George Wingate were appalled by what terrible shots their fellow soldiers were. It was estimated that for every one bullet that hit a Confederate soldier, Union soldiers shot one thousand bullets.[2] That's a lot of wasted ammo.

And so, the NRA was born. Church and Wingate's goal was to teach Americans how to shoot better and more safely, either for the next war or for hunting and recreational shooting. This is still part of what the NRA does—the organization runs firearm-training classes all over the country.

For nearly one hundred years, the NRA was all about promoting safe and proper gun use, often in cooperation with the government. The US Army donated extra equipment to the NRA. The state of

AMERICA'S SAFEST TIME OF YEAR

According to a 2018 study conducted by Harvard Medical School, gun injuries in America drop 20% during annual NRA conventions, which are attended by more than eighty thousand gun owners.[1]

s the NRA Get the Big Bucks?

RA's pockets are filled by gun manufacturers. Guns
in America. Makers of guns and ammo earned $13.3
while the stores that sell them earned $85 billion!
with a capital B, people! (That's more than Costa
oss domestic product, the measure of the country's
)[12] Since 2005, gun manufacturers have donated up
n dollars to the NRA each year. And the NRA
t of its money ($20.9 million) from selling ads in its
s—again, to gun manufacturers. And many of the
te partners" (aka gun and gun accessory companies)
of each sale back to the NRA. Top NRA donors
ton (maker of the Bushmaster assault rifle used in
Elementary School massacre), Smith & Wesson,
er. All of this corporate sponsorship adds up to the
's money.[13]

A is a virtual subsidiary of the gun industry," said
executive director of the Violence Policy Center.
portrays itself as protecting the 'freedom' of indi-
s, it's actually working to protect the freedom of
o manufacture and sell virtually any weapon or

Influences Politicians

w who is funding the NRA, let's look at what
doing with all that gun money. The NRA spent
bying in 2016 and $4.1 million in 2017. That's
k of change, but it's small beans compared to
ps like the Dairy Association and the National
ors.[15]

New York helped the NRA buy its first shooting range. The NRA and the government were buds.[3]

But even back then, guns had a dark side. Although guns were commonplace in early America, when the NRA started, they were already controversial. The controversy started when President Lincoln was shot and killed in 1865. In quick succession, three more presidents were shot—James Garfield in 1881, William McKinley in 1901, and Theodore Roosevelt in 1912. Only Roosevelt survived. Even back then, Americans thought adding some restrictions on guns would be a good idea.

Believe it or not, the NRA wasn't always opposed to gun restrictions. In fact, back in the day, the NRA actually supported commonsense gun safety and worked with the government to make laws to protect the safety of all Americans. The NRA of the past worked to limit access to guns by ex-convicts and people with severe mental illness. Its leaders supported permits for concealed weapons.[4]

In the aftermath of a wave of gun violence during Prohibition, the NRA supported and enforced the National Firearms Act of 1934 and the Gun Control Act of 1938, which regulated guns, banned some buyers, and made gun dealers register with the government. They worked to add more gun regulation again after the assassinations of President John F. Kennedy, Martin Luther King Jr., and Senator Robert Kennedy, supporting and enforcing a 1968 gun bill.[5]

Doesn't sound much like the NRA of today, does it? So, what happened?

There was a coup in the NRA.

The Takeover That Led to the Dark Side

Just like when Anakin got brainwashed by Emperor Palpatine and killed all those adorable Padawans, the NRA got turned to the Dark Side by nefarious forces within its own ranks. Here's how it went down. The 1960s, when all those American leaders got assassinated, was a time of social unrest and upheaval. Activists were protesting and even rioting. Hippies were roaming the streets. The civil rights and women's rights movements were in full swing.

Much like today, some people panicked and thought more guns were the answer. The majority of NRA leadership wanted to stay out of politics and stick to teaching marksmanship and gun safety, as they always had. But a smaller faction of members thought the NRA should shift their focus to crime and personal safety as their core issues.

In 1971, there was a turning point. Federal agents killed an NRA member who was hiding a bunch of illegal weapons. Hard-liners within the NRA went ballistic and created a lobbying group to advocate for NRA issues.[6] Harlon Carter of Texas ran the new NRA lobby. He believed, "You don't stop crime by attacking guns; you stop crime by stopping criminals."[7] Sound familiar? Carter was

a bit much for the more mo
to decrease his powers. Cart
up his power.

At the 1977 NRA conv
other hard-liners kicked ou
took over. Their new miss
gun violence prevention ad

For the past forty years,
Decades after the coup, th
"Your support will help
doms whenever and whe
on, the NRA's focus shif

Who Controls the

Today's NRA still trai
thanks to Harlon Cart
organization's attentio

According to its w
million members[9] (in
the main lobbying g
same membership nu
year and gets you a c
magazine. You also
and free admission

Whereas the old
bership dues and cl
from corporate inf
money from other

So, who is giv
is funding all thi
whispering in the

Where Doe

Mostly, the N
are big business
billion in 2017
That's billions
Rica's entire g
entire economy
to $52.6 millio
makes 10 percer
NRA magazine
NRA's "corpora
donate a portion
include Remin
the Sandy Hook
Beretta, and Rug
bulk of the NRA

"Today's NRA
Josh Sugarmann,
"While the NRA
vidual gun owner
the gun industry
accessory."[14]

How the NRA

Now that we kno
the organization is
$3.1 million on lob
a pretty good chur
other lobbying grou
Association of Real

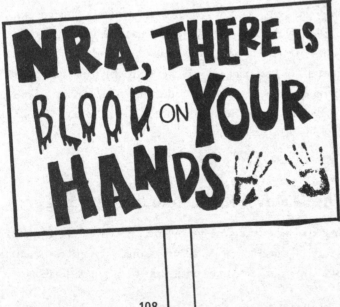

Don't be fooled—that's not *all* the money the NRA is spending to influence politics. Thanks to the US Supreme Court's ruling on the Citizens United case (where they decided that corporations are people too!), there is now no limit on how much the NRA can spend for or against individual candidates in an election. So that's where they're spending the big bucks.

CITIZENS UNITED V. FEDERAL ELECTION COMMISSION

In 2010, this case went before the Supreme Court, which ruled that political spending is a form of protected speech under the First Amendment, and therefore the government may not keep corporations or unions from spending money to support or denounce individual candidates in elections.[16] This ruling opened the floodgates for companies and other interest groups to spend unlimited amounts of money to influence politics. Including the NRA and gun companies.

In 2016, the NRA gave $21 million dollars to Trump's presidential campaign through these "independent expenditures"—the most they've ever given to any presidential candidate in history. This money paid for some very expensive attack ads against Hillary Clinton. And they worked. "You have a true friend and champion in the White House" was Trump's thank-you in a postelection speech to the NRA.[17]

That same year, the NRA also spent $14.4 million supporting forty-four candidates who won and $34.4 million opposing nineteen candidates who lost.[18] Of course, they opposed candidates who were for gun safety and supported candidates who were against it—senators, representatives, governors, and so on, from the president on down the line. Every candidate the NRA donates to who wins, owes them. That's how the NRA buys its political influence.

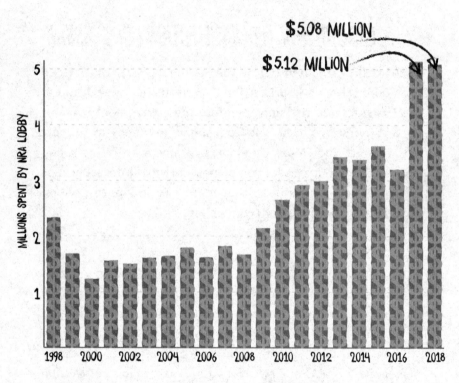

ANNUAL LOBBYING MONEY SPENT BY NRA

Source: "National Rifle Association," Center for Responsive Politics, accessed February 9, 2019, https://www.opensecrets.org/lobby/clientsum.php?id=d000000082.

To find out if your senator, representative, governor, or other elected official took money from the NRA, go to: opensecrets.org/orgs/recips.php?id=d000000082.

GUN RIGHTS SUPPORTERS THREATEN LAWMAKERS AND ACTIVISTS

It's not just the young activists profiled in this book who endure threats from gun rights supporters. Activists working for gun violence prevention and lawmakers do as well. "We are bullied and followed by folks practicing open carry on a regular basis," said Miranda Viscoli, copresident of New Mexicans to Prevent Gun Violence. "Democracy should not be defined by who carries the biggest gun into committee hearing rooms."[19]

Yet the people who work to uphold our democracy every day are some of the most threatened. When state legislators vote on gun bills, it is common to see gun rights supporters on the steps of the capitol or even inside the building where the testimony or voting happens, with their weapons in plain view. It is concerning to lawmakers, to say the least.

The intimidation got so bad in New Mexico that in 2019 lawmakers made it illegal for anyone but police officers and people with concealed-carry licenses to have a gun in the state capitol. "It's very intimidating with guns being openly carried," said New Mexico Senate Majority Leader Peter Wirth, from the Democratic Party. New Mexico State Senator Bill Sharer, from the Republican Party, went further, stating, "When someone's in the back of the [committee] room waving a gun around, I want to say, 'You're not helping, jackass.'"[20]

On top of those very visible threats, lawmakers working for gun violence prevention are flooded with threatening emails and phone calls. In 2013, when New York Congresswoman Carolyn Maloney (Democrat) introduced a gun violence prevention bill, she got three death threats in one day. "They said they were going to kill me," she remembered. So, she canceled her dinner plans that night. "I couldn't go. Who knows what could happen? I think any member of Congress would be scared after what happened to my good friend Gabby Giffords."[21] Representative Gabrielle Giffords (a Democrat from Arizona) was shot during a meeting with her constituents in 2011.

After Colorado State Representative Rhonda Fields (Democrat) sponsored a bill reforming gun policies in her state, she received a letter that read, "There will be blood," and saying they hoped someone would "Giffords" her. The writer was arrested for the harassment.[22]

In Santa Clara, California, a man was charged with threatening to kill State Senator Leland Yee (Democrat) after he proposed legislation that would limit the rapid reloading of assault weapons. Police discovered twenty-six guns and thousands of bullets in the man's home.[23]

The NRA Is the Squeakiest Wheel

As much as the NRA spends to influence America's politicians, its real power comes from something besides cold, hard cash. "The NRA is not successful because of its money. The NRA has money that it uses to help its favored candidates get elected. But the real source of its power . . . comes from voters,"[24] said Adam Winkler, author of *Gunfight: The Battle Over the Right to Bear Arms in America.*

Yep, the NRA's Force lightning comes not from its money but from using its supporters to influence races.

While their member numbers aren't huge (five million), the NRA gets its people fired up. The leaders can and do inspire their supporters to get out and vote for pro-gun candidates and against any candidate who voices support for gun violence prevention.

Robert Spitzer, author of five books about guns, has described the NRA's technique this way:

They have a very powerful ability to mobilize grassroots support and to engage in politics when most Americans can barely be bothered to vote. I mean more than voting. I mean going to a meeting, writing a letter, contacting a friend. And because so few Americans do those things, if you get a bunch of people in a locality who are all prepared to go out to a meeting, they can have a big effect. Elected officials feel the impact of constituents when they hear their voices. Politics is often about the squeaky wheel—who makes the loudest noise, who gets the most attention.[25]

A Final Word

NRA supporters are very squeaky wheels. So they get outsized attention from politicians, despite their smaller numbers. If a politician votes for a gun safety measure, she knows she's going to have thousands of angry voice mails waiting for her the next day. And probably some very angry gun owners sitting outside her office.

Gun money is a factor in the success of the NRA's agenda, for sure, but the real reason the NRA and gun companies control our country right now is that their supporters make more noise than gun sense supporters. If we want to succeed in changing our country's gun laws, we need to learn from the NRA and their supporters. We need to make more noise than they do and get more active. See part 4 to find out how!

GET SQUEAKY!

Here's an Everytown website where you can find out if your member of Congress has been accepting NRA money. If they have been, this website, https://every.tw/2Syh8Bj, tells you how to contact them and tell them: "Enough is enough!" Get squeaky, just like the NRA.

GUN OWNERS TAKING A STAND

PAUL KEMP, COFOUNDER OF GUN OWNERS FOR RESPONSIBLE OWNERSHIP[1]

Paul Kemp was born and raised in Michigan, a state where hunting was and is a popular sport. "Growing up there," he says, "opening day of deer season was a big deal. We would go hunting for rabbit, deer, pheasant, duck, and all that." Paul hunted with the men in his family. "It was an important rite of passage," he explains. "Gun safety was a big deal for my grandfather, as it was with all my uncles and my stepdad. I learned that guns should be stored locked up and unloaded at home. That's how I was brought up."

As an adult, Paul moved to Oregon and married a woman who also grew up hunting, and they started a family together. When his son was old enough, Paul took him hunting and set up a target range on their property, where they could practice shooting. And he passed on his grandfather's lessons about gun safety to his own children.

One tragic event showed Paul that he needed to share his beliefs about gun safety with others beyond his own family.

In 2012, his brother-in-law, Steve Forsyth, was killed in a shooting at Clackamas Town Center. The shooter entered the mall at 3:28 p.m. and within two minutes, he fired off seventeen bullets, killing Steve Forsyth and Cindy Yuille (see profile on Hunter Yuille) and seriously wounding 15-year-old Kristina Shevchenko. He had 145 bullets in five thirty-round magazines on him, and there were nearly ten thousand people in the mall that afternoon. Luckily, after firing those first shots, his gun jammed. He ran into a stairway and shot himself.[2]

Paul had planned to visit Steve at the mall that evening. After receiving a frantic call from his sister, Paul left work to meet her and his niece outside the mall. They could not reach Steve on his cell phone. Paul was with his sister and niece when they got the terrible news about their husband and father. Talking about that day still brings Paul to tears, nearly seven years later.

Police later discovered the shooter had stolen the weapon he used, a Stag-15 semiautomatic rifle, from a friend's apartment the day of the shooting. That friend had purchased the rifle legally, then left it out, unlocked and loaded. He noticed the gun and his friend (the shooter) were both missing before he went to work, but he did not call police to tell them about the theft. The gun owner did not call police until the mass shooting was already national news.[3]

When Paul learned about this gun that had killed his brother-in-law, he was angry. "Doesn't Oregon have a safe storage law?" he asked police officers. He was surprised to hear the answer was no.

WHAT ARE SAFE STORAGE LAWS?

Safe storage laws promote responsible gun ownership by requiring gun owners to store their guns out of the reach of others, such as children or others prohibited from using guns. These laws help prevent tragedies—like unintentional shootings, suicide, and mass shootings—by ensuring guns are used only by their rightful owners. Only eleven states have laws about how to store guns safely. Massachusetts is the only state that requires all guns be locked when stored.[4]

Just three days after the Clackamas Town Center shooting, Sandy Hook happened—six adults and twenty children were murdered. "I couldn't stay silent anymore," Paul said. "I had to speak up. It's all I could do for Steve." He and other gun owners formed a group called Gun Owners for Responsible Ownership (GOFRO). The advocacy group supports Americans' right to own guns but urges gun owners to store their weapons safely—specifically, to store firearms and ammunition locked and separate and to support universal background checks.

Here's the organization's mission:

We are gun owners, sportsmen, veterans, mothers and fathers, daughters and sons who seek reasonable and responsible solutions to preventing gun violence.

We envision an America where all are safe from gun violence and where responsible gun owners take the lead to promote safe gun ownership and sensible laws and regulations.

We believe our Second Amendment rights come with responsibilities.

We believe in commonsense efforts to reduce gun violence and promote gun safety including:

- Universal background checks to keep firearms out of the hands of dangerous people

- Safe and secure storage of firearms to prevent access by children or any unauthorized person[5]

DID YOU KNOW?

89% of unintentional gun deaths of children happen in the home. Most of these deaths occur when children are playing with a loaded gun while their parents are gone.[6]

Paul and his group are advocating for stronger gun safety laws in Oregon and nationwide. Although he has a full-time job, Paul devotes a lot of time to speaking at rallies, as well as lobbying lawmakers in Salem, Oregon's capital, and Washington, DC. He says, "There are groups on the right and groups on the left. We are a voice in the middle, for gun owners to speak up." Paul thinks groups like his are good alternatives to the NRA because they are true supporters of gun safety—not lobbyists for gun manufacturers.

Paul does this work to honor his brother-in-law, who he describes as "the most positive guy I've ever known." Steve was a husband, father, entrepreneur, youth sports coach, and beloved member of his community. If Oregon had had a safe storage gun law on the books in 2012, it's possible he would still be alive today.

Paul's advice to young activists:

"TALK TO YOUR LEGISLATOR. CALL. EMAIL. GO TO YOUR STATE CAPITOL."

◎ ◎ ◎

Learn more about what Paul is working on and get involved at responsibleownership.org.

CHAPTER 8

CHANGING LAWS: HOW THE NRA MESSES WITH THE RULES

Not only does the NRA influence politicians through financial contributions and threats to unleash its followers, but it also supports some frightening legislation. These NRA-sponsored laws are some of the biggest obstacles to gun reform.

The Dickey Amendment (or Why We Can't Study Gun Violence)

Every time there is a mass shooting, there is an outcry for gun safety measures. The NRA and other pro-gun activists counter, *Hey, there's no research proving gun regulation works to stop gun violence, so suck it.* And they're right. There is not much research on it. Why not? Because Congress made it nearly impossible for our government to research gun violence.

Even though gun violence is one of the top killers of young people,[1] is a plague in low-income communities, and kills more Americans than all kinds of things the government is able to research (like rabies or meningitis), scientists are not allowed to study or report on gun violence as a health issue.

Why is that?

If you guessed the NRA, you're right. Here's the story. Back in the 1990s, public health researchers did a bunch of studies on gun violence and found that having a gun in your house dramatically increased the risk of homicide and suicide (see chapter 4)—basically having a gun can be super dangerous for your health.[2]

Of course, the NRA didn't like those results and didn't want gun owners to hear that kind of bad PR, so its leadership put the squeeze on their buddies in Congress.

In 1996, Congress added a sneaky amendment to a spending bill. The Dickey Amendment, as it was called, made it illegal for the Centers for Disease Control and Prevention (aka the CDC—America's top health research organization) to use federal money to "advocate or promote gun control."[3] Is researching gun violence the same as advocating for gun control? The wording is about as vague as the Second Amendment's, but it did the job. The CDC, fearing its research funds would be cut off, stopped all research into gun violence. The amendment had a chilling effect on nongovernmental research into gun violence as well.[4]

Well done, NRA. Well done.

The Protection of Lawful Commerce in Arms Act (or Why We Can't Sue Gun Manufacturers or Sellers)

Another law the NRA pushed through Congress impacts our ability to hold gun manufacturers accountable for the dangerous products they make and sell. Nearly every American industry and product can be sued if their product causes harm to anyone. Take swings, for example. It used to be that every school playground had swing sets. Now it's nearly impossible to get a school to install this seemingly harmless play equipment. Why? Too many lawsuits. Parents whose children flew off and broke their arms could and did sue schools, swing set manufacturers, and anyone else they could get their hands on.

The result? No new swing sets on American playgrounds. Too risky for schools.

That seems kind of crazy, yet we don't hold gun manufacturers or sellers to the same standard. When children at Sandy Hook Elementary School were attacked by a shooter using three different guns, parents of the twenty 6- and 7-year-olds who were murdered were not able to sue the manufacturers of those guns—Bushmaster, Glock, and SIG Sauer—for creating such a deadly product. They couldn't sue the store where the shooter's mother bought the gun. They wanted to, but they couldn't.

Why the double standard?

Because in 2005, the NRA pushed for, and Congress passed, the Protection of Lawful Commerce in Arms Act. This law makes gunmakers and gun sellers immune from nearly all lawsuits.[5] Schools won't install new swing sets because they fear potential lawsuits, but the gun industry has no fear and, therefore, no motivation to change their practices.

Lawsuits are an important way we Americans protect ourselves from injury and death. At least with swing sets. But not with guns. To read the entire bill, go to govtrack.us/congress/bills/109/s397/text.

GUNS ARE LEGAL, BUT THESE ITEMS ARE BANNED IN THE US

We can't sue gunmakers or gun owners, so even though guns are deadly as can be, we are having a heck of a time getting even the smallest of protections passed. But thanks to lawsuits that aren't banned by Congress, Americans are safe from these terrifying items:

Kinder Surprise eggs: These chocolate eggs, popular and legal all around the world, are banned in the US because they have a toy inside the chocolate eggs and could pose a choking hazard for young kids.

UK books printed before 1985: These can't be sold in the US due to worries they might have lead in the ink.

Some cheeses: Cheese made from unpasteurized milk is illegal in America.

Bad breath: Yep, in Indiana it's illegal to go to a public event or use public transport if you've eaten garlic or onions within the past four hours.

High heels: In Carmel, California, you can't walk in heels that are taller than two inches or with less than a square inch of heel surface unless you have a special permit.

Haggis: This popular Scottish dish—made from sheep's heart, liver, lungs, and stomach—has been banned for more than twenty years in the US.

Hairy women: That's right, in New Mexico (which gets an F from Giffords Law Center on its gun laws), where you are not required to get a license to own or sell guns, it's illegal for women to appear unshaven in public. Whaaaaat?

Goatees: Sure, you may think goatees are ugly facial hair, but illegal? In Louisiana, you need permission from the state to sport one. And you have to pay a fee too!

Snowball fights: Believe it or not, these beloved winter battles are illegal in Aspen, Colorado, where snowballs are considered "missiles" that can't be fired at another person.[6]

NRA-Backed State Laws

These big NRA-backed laws impact us on a national level. But the NRA is also pushing forward smaller laws—laws to loosen gun regulation, laws to increase access to guns—in every state, all the time. Since the 2012 Sandy Hook shooting, nearly two-thirds of all state gun laws that have been passed were backed by the NRA and actually loosened gun restrictions, not the other way around. It's ironic (and scary) that after every mass shooting, there is a spike in laws that *loosen* gun restrictions, not tighten them.[7]

Here are a couple of state examples. Governors in Texas, Kansas, Idaho, Georgia, and Arkansas signed bills allowing people with a carrying concealed weapon (CCW) permit to bring guns onto college campuses (seven other states already allow that). North Dakota, Missouri, Maine, and West Virginia decided it's a good idea to let gun owners carry loaded firearms without any permit or training whatsoever.[8]

When Republicans took control of a majority of state governments and governors in 2010, the NRA gained allies and more power to change state laws in its favor. And the organization has been going for it. Their goal is to enact laws that allow people to carry guns in places they've never been able to carry them before: churches, bars, colleges, day care centers, government buildings. The NRA wants guns to become as normal an accessory as purses and backpacks.[9]

A Final Word

The NRA is sponsoring laws that increase the number of guns on our streets and loosen safety regulations all over the country, all the time.

What are they pushing for in your state? To find out, go to Giffords Law Center to Prevent Gun Violence's Annual Gun Law Scorecard: lawcenter.giffords.org/scorecard/.

STUDENTS TAKING A STAND

JAZMINE WILDCAT, AGE 15, GUN VIOLENCE PREVENTION ACTIVIST AND AMBASSADOR WITH THE CENTER FOR NATIVE AMERICAN YOUTH[1]

Fifteen-year-old Jazmine Wildcat has a lot on her plate for a girl her age. She is a percussionist in the Wyoming all-state marching band, a swimmer, a soccer player, a Science Olympiad member, and a Special Olympics coach. She is creative, too, and loves to make things with her hands: stained and fused glass, knit and crocheted pieces, and even balloon animals and duct-tape creations. She is also a member of the Northern Arapaho and serves as an ambassador with the Center for Native American Youth. Recently she has added a particularly challenging new task to her already full plate: advocating for gun violence prevention.

"Everyone I know has guns," she explains. "I come from a hunting family, and my family owns a lot of guns. Everyone at my school hunts too. It's a big part of their identity."

Jazmine used to live on Wyoming's Wind River Reservation, but now she and her family live in Riverton, a town just outside the reservation. Geography gives Jazmine a unique perspective on the dangers of guns—she has seen gun violence impact her own family, her tribal community, and the non-Native people of Riverton and Wyoming.

She knows firsthand that gun violence in Native communities is a unique problem. Native Americans have the highest suicide rate compared to all other groups in America. This is especially dangerous for young Native Americans (ages 15 to 24), who are three and a half times more likely to die by suicide than other young people.[2]

As you already know, guns make suicide much easier to accomplish. Jazmine has two uncles and a grandfather who served in the US military and suffer from post-traumatic stress disorder (PTSD). They also own guns. "My family had to take their firearms away because they threatened to take their lives," Jazmine says.

She also points out that domestic violence—a key area of gun violence prevention—is a big issue in Native communities. "Did you know that four out of five Native women will experience violence in their lifetime?" she asks. That's twice as high as it is for white women.[3]

Jazmine also worries about guns and police violence. "An overlooked fact is that Native Americans are killed in police shootings at a higher rate than any other minority group." She's right: from 1999 to 2015, police shot and killed more Native Americans than black Americans (2.9 out of one million versus 2.6 out of every million, respectively).[4]

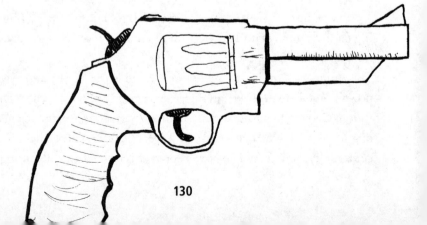

Jazmine has been writing letters and speaking out, urging Wyoming lawmakers to pass sensible gun laws that will protect Native people and non-Native people from violence. In 2018, after hearing about her activism, the Center for Native American Youth asked Jazmine to be their representative on gun reform. She was profiled with other young activists in *Teen Vogue* and participated in the March for Our Lives.

She says, "There were no marches in Wyoming. The closest one was in Denver, so I went there. It was really cool to see what we can do when we work together. To see how everyone was so accepting of our ideas. That was a big change of scenery for me."

Advocating for gun safety in Wyoming—a rural, conservative state—has been challenging for Jazmine. The state earned an F on the Giffords Law Center to Prevent Gun Violence's Annual Gun Law Scorecard for its weak gun laws (it is number forty-five out of fifty states) and high gun death rates (number eleven out of fifty). It also has the second-highest gun suicide rate in America. Wyoming has no gun regulations regarding background checks, domestic violence, or child access prevention. In Wyoming, you don't need a permit to carry a concealed weapon, there are no Red Flag Laws, and military-style weapons are legal. In 2017, they passed a law allowing K–12 school employees to carry hidden, loaded firearms into schools.[5]

Jazmine knows she is fighting an uphill battle: "Wyoming has one of the highest guns per capita in the nation. [People here] are quick to think that 'gun control' means taking guns away. But that's not what gun control is." She is advocating for commonsense gun laws in Wyoming: more background checks and safety training for gun owners, permits for carrying concealed weapons, and Red Flag Laws to remove guns from people who are a danger to themselves or others.

Jazmine is the only student at her school working for gun reform, and speaking out amid strong opposition has taken real courage.

No one really listens to me when I try to talk about stuff like this. I've gotten threats against me, even from students in my school. There probably are some other people like me around the state, but locally at my high school, there are just one or two others. I guess they're not as confident to speak out because it's so disheartening. Even my friends are scared to speak out. They don't want to be threatened as well.

But Jazmine isn't giving up. She plans to keep advocating for gun violence prevention, for her own family and community, and for the state of Wyoming. She'll be going off to college soon, where she plans to study politics and public policy. With any luck, we might see Jazmine run for office herself someday. She would make a great gun sense candidate! "I have my work cut out for me," she says. "We cannot just sit here and wait for the next violent event to happen."[6]

Her advice to students who live in communities with less support for gun violence prevention:

"STICK WITH IT. THINK ABOUT THE FUTURE AND THE CHANGE YOU WILL MAKE. STAY CONFIDENT IN YOURSELF, AND THINGS WILL GET BETTER."

◎ ◎ ◎

Learn more about what Jazmine is working on at cnay.org.

PART 3

THE SOLUTIONS

It is not conservative or liberal. It's about making sure children don't get harmed in school and we don't live in a country that has institutionalized fear. No child should have to learn how to hide from a shooter.

—LANE MURDOCK, ORGANIZER OF THE NATIONAL SCHOOL WALKOUT

CHAPTER 9

Reasons to Hope

Americans have been working on gun reform for decades. The Brady Campaign to Prevent Gun Violence, America's first major gun reform group, was founded in 1974. Decades have passed, thousands more Americans have been killed in gun violence, yet we now have more guns in America, not fewer. Our country is more dangerous, not less. It can feel like an uphill battle.

But things are finally shifting and there are changes to get excited about.

Gun Owners and Gun Sense Advocates Agree!

Americans are actually very united on wanting gun reform. Surprisingly so. It is politicians who are taking money from the NRA or are afraid of gun rights supporters who are standing in the way.

AGREEMENT BETWEEN AMERICANS WHO OWN GUNS AND THOSE WHO DON'T

AGREE WITH THE FOLLOWING

	🔫	🚫🔫
BAN ON GUN SALES TO PEOPLE WITH MENTAL ILLNESS	89%	89%
REQUIRE UNIVERSAL BACKGROUND CHECKS FOR GUN PURCHASES	85%	89%
REQUIRE BACKGROUND CHECKS FOR PRIVATE AND GUN SHOW SALES	77%	87%
REQUIRE MORE SAFETY TRAINING FOR CONCEALED CARRY PERMIT HOLDERS	83%	85%
BAN ON GUN SALES TO PEOPLE ON NO-FLY OR WATCH LISTS	82%	84%
BAN ON GUN SALES TO PEOPLE WITH DOMESTIC VIOLENCE RESTRAINING ORDERS	77%	82%
PASS RED FLAG LAWS	75%	80%
CREATE FEDERAL DATABASE TO TRACK GUN SALES	54%	80%
BAN ON ASSAULT-STYLE WEAPONS	48%	77%
BAN ON HIGH-CAPACITY MAGAZINES	44%	74%

Source: Ruth Igielnik and Anna Brown, "Key Takeaways on Americans' View of Guns and Gun Ownership," Pew Research Center, June 22, 2017, http://www.pewresearch.org/fact-tank/2017/06/22/key-takeaways-on-americans-views-of-guns-and-gun-ownership/; Colleen L. Barry, Daniel Webster, et al, "Public Support for Gun Violence Prevention Policies Among Gun Owners and Non-Gun Owners in 2017," *American Journal of Public Health*, June 6, 2018, https://ajph.aphapublications.org/doi/10.2105/AJPH.2018.304432.

Even the majority of NRA members believe that some reform is needed:

69% OF NRA MEMBERS SUPPORT COMPREHENSIVE BACKGROUND CHECKS FOR ALL GUN SALES.[1]

There's a lot of agreement about gun safety between people who own guns and those who don't. It's time we start working together.

You, the Young People, Will Change Our Country!

While many of us picture grown-ups when we think about societal change and revolution—John Kennedy, Martin Luther King Jr., Nelson Mandela—historians know it's actually you, young people, who initiate and fight for big changes in our world.

Sasha Costanza-Chock, an associate professor at MIT, argued in her paper "You and Social Movements: Key Lessons for Allies" that "whenever we have had a movement with widespread mobilization through history, young people are at the forefront."[2]

Here are some young activists who launched national movements:

Dora Thewlis, a 16-year-old suffragette, got arrested in a protest and helped turn the tide in the battle for women's right to vote.

Claudette Colvin was 15 when she refused to sit at the back of the bus in Montgomery, Alabama, inspiring Rosa Parks (who did the same nine months later) and helping launch the civil rights movement.

Malala Yousafzai was 13 when she began speaking out against the Taliban's oppression of girls. She was shot in the face for her troubles, which only spurred her to greater action fighting for the rights of girls and women.

Students from Marjory Stoneman Douglas High School ratcheted up gun violence protests to levels never seen before after the Parkland shooting. And they're not quitting anytime soon.

Those taking action and demanding change have always been and continue to be young people. In the gun violence battle, you have young leaders in place already—just check out all the profiles in this book. *You* will get rid of those in power who continue to block change. History is on your side.

TWO-THIRDS OF AMERICANS UNDER AGE 30 SUPPORT STRONGER GUN LAWS.[3]

Thoughts & prayers Don't STOP BULLETS

The Tide *Is* Turning

Things are finally changing, thanks to young people getting involved. After the Parkland shooting in February 2018, the public outcry from students at Marjory Stoneman Douglas High School, and the media attention, gun safety groups saw a surge in donations and volunteers far beyond anything they'd seen after past shootings.

- Moms Demand Action (the largest national grassroots group) had seventy-five thousand new volunteers attend a meeting or volunteer in a substantial way (beyond signing up).

- The Brady Campaign had a large increase in donations and enough new members sign up to start three new chapters.

- More than 450,000 people signed a "Vote for Courage" pledge by the Giffords Courage to Fight Gun Violence group (started by former Congresswoman Gabby Giffords after she was shot in a mass shooting), promising to vote for gun sense candidates in upcoming national and local elections.

- Giffords Law Center to Prevent Gun Violence also saw an uptick in donations: 43,000 people donated $1.2 million (average donation $27).[4]

Important Allies Join the Gun Safety Cause: Police and Doctors

Another development that should cheer everyone working for gun violence prevention is that police and doctors are stepping into the spotlight and demanding change. These two groups are well respected and powerful advocates.

POLICE CHANGE THEIR TUNE, URGE GUN REFORM

The gun violence prevention movement has a powerful new ally: America's police force. Nobody knows more about the problem of gun violence—police are the first responders to America's epidemic of suicides, murders, domestic violence, and school and mass shootings; they put their lives on the line every day facing an armed citizenry.

FROM 2006 TO 2015, **521 LAW ENFORCEMENT** OFFICERS WERE FATALLY SHOT IN THE US.

IN 2013, OVER 91% OF POLICE KILLED IN THE LINE OF DUTY WERE KILLED WITH GUNS.[5]

In the face of growing violence and mass shootings, police leaders are taking a stand on gun reform, joining the loud chorus of voices demanding that politicians strengthen our gun laws.

America's police force was split on the gun issue until recently. Jim Bueerman, a former police chief and president of the Police Foundation, a research and training group, explained the division:

Police officers are in many, many ways no different than everybody else. Depending on where they are in the country their perspectives might be in line with what the average person feels about gun control in their area.[6]

Like the rest of America, police chiefs and officers in larger cities tend to favor stricter gun laws, while sheriffs and officers in small towns and rural areas tend to lean the other way. Rural and urban police each make up about half of America's law enforcement, so it's been a pretty even split for decades.

But opinions in the law enforcement community have shifted since the Parkland shooting in 2018. Several national police organizations are now teaming up with gun violence prevention groups to demand action. The National Law Enforcement Partnership to Prevent Gun Violence represents police chiefs from major cities, as well as black, Hispanic, and female law enforcement executives. The Law Enforcement Coalition for Common Sense is another group of law enforcement officials from across the country. These two groups are publicly advocating for a host of gun law reforms, including:

- Require and improve background checks for all firearm purchasers.

- Limit high-capacity magazines to ten rounds.

- Ban new semiautomatic assault weapons.

- Oppose federal law that would make it legal for gun owners to carry concealed weapons into states that don't allow it.

- Oppose federal law that would make it easier to purchase silencers.

- Strengthen penalties for straw purchasing and firearms trafficking.[7]

While there are still differences of opinion within our national police community, leaders are taking a public stand to show their support for gun reform.

#THISISOURLANE: DOCTORS STAND UP TO THE NRA

Another group that experiences the fallout from gun violence daily is doctors. That group has also joined the gun violence prevention movement in a big way.

This issue is extremely personal for Dr. Joseph Sakran. In 1994, when he was 17 years old, he was shot in the throat after a high school football game. The bullet wasn't aimed at him—it was a stray fired into the crowd during a fight between other teenagers—but nonetheless, it punctured his trachea and severed his carotid artery. He nearly bled out and died in the ambulance. Luckily, trauma surgeons at the hospital managed to save his life. They also inspired him.[8]

He went to med school and trained with the same surgeons who had saved his life years before. "It was awe-inspiring to say the least," he said. "For me the most gratifying opportunity was to give some-one else the same second chance that those surgeons gave me."[9]

Dr. Sakran is now a trauma surgeon at Johns Hopkins Hospital in Baltimore, Maryland. For years he was a quiet activist, speaking to groups of students about his experience with gun violence and starting Docs Demand Action, a gun violence prevention group. But in October 2018 he stepped into the national spotlight by tak-ing on the NRA.

It happened when the American College of Physicians published a paper titled "Reducing Firearm Injuries and Deaths in the United States." The paper called gun violence a "public health crisis" and recommended immediate political action, including "a public health approach to firearms-related violence."[10] The NRA was not happy and responded on Twitter with some pointed comments: "Someone should tell self-important anti-gun doctors to stay in their lane," and, "Everyone has hobbies. Some doctors' collective hobby is opining on firearms policy."[11]

Instead of shaming doctors into silence, the NRA's tweets had the opposite effect. They opened the floodgates. Dr. Sakran launched a hashtag #ThisIsOurLane, that more than ten thousand doctors used to respond with photos of bloody scrubs and operating rooms and grim stories like these: [12]

"I am not anti-gun, I own firearms. I am anti–bullet hole," wrote Dr. Richard Sidwell, a trauma surgeon from Des Moines, Iowa.[13]

"When you work at a major trauma center, that means fixing blood vessels shredded by bullets. My lane is paved by the broken bodies left behind by your products," wrote Dr. Westley Ohman, a vascular surgeon in Saint Louis, Missouri.[14]

"Let me mention lifetimes in wheelchairs with SCI [spinal cord injury], useless arms from brachial plexus destruction, colostomies from belly destruction, and years of dependence with TBI [traumatic brain injury]," wrote Dr. Kathleen Bell, a rehab specialist at the University of Texas.[15]

"Do you have any idea how many bullets I pull out of corpses weekly? This isn't just my lane. It's my f**ing highway," wrote Dr. Judy Melinek, a forensic pathologist in Oakland, California.[16]

Dr. Sakran and his colleagues are urging these changes to our gun laws:

- Expand universal background checks.

- Require safe storage and education.

- Provide federal funding for research on gun violence so we can find data-driven solutions.[17]

Doctors know that in order to understand the scope of this public health crisis and find the best solutions, they must be able to research the problem, as they do for other deadly killers, such as car crashes, cancer, and tuberculosis. But the 1996 Dickey Amendment—which banned federal funding for gun violence research—makes that impossible (see chapter 10 for a full explanation of this amendment). "It's the most reprehensible piece of legislation ever written," said Dr. Cathleen London, a primary care doctor in rural Maine. "It's disgusting and needs to go away."[18]

In spite of the Twitter battle, doctors are not at war with the NRA. "People want to polarize this debate. But no one wants to take away the guns," said Dr. Sakran. "There's not one solution to this. Part of it is developing the right data and the right research in order to understand what solutions we need to implement."[19] Dr. Heather Sher, a radiologist in Fort Lauderdale, Florida, seconded that "it is not an 'us versus them' issue. What we are truly asking for is a coming together of both sides to find a solution to this national health problem." Following the Twitter battle, Dr. Sher drafted a letter inviting the NRA to join doctors in their efforts to decrease gun violence. Within two days, more than twenty-three thousand doctors had signed it. "It is in the NRA's best interest to help us be part of the solution," Sher said.[20]

Having so many police and doctors publicly join the side of gun reform is a powerful development. It is difficult for the NRA to demonize these groups that do so much good for our country. It is also good to know that the people who really see and experience the end results of gun violence—the true experts—agree that enacting commonsense gun laws is the best solution.

A Final Word

It should give you hope that most Americans agree on the need for commonsense gun reform, and that your generation is more united about this issue than any generation before you. More than two million Americans joined the 2018 student-led March for Our Lives protests, demanding change. That's a lot of Americans united toward a single goal. With the police and doctors on our side, nothing is impossible!

STUDENTS TAKING A STAND

THE PARKLAND SURVIVORS, FOUNDERS OF #NEVERAGAIN AND MARCH FOR OUR LIVES

CAMERON KASKY

For decades before the Parkland massacre, there would be a school shooting or a mass shooting nearly every month, followed by a few days of mourning when politicians would offer "thoughts and prayers," but no gun laws were passed. Then the media and the nation's attention would move on and nothing would change.

But in the days following the Parkland shooting—when seventeen high school students were murdered by a former student armed with an AR-15—something different happened. The Marjory Stoneman Douglas students essentially grabbed the microphones away from the adults and shouted out to America, "Hey, we are *done* with this!" Instead of disappearing into teary candlelight vigils, they got angry and made their voices heard.

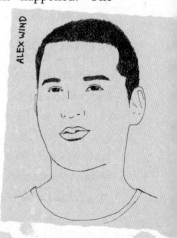

ALEX WIND

Parkland students took over the media spotlight, publicly condemning the NRA for its influence on politics and its role in the unending shootings and shaming America's leaders for their inaction on gun law reform.

Although most were not old enough to vote, a group of these students became the leaders of one of the most powerful gun reform movements in history.

Cameron Kasky, Alex Wind, and Jaclyn Corin

The day after the shooting, Cameron Kasky, Alex Wind, and Jaclyn Corin got together and launched #NeverAgain on Twitter.[1] Jaclyn also organized one hundred students to travel to Florida's capitol to

lobby the state legislature.[2] #NeverAgain evolved into a student-led political action committee and a national movement that fired up hundreds of thousands of students across the country. #NeverAgain led to annual protests, marches, and die-ins in every state, shining a much brighter light on our country's gun problem.

Emma Gonzalez

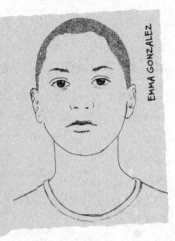

Three days after the shooting, Emma Gonzalez gave an eleven-minute speech at a Florida gun violence rally. Her tearful, angry, unflinching words voiced the frustration and rage of her generation (which the Parkland group has dubbed "the mass shooting generation").[3] With that speech, Emma became the face and voice of the student movement. Before the shooting, Emma didn't have a Twitter account. After her speech, she had more followers than the NRA.[4] When a candidate running for the House of Representatives in Maine called her a "skinhead lesbian," the backlash was so furious he had to drop out of the race.

David Hogg

Before the shooting, David Hogg was a student journalist. As the shooter roamed his school killing his classmates, David crouched in a locked room with other students and filmed the terrifying experience. He left the building alive and immediately went on the offensive, publicly attacking politicians who accept money from the NRA and others who won't take action on gun violence. Days after the shooting, someone posted a video on YouTube claiming David was an actor paid by left-wing activists trying to get rid of the Second

SURVIVOR PTSD AND SUICIDES

nother heart-breaking challenge for gun violence survivors
the post-traumatic stress disorder (PTSD), depression, and
uicide risk they struggle with after the shootings. Survivors
ften feel responsible for the deaths or believe they could have
one more to stop the shooting. Years after the shootings at
andy Hook and Columbine, several family members of victims
ied by suicide; and two students who survived the Parkland
assacre took their own lives within a year of the tragedy.
 2017 research review found that survivors and community
embers impacted by gun violence showed increased signs
f PTSD and depression, two prime risk factors for suicide.
he closer a person was to the shooting (a survivor or family
ember), the greater the risk for long-term mental health
roblems. Sadly, even those who *survive* gun violence are
traumatized, their invisible scars lasting a lifetime.[16]

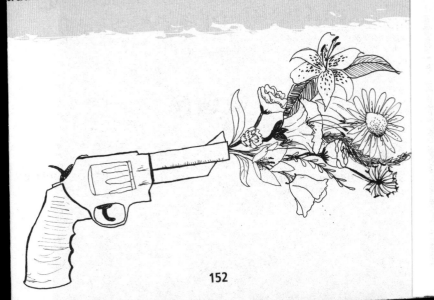

Amendment.[6] David isn't letting the haters slow him down, and he isn't going to wait for adults to change gun laws—he plans to run for a Senate seat when he turns 25, the minimum age to run. "I want to be at least part of the change in Congress," he says.[6]

These Parkland students have made a real impact in the gun violence movement. They raised more than $4 million for their cause from small donors on GoFundMe, plus a few million more from celebrities like George Clooney, Steven Spielberg, and Oprah Winfrey.[7] On March 14, 2018, just one a month after the shooting, nearly a million kids across the country walked out of their schools to join the National School Walkout, protesting the school shooting epidemic. It was one of the largest school walkouts in history. March for Our Lives, a nationwide protest that included a march in Washington, DC, also had hundreds of thousands of protesters in every state demanding an end to gun violence.

After Parkland, national support for stronger gun laws went up and support for the NRA dropped to an all-time low of 37 percent.[8] Well-known companies cut their ties with the NRA, and many big-box stores that sell guns will no longer sell assault rifles and even raised their minimum age requirements. And gun reform that politicians haven't been able to accomplish in decades, the Parkland activists got done in weeks.

Over the summer of 2018, the Parkland group tackled voter registration. They launched a cross-country bus tour to register young voters: seventy-five cities, twenty states, in two months. They are making gun reform the central issue for those newly registered voters. "We're going to show these politicians that we're coming for them," says David Hogg.[9]

DEATH THREATS

Even gun violence survivors and activists who are just kids have to deal with bullying and abuse from gun rights supporters. Every teen I interviewed for this book complained about online trolls they have to deal with on a daily basis, and most have received death threats. The Parkland students, especially David Hogg and Emma Gonzalez, had to hire private security guards to protect them 24/7. "We get people armed to the teeth showing up and saying, 'Where's David Hogg?'" explains Matthew Deitsch, a Stoneman Douglas graduate who was on the bus tour with the Parkland survivors. Throughout the two-month bus tour, a pro-gun group called the Utah Gun Exchange followed the teens to every event in a tank-like armored vehicle topped with a machine-gun turret.[10]

The students' anger highlights a generation gap on the gun issue. Among voters ages 18 to 29, 77 percent say gun control will be an important factor in deciding how they will vote. Nationally, the number of young registered voters has gone up 2 percent since the Parkland shooting. In Florida, where the shooting took place, youth voter registration is up an incredible 41 percent.[11]

"This youth movement is unprecedented," says Kris Brown, copresident of the Brady Campaign to Prevent Gun Violence. "What's different here is that the children who are impacted are older, and they are able to give voice in a way that could not happen before."[12]

The Parkland students have been incredibly savvy in how they use social media too. They've been able to organize more quickly and broadly through Twitter and other platforms. Jaclyn explains their young approach: "People always say, 'Get off your phones,'

but social media is our weapon. Without it the move have spread this fast."[13] They are also leading themse ing on adults to tell them what to do. They are gett only to do things teenagers legally can't do, like signii they are too young to sign for. When their parents asl could help, the Parkland group answered, "Order pizz

These young Parkland activists realize that chang laws will take time, and they are in it for the long ing to get more young people behind them. They hop the number of young voters, making them a group wit power. And it won't be long before they are running themselves and leading our country—you can be sure th what's broken once they take power.

David Hogg's reminder to young activists:

"iT'S THE INDIVIDUAL EFFORT OF EVERYBODY WORKING TOGETHER TOW. A COLLECTIVE GOAL THAT CAUSES REA EFFECTIVE CHANGE IN AMERICA AND iN THE WORLD."[15]

◎ ◎ ◎

Learn more about what the Parkland survivors are working on involved on Twitter @#NeverAgain.

CHAPTER 10

How to Fix It: Six Steps to Protect Ourselves from Gun Violence

The gun problem in America can seem overwhelming and even hopeless at times. But there are smart, passionate people out there who have great ideas for how to fix the problems—including the young activists profiled in this book. Now that you know the details of America's gun problem, learning about possible solutions is the next step in getting prepared for action. Here are six urgent priorities that would immediately start saving lives.

1. Require Background Checks for *All* Gun Sales

Background checks are one of the most important pieces of gun violence prevention. When states require a background check for all gun sales, it leads to big drops in gun homicide and suicide rates. After Connecticut passed its law requiring background checks on all guns sales, gun homicides in the state dropped by 40 percent, and gun suicides dropped by 15 percent (see chapter 11).[1]

The good news is that nearly all Americans—including gun owners and NRA members—support background checks. A poll conducted by Quinnipiac University in 2018 showed that 97 percent of Americans support criminal background checks for all gun sales.[2]

Yet fewer than half of US states have comprehensive background check laws. Due to pressure from the gun lobby, Congress and most states have failed to close deadly loopholes in the background check system.

ONE IN FIVE GUNS ARE SOLD IN THE US WITHOUT A BACKGROUND CHECK BECAUSE OF GAPS IN FEDERAL LAW.[3]

PRIVATE SALE LOOPHOLE

According to federal law, only licensed gun dealers need to do background checks. That means millions of guns are bought and sold each year without any background checks—through online sales, at gun shows, or through unlicensed private sellers. Through these loopholes, people with felony convictions or serious mental illness as well as domestic abusers are able to buy guns legally, no questions asked.[4]

CHARLESTON LOOPHOLE

Ninety percent of background checks take a matter of seconds. But around 10 percent take more time. Federal law says if a background check takes more than three days, the sale can go through without knowing the result. Because of this loophole, nearly three thousand people who were not supposed to have guns (people with criminal records, mental illnesses, and so on) were able to purchase them, including some mass shooters.[5]

NEVER FORGET: CHARLESTON CHURCH SHOOTING

When: June 17, 2015
Where: Charleston, South Carolina
How many died? Nine
What happened? A white supremacist entered a church and shot and murdered nine black churchgoers during prayer service. The shooter's goal was to start a "race war" with his actions, and he was eventually convicted of thirty-three federal hate crimes, in addition to the murder charges. On his website, the shooter posted photos of the Confederate flag, which sparked national debate on the morality of displaying the flag and led South Carolina to remove it from the state capitol grounds.

WHAT'S IN A NAME?

This loophole is technically called "delayed denial," but it's been dubbed the "Charleston Loophole" because in 2015 a white-supremacist shooter killed nine black people in a church in Charleston, South Carolina. The shooter had an arrest record that should have prohibited him from buying a gun, but law enforcement had trouble sorting out his paperwork, and it took more than three days, so the shooter was able to purchase his gun and kill people with it.[6]

BOYFRIEND LOOPHOLE

Federal law stops anyone with domestic violence misdemeanors from having a gun, but that doesn't include partners who aren't married, don't live with their partner, or don't share a child with them. This means thousands of dangerous people can buy guns when they shouldn't be able to. When states pass laws closing this loophole, domestic violence homicide rates declined by 7 percent.[7] You can read more about the problem of domestic violence and guns in chapter 4.

In 1993, Congress passed the Brady Law, requiring background checks for every gun sold at a licensed gun dealer. This law has vastly improved safety in America, but there is more still to be done to strengthen it. Closing deadly loopholes is a big part of that.

SINCE 1993, BACKGROUND CHECKS HAVE BLOCKED MORE THAN 3 MILLION GUN SALES TO PROHIBITED PEOPLE.[8]

2. Require Gun Owners to Store Guns Safely

This area of gun safety is a great place for gun owners to get involved in reform. Requiring gun owners to safely store their guns would reduce the body count significantly. About a third of American children live in homes with guns. That wouldn't be a problem if all the guns were stored safely, but nearly two million of those children live in homes where guns are left loaded and accessible. American kids are sixteen times more likely to be accidentally shot and killed than kids in other developed countries. The majority of those deaths happen when children are in their own homes, unsupervised, playing with a gun.[9]

68% OF SCHOOL SHOOTERS GOT THEIR GUNS AT HOME OR FROM THE HOME OF A RELATIVE—INCLUDING THE PARKLAND AND SANDY HOOK SHOOTERS.[10]

Many gun owners think it won't happen to them—that their children either don't know where the guns are kept or know better than to play with them. But studies show that more than two-thirds of kids know where their parents keep their guns, even when parents think they don't. And more than one-third have actually handled the gun.[11] Gun storage is also a big problem when it comes to teen suicide. One study found that of teens who had already attempted suicide in the last year and who had guns in their home, 40 percent had easy access to those guns.[12]

Safe storage laws require that guns and ammunition be stored in a locked container or gun safe or that they be disabled with a gun lock when not in use. According to Gun Owners for Responsible

Ownership (see profile in chapter 7), "There are so many options for gun owners depending on the situation: trigger locks, cable locks, and quick access safes."[13]

There are also "smart guns" being developed, which could be on the market as early as 2019. Smart guns use fingerprint recognition and other technology so only their owners can fire them.[14]

And safe storage laws work! In Massachusetts, which has the strongest safe storage laws in the US, guns are used in just 9 percent of youth suicides, compared to 42 percent in the rest of the country. Massachusetts's youth suicide rate is 38 percent lower than the national average.[15]

YOUTH SUICIDE BY GUN 2000–2016

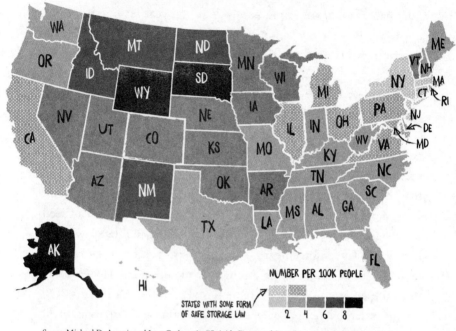

NUMBER PER 100K PEOPLE

STATES WITH SOME FORM
OF SAFE STORAGE LAW

2   4   6   8

Source: Michael D. Anestis and Joye C. Anestis, "Suicide Rates and State Laws Regulating Access and Exposure to Handguns," *American Journal of Public Health* 105, no. 10 (October 2015), https://www.ncbi. nlm.nih.gov/pmc/articles/PMC4566524/; "Child Access Prevention," Giffords Law Center to Prevent Gun Violence, accessed February 10, 2019, https://lawcenter.giffords.org/gun-laws/policy-areas/child-consumer-safety/child-access-prevention/.

Safe gun storage needs to be the law in every state and the new norm in America.

3. Pass Red Flag Laws

The Arizona shooter who killed six people and wounded thirteen more, including Congresswoman Gabby Giffords, in 2011 showed all kinds of signs he was dangerous. His parents were so worried they took his shotgun away, but they couldn't keep him from buying more guns. Which is exactly what he did.[16]

The shooter who attacked Marjory Stoneman Douglas High School in 2018, killing seventeen students, was described by his guardian as a "ticking time bomb."[17] In the year leading up to the massacre, Florida law enforcement received at least eighteen calls describing the shooter's threats of violence and access to guns, including specific concerns that he planned to shoot up the school. Some callers even asked the police to take his guns away. Law enforcement did nothing.[18]

Thirty-eight out of the sixty-two mass shooters in the past twenty years displayed signs of violent intentions prior to the massacres. An FBI study of preattack behaviors from 2000 to 2013 found that the average shooter showed four to five concerning behaviors.[19]

In most mass shootings, people who knew the shooter had seen these signs and were already worried, but federal and state laws gave family and law enforcement no way to restrict access to guns, even temporarily. Red Flag Laws give family members and law enforcement the ability to seek an Extreme Risk Protection Order (ERPO), a court order that temporarily restricts a person's access to guns when they pose a danger to themselves or others. It is a way for family and police to act before warning signs escalate into deadly violence.[20]

Currently, just thirteen states have Red Flag Laws. California's Red Flag Law has been used to disarm domestic abusers, people on the FBI's terror watch list, and suicidal family members. On April 12, 2018, the day after Vermont passed its Red Flag Law, law enforcement was able to remove guns from an 18-year-old who had planned a mass shooting at a high school.[21]

Red Flag Laws help prevent suicides as well. Indiana's Red Flag Law led to a 7.5 percent drop in suicides over the ten years after it was passed in 2005. Connecticut's Red Flag Law led to a 13.7 percent reduction in suicides after 2007.[22]

Red Flag Laws are a commonsense option that will reduce suicides and limit gun access to people who are in mental health crisis.

4. Ban Assault Weapons and Large-Capacity Magazines

The Las Vegas concert massacre.

The Pulse nightclub massacre.

The Aurora movie theater massacre.

The Sandy Hook Elementary School massacre.

The Marjory Stoneman Douglas High School massacre.

What do these—the highest-casualty shootings in American history—have in common? They were all done with semiautomatic weapons—the AR-15, to be exact.[23]

NEVER FORGET: AURORA MOVIE THEATER SHOOTING

When: July 20, 2012
Where: Aurora, Colorado
How many died? Twelve
What happened? During a midnight screening of the movie *The Dark Knight Rises*, a shooter opened fire on the audience inside a movie theater, killing twelve and wounding fifty-eight more. It was the deadliest Colorado shooting since the Columbine High School massacre thirteen years earlier.

AR-15s ALLOW SHOOTERS TO SPRAY BULLETS INTO A CROWD WITHOUT NEEDING TO PAUSE TO RELOAD.

Research shows that semiautomatic weapons with high-capacity magazines are more dangerous than other types of guns during shooting events. In a 2017 study of two hundred mass shootings in the US, researchers at Brigham and Women's Hospital found that if a shooter uses a semiautomatic instead of another type of gun, it doubles the chances of people being wounded or killed.[24] Assault weapons and guns equipped with high-capacity magazines, together, make up nearly 40 percent of guns used in crimes, especially violent crimes.[25]

One major challenge to banning assault weapons is that they are very popular guns in in America right now. The NRA estimates there are between 8.5 million and 15 million assault rifles owned by Americans.[26] Could the government ban them even if it wanted to?

When you read the Second Amendment (see chapter 6), you understand that there is nothing in there about what kinds of guns people can have. In fact, it wasn't until 2008 that the Supreme Court interpreted the Second Amendment as referring to an individual's right to have a firearm in the home for personal reasons, like self-defense (*District of Columbia v. Heller*). Before that, it was interpreted to protect guns that were for military/militia use. And even in that ruling, the late conservative Justice Antonin Scalia wrote that this right was not "unlimited." He wrote that there would be no constitutional problem with banning "dangerous and unusual" firearms. According to this ruling, the Second Amendment only guarantees the right of a person to possess guns that are commonly used by law-abiding citizens for lawful purposes.[27]

Also, seven states plus Washington, DC, already ban the sale or importing of the AR-15 and other assault weapons.[28] And while those laws have been challenged in court, the Supreme Court has not voted to overturn any of them.

So, is a ban possible? Sure is.

1994 FEDERAL ASSAULT WEAPONS BAN (AWB)

America did at one time ban the manufacture and use of certain assault weapons and large ammunition magazines. In 1994, after a series of mass shootings with these weapons, Congress voted into law the Federal Assault Weapons Ban. The ban was supported by 77 percent of the public, signed into law by then-President Clinton, and endorsed by former presidents Bush, Ford, Carter, and Reagan. When the ban expired in 2004, Congress did not renew it.[29] A new ban was introduced to Congress in 2015 but failed to pass. This refusal to reinstate the ban coincides with a sharp increase in NRA contributions to Congress. Coincidence?

Other Federal Gun Regulations to Know

Title II and National Firearms Act: Certain weapons are heavily regulated under these federal laws, including short-barreled shotguns, short-barreled rifles, automatic shotguns, submachine guns, machine guns, rocket launchers, grenade launchers, grenades, and homemade bombs (among others). To buy one, you must get approval from the federal Bureau of Alcohol, Tobacco and Firearms (ATF).

1968 Gun Control Act: These are the rules American gun dealers currently follow when selling a gun to a private buyer. There are restrictions on the types of people who can purchase guns (no felons) and on interstate trading, since each state has different laws about gun ownership.

1986 Firearm Owners Protection Act: A response to the 1968 Gun Control Act, this loosened laws on interstate transfer, long-barrel sales, and record keeping.

1993 Brady Handgun Violence Prevention Act: This requires gun dealers to do a federal background check for every gun buyer. It flags people who cannot legally own firearms due to previous illness diagnoses or felony convictions. Using the FBI's National Instant Criminal Background Check System (NICS), the check takes no more than a few minutes.[30]

5. Treat Guns Like We Treat Cars

Believe it or not, we already have a great model for how we could regulate gun safety: cars! We Americans love our cars just about as much as we love our guns. But we don't let people drive them without a license or without insurance. We make people take safety classes and pass tests before we let them behind the wheel of this potentially deadly item. We have age requirements about who can drive. If you violate car regulations, you must stop driving. And you have to use seat belts to protect yourself and others in the car.

Even though cars kill a lot of Americans, we don't ban them. But we do regulate the heck out of them to try to make them as safe as possible. This is how we could and should treat guns.

In fact, cars give us a great model showing the success of regulation in reducing death. If you look at this chart showing the history of car regulation since 1945, you can see just how many lives these laws have saved.

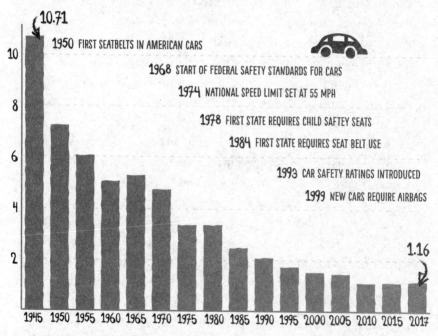

INCREASED CAR SAFETY FROM 1945 TO 2017

FATALITY RATES PER 100 MILLION VEHICLE MILES TRAVELED

10.71

1950 FIRST SEATBELTS IN AMERICAN CARS

1968 START OF FEDERAL SAFETY STANDARDS FOR CARS

1974 NATIONAL SPEED LIMIT SET AT 55 MPH

1978 FIRST STATE REQUIRES CHILD SAFTEY SEATS

1984 FIRST STATE REQUIRES SEAT BELT USE

1993 CAR SAFETY RATINGS INTRODUCED

1999 NEW CARS REQUIRE AIRBAGS

1.16

1945 1950 1955 1960 1965 1970 1975 1980 1985 1990 1995 2000 2005 2010 2015 2017

Source: "Motor Vehicle Traffic Fatalities and Fatality Rates, 1899–2015," National Highway Traffic Safety Administration, February 14, 2017, https://cdan.nhtsa.gov/TSFTables/Fatalities%20and%20Fatality%20 Rates%20(1899-2015), pdf; "Fatal Crash Totals: 2017," Insurance Institute for Highway Safety, accessed February 10, 2019, https://www.iihs.org/iihs/topics/t/general-statistics/fatalityfacts/state-by-state -overview#Fatal-crash-totals; "A Drive Through Time," National Highway Traffic Safety Administration, accessed February 10, 2019, https://one.nhtsa.gov/nhtsa/timeline/index.html.

Requiring safety measures like national speed limits, seat belts, child safety seats, and airbags has led to a dramatic drop in car deaths over the past seventy years. Those changes didn't come about just because our government wanted to protect us and keep us safe. Those changes came about because Americans sued carmakers when they believed cars could be and should be safer.

Currently, we can't do the same with guns because there is a special protection just for guns, gunmakers, gun sellers, and gun owners. They cannot be held liable for the many deaths their guns cause. That must change. In order to regulate guns the way we do cars, Congress has to repeal the Protection of Lawful Commerce in Arms Act, which the NRA pushed through in 2005 (see chapter 8). This law makes gunmakers and gun sellers immune from nearly all lawsuits. With this protection in place, our lawmakers cannot work with the courts to fight for our safety in the same way they can with any other item we use (cars, swing sets, paper clips, etc).

We even have a couple of state models that show how regulating guns works to reduce gun violence and improve safety. In Connecticut, lawmakers required people to get a license and do some safety training before buying a gun, just like we do for cars. Over the next ten years, gun homicides and suicides in Connecticut dropped at faster rates than other states without such laws.[31] In Missouri, lawmakers repealed its licensing requirements in 2007 and saw an increase in homicides and suicides in the years after.[32]

Representative Jennifer Williamson, a Democrat from Oregon and a gun sense politician, had this to say about how the Protection of Lawful Commerce in Arms Act hurts gun safety:

It's a huge barrier. For so many products, like cars, when people got hurt in car crashes, lawsuits were how we got seat belts mandated. The courts help define what we need to be doing to make people safer—whether it's safer guns or how people store their guns or sellers being held accountable for being negligent or reckless. The court is set up to do that and we don't have that ally in this fight. It limits our ability to address fundamental issues—like smarter guns. If a gun manufacturer got sued because they're not using the best technology for smarter guns, then they would change that. The market would change that. But they're never held accountable by the courts. That's a huge problem.[33]

WHAT ARE LARGE-CAPACITY MAGAZINES?

A magazine is a storage and feeding device for bullets. It is either inside the gun (internal/fixed) or attached to the outside (detachable) of a gun that shoots multiple bullets. Mass shooters commonly use large-capacity magazines because they make it possible to fire at large numbers of people without taking the time to reload. Victims have no chance to escape, and law enforcement has no chance to come to the rescue. Large-capacity magazines dramatically increase the number of people killed in mass shootings. There is no reason they should be used for hunting or self-protection.[34]

6. Let There Be Research

In 2016, the US government was worried about the Zika virus, so the Department of Health and Human Services, along with state officials, got busy. They tested mosquitos, sprayed mosquito-heavy areas, launched an education campaign to get Americans to use DEET, and worked on developing a vaccine.

HOW MANY AMERICANS DiED FROM THE ZiKA VIRUS iN 2016? ONE. [35]

HOW MANY AMERICAN DiED FROM GUN VIOLENCE THAT SAME YEAR? OVER THIRTY THOUSAND. [36]

So, what was the government's response to an obvious larger health crisis?

Nothing.

That's because in 1996 Congress tied the hands of researchers at the Center for Disease Control and Prevention (CDC), our government's top health research organization. A spending bill rider, dubbed the Dickey Amendment (read more about it in chapter 9), stated that "none of the funds made available for injury prevention and control at the CDC may be used to advocate or promote gun control." The CDC, fearing a cutoff of funding, stopped nearly all research into gun violence. Other research groups were equally scared. As a result, research into gun violence—its causes and impacts—has dropped significantly.[37]

Here is a chart showing how many Americans died from four diseases and gun violence from 1973 to 2012, compared to the number of research awards granted to study each problem, by the National Institutes of Health (NIH).

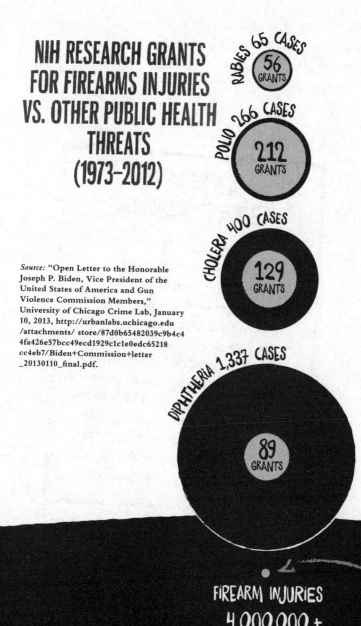

NIH RESEARCH GRANTS FOR FIREARMS INJURIES VS. OTHER PUBLIC HEALTH THREATS (1973–2012)

RABIES 65 CASES
56 GRANTS

POLIO 266 CASES
212 GRANTS

CHOLERA 400 CASES
129 GRANTS

DIPHTHERIA 1,337 CASES
89 GRANTS

Source: "Open Letter to the Honorable Joseph P. Biden, Vice President of the United States of America and Gun Violence Commission Members," University of Chicago Crime Lab, January 10, 2013, http://urbanlabs.uchicago.edu /attachments/ store/87d0b65482039c9b4c4 4fa426e57bcc49ecd1929c1c1e0edc65218 cc4eb7/Biden+Commission+letter _20130110_final.pdf.

FIREARM INJURIES
4,000,000+

3 GRANTS

We should repeal the Dickey Amendment and let the CDC research gun violence as the public health crisis that it is. If the government is going to figure out solutions to the gun violence epidemic that plagues our country, it first must research and understand the problem.

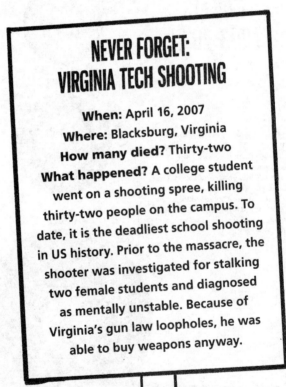

NEVER FORGET: VIRGINIA TECH SHOOTING

When: April 16, 2007
Where: Blacksburg, Virginia
How many died? Thirty-two
What happened? A college student went on a shooting spree, killing thirty-two people on the campus. To date, it is the deadliest school shooting in US history. Prior to the massacre, the shooter was investigated for stalking two female students and diagnosed as mentally unstable. Because of Virginia's gun law loopholes, he was able to buy weapons anyway.

More Ideas to Explore

While these six are some of the most crucial changes being proposed by gun sense lawmakers, there are a *lot* more ideas out there for how to solve America's gun violence problem. The Giffords Law Center to Prevent Gun Violence (lawcenter.giffords.org) has a comprehensive list of policy areas they are working on, including:

- Improve the National Instant Criminal Background Check System (NICS) so that all records are accessible, across state lines, quickly and efficiently.

- Close loopholes that allow people experiencing mental health crises access to guns.

- Make sure the reasons why people get banned from buying a gun—the reasons they are considered a "prohibited person"—are consistent across all states.

- Ensure people on the US terrorist watch list are not able to purchase or possess guns.

- Raise the minimum age for purchasing and possessing a gun.

- Increase oversight and regulation of gun dealers.

- Improve record keeping for all gun sales.

- Add waiting periods for gun sales.

- Tighten regulation of sales at gun shows.

- Require gun owners to get a license and registration for their guns and to report any stolen weapons, which will decrease illegal gun trafficking.

- Require all new guns be made using smart technology safety features, like a key or fingerprint match, before they can fire.

- Require good cause or safety training for someone to obtain a carrying concealed weapons (CCW) permit.

- Restrict open carry practices to ensure public safety.

- Repeal state "stand your ground" laws, which allow a person to use deadly force in self-defense in public, even if such force can be safely avoided by retreating.

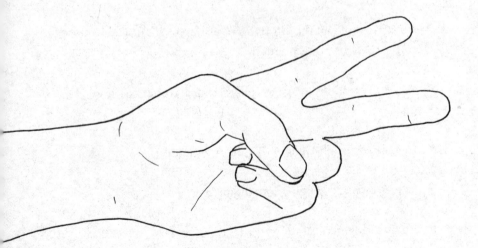

- Keep guns out of schools, including armed teachers.

- Mandate background checks and regulate all ammunition purchases.

- Ban silencers, which make active shooters even more deadly.

- Strengthen laws to eliminate illegal gun trafficking.

- Limit the number of guns and ammunition a person can buy.

- Create intervention programs to stem gun violence in communities where it is happening most often.[38]

A Final Word

To learn more about gun violence solutions that ar
check out the websites of gun sense groups in cl
at the social media of young activists in this h
the charge and have great ideas for fixing A

STUDENTS TAKING A STAND

COLIN GODDARD, AGE 32,
GUN VIOLENCE SURVIVOR AND ACTIVIST

Colin Goddard was a typical college student—his main concern was what he was going to do with his life. And on April 16, 2007, he was late for French class. Also typical.

But the rest of April 16 was not a typical day. A few minutes after settling at his desk, Colin heard a weird banging down the hall. His teacher, Madame Couture, peeked out the door, then quickly shut and ordered her seventeen students to hide under their desks. moments later, bullets were flying through the door and into the room. Then the shooter entered the room and began killing

massacre at Virginia Tech ended when the attacker shot in that classroom, but not before killing thirty-two people, Madame Couture and most of the students in Colin's was shot four times—once in the knee, twice in the once in the shoulder—but he survived. At the time, this st mass shooting in US history, but it has since been he Pulse nightclub massacre in Orlando (forty-nine e concert massacre in Las Vegas (fifty-eight).[1] was the end of one life and the beginning of another.

The shooting really opened my eyes to a world I knew very little about. I assumed, like most people in this country, that we do everything we can to keep guns away from dangerous people. But when I learned that we don't even do a background check on every gun sale, I was like "Whoa, wait a minute. We don't even have that as basic policy?" We're in this situation because the gun industry has written our laws and we need the American public to stand up and say, "We're not going to do it this way anymore."[2]

He didn't join the gun safety movement immediately. Five years later, as he watched the Sandy Hook shooting coverage on TV, something shifted for him. He calls it his "Newtown moment"—the moment when he got fed up with gun violence. The next day, he packed up and moved to Washington, DC. He first went to work for the Brady Campaign and then Everytown for Gun Safety as a senior policy advocate.

Colin is now in his thirties and has a child of his own. He wants his child to grow up in a safer country: "I spent my life since [the Virginia Tech shooting] trying to advocate for better gun laws."[3]

Colin's advice to student activists:

"WHAT WAS YOUR NEWTOWN MOMENT? IF IT HASN'T HAPPENED YET, WHAT IS IT GOING TO TAKE?"[4]

◎ ◎ ◎

Learn more about what Colin is working on and get involved at
bradycampaign.org and everytown.org

CHAPTER 11

US Models: What's Working in States with Strong Gun Laws

Those who oppose gun reform in America say, "Nothing can be done. It can't be changed. It can't be fixed."

That's BS. There are already states in the US that have strengthened their gun laws. The results are conclusive—states that passed comprehensive gun reform have seen drastic reductions in gun deaths as a result. Let's look at the two most famous examples: Connecticut and Massachusetts.

The Connecticut Model

After the Sandy Hook massacre in Connecticut, the state did something radical, something beyond sending "thoughts and prayers" to the victims' families. They took action. Connecticut lawmakers passed a package of new gun laws:

- Banning assault weapons

- Banning sales of magazines that hold more than ten bullets

- Requiring owners to register with the state

Almost immediately, gun deaths began to drop. According to Connecticut's chief medical examiner's office, the number of gun deaths (including homicides, suicides, and accidents) fell from 226 in 2012 to 164 in 2016. That's a 27 percent drop in just four years.[1] Connecticut is now ranked in the lowest states for gun death rates, according to the Giffords Law Center to Prevent Gun Violence, which tracks gun deaths by state. They give Connecticut an A- for its new gun laws.[2]

Check out your state's score at lawcenter.giffords.org/scorecard/.

The Massachusetts Model

Massachusetts, another A- state on the Giffords scorecard, has the lowest gun death rate in the US. It's no coincidence that it also has the strictest gun laws in the country. In 2016, 3.4 people per one hundred thousand died by gun violence in Massachusetts, according to the CDC.[3]

By comparison, in Tennessee (a D- state), the gun death rate was nearly five times higher: 17.3 per one hundred thousand. The safe storage laws enacted in Massachusetts had a dramatic effect on youth suicides as well. Guns are used in just 9 percent of youth suicides, compared to 42 percent nationally. The suicide death rate in Massachusetts is 38 percent below the national average.

Thanks to these impressive statistics, activists and lawmakers have been calling on DC lawmakers to adopt the "Massachusetts Plan" as a model for national gun reform. In March 2018, US Senator Ed Markey (a Democrat from Massachusetts) introduced a bill that would encourage other states to adopt Massachusetts's gun laws by giving them $20 million in grants.[4]

Just what's in this "Massachusetts Plan" anyway? Here's what it does:

- Assault weapons are banned. Republican Governor Mitt Romney signed this into law in 2004.

- All gun dealers must conduct background checks.

- Private sellers must verify that buyers have a valid gun license.

- People with mental illness are banned from owning guns.

- Rapid-firing bump stocks are banned. In 2017, Massachusetts became the first state to do so after the Las Vegas shooting.

- It requires weapons be unloaded and locked away when not in use.

- Police chiefs can deny, suspend, or revoke gun licenses.[5]

A Final Word

When you hear politicians say, "We can't," in response to demand for stricter gun laws, remind them of Connecticut and Massachusetts, where politicians said, "We can." And then they did. If these states can do it, there's no reason other states can't follow suit. There's no reason the whole country can't do it.

POLICE IN CHARGE OF GUN LICENSES

This last Massachusetts law is unusual and interesting. Gun policy experts believe it has been instrumental in keeping guns out of the hands of dangerous people. "There are lots of cases where the police will go to a house multiple times for domestic violence, but there will be no charges or restraining order," said Jack McDevitt, who helped write the law when he was chair of the Massachusetts Committee to Reduce Gun Violence. "That person is not federally prohibited, but the police know this is a dangerous person. So they could turn his license application down."[6]

STUDENTS TAKING A STAND

ELI COUNCE, AGE 16, AND PENELOPE SPURR, AGE 15, FOUNDERS OF STUDENTS FOR CHANGE[1]

ELI COUNCE

Lake Oswego and Lakeridge High Schools are rivals. Because they are the only two high schools in their small, suburban Oregon town, the rivalry runs deep. But in 2018, these two student bodies put aside their differences and came together to work on gun reform.

Students for Change, like many political action groups, started small, with one upset teen: Eli Counce. Eli is a sophomore at Lakeridge, where he does speech and debate and robotics and earns money coding and designing websites. He's lanky and super laid-back—the last guy you would suspect of being a political powerhouse.

But after the February 2018 massacre at Marjory Stoneman Douglas High, Eli was angry. And scared. He wanted to do something to express his frustration, but he didn't know exactly what. "I talked to one of my favorite teachers about it, and he put me in contact with some [politically active] students at Lake Oswego High School," Eli begins. "Originally, I was just going to do a walkout. Then I decided we should go to Salem [the state capital]."

When Eli told his school administration about the plan, he expected to get some pushback. "I asked, 'Do we need to go around you and get unexcused absences?' But they said, 'No, just do this,' and they were super supportive."

The school was supportive of students leaving in protest—thousands of students across the country were planning walkouts—but that didn't mean they could pay for buses to Salem. Eli had no idea how he would get hundreds of students down to the state capitol, which is forty miles away. That's when he got serious about joining forces with students at Lake Oswego High, including Penelope Spurr, who helped him move the plan forward. "The Lakeridge students started a GoFundMe campaign," Penelope remembers, "and in just one day they raised thousands of dollars." It was enough to rent all the buses they needed.

PENELOPE SPURR

Penelope is 15 and a sophomore, like Eli. She's more intense and enjoys debate, art, and all things outdoorsy. She is also smart, organized, and determined. Together, she and Eli make a potent team.

On March 5, less than a month after Parkland, Eli, Penelope, and more than 250 teens walked out of school and rode buses to Salem, where they protested on the capitol steps and talked to state lawmakers, like Governor Kate Brown, Representative Andrea Salinas (a Democrat from Lake Oswego), and state Senator Rob Wagner (also a Democrat). The politicians, who for years had struggled to pass gun safety legislation, were excited about the student activists and encouraged them to do more.

More is exactly what they did. Days after their trip to Salem, students from both schools gathered at Penelope's house and got to work. They called their group Students for Change and brainstormed ideas for gun reform. This brainstorming turned into a plan for the state, which they formally presented to state lawmakers a month later. Their bill, called SB 501, is currently working its way through Oregon's legislative process and will be voted on (and hopefully passed) soon. Gun violence prevention group Ceasefire Oregon calls the bill "one of the most exciting and effective gun violence prevention bills [we've] seen."[2]

OREGON'S STUDENTS FOR CHANGE BILL (SB 501)

This bill, written by Oregon students, requires gun buyers to secure a permit before receiving a firearm. Requirements include:

- Increases the minimum age for purchasing firearms from 18 to 21.

- No prior criminal convictions (including misdemeanor violence).

- No restraining order or court protective orders (Extreme Risk Protection Order, ERPO).

- No unlawful use of drugs.

- Must pass firearm safety course.

- Eliminates bulk sales of weapons by limiting purchases to one gun and twenty rounds of ammunition every thirty days.

- A sheriff may deny permit if sheriff has reasonable grounds to believe applicant is threat to self or others.

- Receipt of firearm without permit is punishable by significant jail time and/or fine.

- Requires person who owns or possesses firearm to secure it with trigger or cable lock or in locked container. Failure to do so is punishable by jail time and/or a fine.

- Requires person who owns or possesses firearm to report to law enforcement any loss or theft of firearm within twenty-four hours; failure to do so is punishable by jail time and/or a fine.

- Bans magazines with capacity to hold more than five rounds of ammunition.

- Requires criminal background check before transfer of ammunition.

- Prohibits transfer of firearm by gun dealer or private party until fourteen days have passed or state police have determined recipient is qualified, whichever is later.[3]

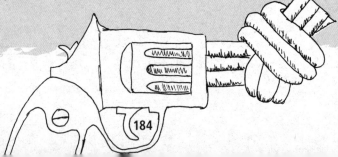

Speaking to reporters soon after writing their plan, Lake Oswego High School senior Robert Vogel explained what it's like to live in fear:

I am no expert. I don't know the perfect solution to this issue. But as I sit in class, I should not be thinking about who I would text, what my last words to my parents would be if, God forbid, someone attacked our school. I'm 19. I can't buy beer; I can't rent a car. But I can walk into a nearby Big 5 and leave in under an hour with an assault rifle.[3]

These students turned their anger and fear into political action. Adults listened and gave them a seat at the table. Students for Change has also inspired other kids across the state, far from Lake Oswego. "There were a bunch of kids in Oregon who were popping up, starting small movements," says Penelope. "Now we are starting to blend together into one larger collective." Their original student-created plan could soon be the law in Oregon. And if SB 501 passes, the rest of the country will have a new state model to follow.

Penelope's advice to young activists:

"REACH OUT TO FRIENDS AND FAMILY AND TEACHERS. THERE ARE PEOPLE OUT THERE WHO WANT TO HELP—YOU JUST HAVE TO FIND THEM."

Eli's reminder to young activists:

"IT TAKES JUST ONE PERSON. THAT COULD BE YOU."

◎ ◎ ◎

Learn more about what Penelope and Eli are working on and get involved by visiting Students for Change on Twitter, @s4cLO.

CHAPTER 12

INTERNATIONAL MODELS: WHY THE REST OF THE WORLD THINKS AMERICA IS NUTS

From the looks of the following chart, America could learn something about gun safety from just about any other country in the world. America is at the bottom of the world heap when it comes to gun violence. We have more gun murders, more gun suicides, more school shootings, and more mass shootings than any other country in the world.

By far.

So which countries are doing a bang-up job combating gun violence? Who can we learn from?

GUN DEATHS IN DEVELOPED COUNTRIES, 2012-2016

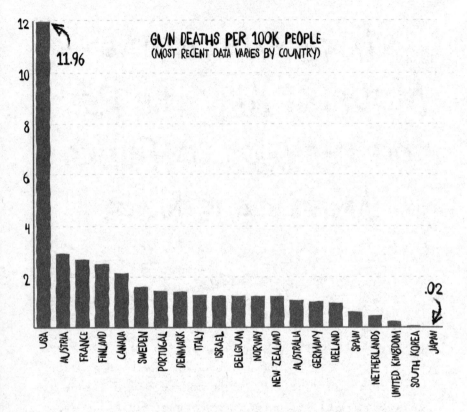

Source: "Compare Your Country to the Rest of the World," Gunpolicy.org, accessed February 10, 2019, https://www.gunpolicy.org.

Australia: Gun Buybacks

In 1996, a man ate lunch in a café in Port Arthur, Australia, then pulled a semiautomatic rifle out of his bag and sprayed the crowd with bullets. Minutes later, thirty-five people were dead, and twenty-three more were wounded. It was the worst mass shooting in Australia's history.[1]

How did the politicians Down Under react? Did they send their thoughts and prayers to the victims, and then continue with business as usual, like we do in America? No, they did not. Australian politicians said, "Enough is enough," and got busy fixing the gun problem in their country.

Twelve days after the shooting, the country's leaders responded with legislation. Conservative Prime Minister John Howard put forward a bipartisan gun plan called the National Firearms Agreement

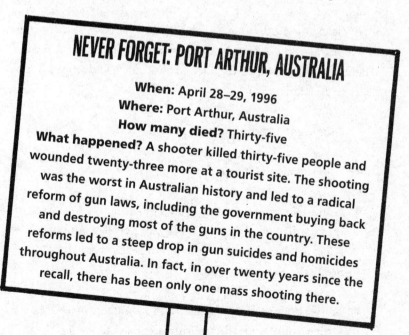

NEVER FORGET: PORT ARTHUR, AUSTRALIA

When: April 28–29, 1996
Where: Port Arthur, Australia
How many died? Thirty-five
What happened? A shooter killed thirty-five people and wounded twenty-three more at a tourist site. The shooting was the worst in Australian history and led to a radical reform of gun laws, including the government buying back and destroying most of the guns in the country. These reforms led to a steep drop in gun suicides and homicides throughout Australia. In fact, in over twenty years since the recall, there has been only one mass shooting there.

(NFA) with new laws banning semiautomatic, self-loading rifles and shotguns, imposing stricter licensing and registration rules, and requiring buyers give a reason for needing a gun (self-defense wasn't an option). The law that gets the most press, however, was the government's mandatory buyback of prohibited guns. The government paid owners fair market value to buy back six hundred thousand weapons, or 20 percent of all guns in Australia, and then destroyed them.[2]

POLLS SHOWED 90% OF AUSTRALIANS SUPPORTED THESE NEW GUN LAWS.[3]

So, did enacting strict gun restrictions result in a safer Australia? The answer is yes! In the decades since the laws went into effect, many academic studies have shown this to be true. A 2011 review of the research by experts at the Harvard Injury Control Research Center showed that gun violence of all kinds had dropped dramatically in Australia:

- Gun homicides dropped 42 percent from 1996 to 2003.[4]

- Gun suicides dropped 57 percent.[5]

- Gun robberies dropped as well. And contrary to fears that not having guns to protect themselves would make Australians more vulnerable to home invasions, there was no increase in those either.[6]

- What about mass shootings? In the eighteen years before Port Arthur, Australia had thirteen mass shootings. In the eighteen years after the stricter gun laws went into effect, there were none. Zero![7]

A 2006 analysis by researchers at the University of Sydney concluded: "Australia's 1996 gun law reforms were followed by more than a decade free of fatal mass shootings and accelerated declines in firearm deaths, particularly suicides."[8]

AUSTRALIA'S ONE MASS SHOOTING SINCE THE BUYBACK

In 2018, Australia had its first mass shooting since it enacted its gun reform policies, and gun rights supporters are claiming, "See? It doesn't work!" But let's examine the shooting carefully. A grandfather shot his family of seven with three guns he owned legally.[9] This was Australia's first mass shooting in twenty-two years. America, by contrast, had eighty-four mass shootings in the same time period. Seven Australians died in that mass shooting while 756 Americans died in ours.[10]

Japan: Tests, Tests, and More Tests

Japan has 127 million people, but fewer than ten gun deaths per year. And they haven't had a single mass shooting. Ever![11]

How do they do it?

Strict gun laws, that's how. For Japanese people who want to own a gun, it ain't easy:

First, there's an all-day class followed by written test.

Then there's a shooting-range test, which they have to pass with 95 percent accuracy.

Then there's a mental health test at a hospital.

And finally, there's a background check and interviews with friends and family.[12]

If a wannabe gun owner actually passes all those tests, they are allowed to buy an air rifle or a shotgun. No handguns—those are illegal. And every three years, gun owners have to take the class and all the tests again!

Norway: Unarmed Police

Like Americans, Norwegians like their guns. The country has about one-third the number of guns per one hundred civilians, but only about one-tenth the rate of gun deaths.[13]

What's their secret?

The Norwegian culture of gun ownership is very different from America's. In Norway, you rarely see guns outside of organized settings like gun clubs or during hunting season. The rest of the time their guns are locked up and stored away.

Their attitude toward the police and guns is also quite different. "The police have not been armed in Norway," said Norwegian journalist Åsne Seierstad. "People in the US could say, 'Well, isn't that scary?' Well, when the police are not armed, the drug dealer is not armed, the criminals are not armed, because no one is armed."[14]

A 2015 study found that the number of fatal shootings by Norwegian police over the previous nine years was less than the number of fatal shootings by American police in one day.[15] And yes, America is a much bigger country than Norway, which makes it challenging to compare the two, so let's try this: Norway has 5.3 million people[16], and Chicago has about half that, with 2.7 million.[17] In Chicago, over six years (from 2010 to 2016), the police engaged in 435 shootings, killing ninety-two people.[18] In Norway, there were zero police killings in that same time period.

THE LAST TIME A NORWEGIAN POLICE OFFICER SHOT AND KILLED SOMEONE WAS IN 2006![19]

Even when a terrorist killed seventy-seven people in Norway's only mass shooting, the police fired just one time. And after the attack, Norway didn't change, crack down, and add *more* guns to their police force. They knew the facts: their lack of guns was still keeping their population much safer.

Instead of using guns and fear to keep people in line, Norwegian police work to build trust in the communities they are protecting, to create a partnership with the people. The idea is that when people feel safe around the police, the police will understand the neighborhood better and be able to tackle problems before they get out of control.[20]

Seems like a model America could learn from.

South Korea: Lock 'Em Up

American visitors to the 2018 Winter Olympics in South Korea were struck by the lack of security at the games. Where were all the police carrying Uzis? It turns out South Korea doesn't need them because they have so little violent crime and almost no shootings at all. A mass shooting in their country is nearly unthinkable.

"In the capital city of Seoul, you can walk around at 1:00 a.m. or 2:00 a.m. and still be safe," said Sung Baik You, a spokesman for South Korea's Olympic committee.[21]

According to South Korea's National Police Agency, in 2016 there were 356 homicides in South Korea, which has fifty-one million people. Compare that to Chicago, which had 762 murders that same year but has just 2.7 million people.[22]

South Korea *does* have guns—nearly half a million. And the majority of Korean men know how to shoot them, thanks to mandatory military service.[23]

So, what's the deal?

While there *are* guns in South Korea, they are really hard to get. South Koreans can use guns for hunting or target practice, but those guns must be registered and stored at a local police station when they not in use. Korean gun owners must go to the police and check out their gun when they want to use it. And even though guns are stored at police stations, like in Norway, most Korean police officers are not armed![24]

A Final Word

Would any of these international models be possible in the US? It's hard to say. America has a lot more guns in circulation than any of these countries, and a population that is decidedly less excited about giving them up. But the examples and evidence are there, all around the world. Perhaps some of these ideas might be possible on a smaller scale, state by state.

STUDENTS TAKING A STAND

NATALIE BARDEN, AGE 17, SANDY HOOK SURVIVOR AND MEMBER OF JUNIOR NEWTOWN ACTION ALLIANCE

On December 14, 2012, something unthinkable happened. A 20-year-old in Newtown, Connecticut, shot and killed his mother while she slept, then drove to Sandy Hook Elementary School, which he had attended years earlier, where he shot and killed six adult staff and twenty 6- and 17-year-old children. Then he shot himself.

Because he used a semiautomatic rifle, the whole thing took less than five minutes.

The Sandy Hook massacre was the deadliest elementary or high school shooting in history, with the youngest, most defenseless victims. Afterward, law enforcement discovered that the shooter had severe untreated mental illness. He also had access to deadly guns and ammo in his home. His mother, a gun enthusiast, legally purchased all the guns he used in the shooting. They were kept in a gun safe, which the shooter had access to.

The town of Newtown was devastated by the shooting, especially the families of the murdered children. Natalie Barden was in the fifth grade when it happened. Her school went on lockdown that day, but she thought it was just a drill, like so many others. When she got home that afternoon, her parents delivered the horrific news: her little brother, Daniel, at just 7 years old, was killed in the shooting. Five years later, Natalie's memory of that moment is crystal clear: "I still remember my [other] brother and I screaming and crying, both in the utmost pain imaginable."[1]

After the shooting, Natalie couldn't fathom trying to fix the gun violence problems that led to her brother's murder. She was a fifth grader. "All I wanted was to be normal and not constantly reminded of my loss. I left the fighting to my dad, who started Sandy Hook Promise, confident that his efforts in gun-violence prevention would create the change that was needed"[2] (see chapter 13). Natalie and the other young survivors focused on healing from their trauma and moving on with their lives.

The town of Newtown moved on too. Sandy Hook Elementary School was demolished a few months after the shooting, and a new school was built. On every December 14 since the shooting, the town has asked media to stay away and teachers at Newtown schools to stick to a regular schedule—just another normal day.

Years passed, and as the youngest survivors started middle school and the oldest went to high school, they realized that the grownups had *not* solved the gun violence problem—in fact, it was getting worse. When Natalie first heard about a gun violence prevention club being started at her high school by fellow students Jackson Mittleman and Tommy Murray, she thought, "Why am I not in that club?"[3]

The first meetings of the Junior Newtown Action Alliance were disappointing, however. Only a few students showed up, and it was emotionally draining to talk about gun violence when they had been through a school shooting themselves and some, like Natalie, had lost loved ones. It was hard to get kids involved.

Then the Parkland shooting happened.

The Sandy Hook survivors watched as Parkland students immediately grabbed the media spotlight and demanded change from America's leaders, even as they were reeling from their trauma.

They watched the Parkland teens launch a national youth-led gun reform movement. Natalie remembers this as a turning point: "I thought, if these kids are able to speak about this topic so soon after this tragedy, I can join them by adding my voice."[4]

She began doing media interviews and writing articles about her brother's death. She was invited to a *Teen Vogue* summit for young leaders in the gun violence prevention movement.

Natalie wasn't the only Sandy Hook survivor inspired by Parkland. The next Junior Newtown Action Alliance meeting was packed—more than one hundred kids showed up ready for action. First, the group focused on beefing up their social media presence, to show other teens who they are. They launched humansofnewtownct on Instagram, where survivors tell their own stories from the shooting.[5]

That summer, just months after the massacre at their school, the Parkland teens embarked on a two-month Road to Change bus tour across America. They met with teens and victims of gun violence, registered young voters, and educated students about the gun issue. Their final stop was at Newtown, where the two groups of survivors met for the first time. It was an emotional meeting. Natalie explains their shared passion: "Parkland was a reminder that what happened in Newtown is still happening, and not nearly enough has changed in the almost six years between the two tragic events."[6]

The Junior Newtown Action Alliance has been busy ever since. They're organizing voter-registration drives and urging young people to vote for candidates who support stricter gun laws. They are asking lawmakers to change current gun laws:

- Ban semiautomatic magazines that can hold dozens of bullets.

- Close loopholes in background check laws.

● Provide a way for courts and law enforcement to temporarily remove guns from people who pose a threat to themselves or others. (See chapter 10 for details on these solutions and more.)[7]

In an essay for *Vice* magazine, Newtown student activist Jenny Wadhwa wrote, "What people need to realize is that we're not scared of mental illness or unarmed guards. We're scared of guns and inaction."[8]

The Sandy Hook survivors, like the Parkland students and other young activists, have found their voices. Their group is harnessing their power to make change happen. They do not want to see another Sandy Hook or Parkland happen ever again.

Natalie's reminder to young activists:

"THIS NEW GENERATION WILL **ENACT CHANGE** BECAUSE WE HAVE NO CHOICE. WE CANNOT SIT BACK AS TOO MANY ARE SLAUGHTERED ON A DAILY BASIS. **WE STAND TOGETHER,** AND WE ARE NOT BACKING DOWN UNTIL WE FEEL SAFE IN OUR OWN COUNTRY."[9]

◎ ◎ ◎

Learn more about what Natalie and the other Sandy Hook activists are working on and get involved at humansofnewtownct on Instagram and on Facebook at facebook.com/JrNewtownAction/.

PART 4

TAKE ACTION!

People call us snowflakes. What happens when all the snowflakes vote? That's called an avalanche.

—DAVID HOGG, PARKLAND SURVIVOR AND GUN VIOLENCE ACTIVIST

CHAPTER 13

Get Organized

There's a lot to know when it comes to the gun issue. Now that you've learned about what's causing the problem and about possible solutions, it's time to take action. It's time to get organized. There are some very basic and easy first steps you can take to get politically active. Starting with . . .

Register to Vote and Be a Gun Sense Voter

Young people (ages 18 to 29) make up roughly 21 percent of the population eligible to vote in the US.

In 2016, there were forty-six million young people eligible to vote compared to thirty-nine million senior citizens. In fact, in the 2016 presidential election, millennials and Gen Xers cast more votes than the baby boomers and other older generations for the first time in decades: 69.6 million versus 67.9 million. This trend—young people outnumbering and outvoting old people—will continue as the older generation ages and dies and more millennials and Gen Zs reach voting age.[1]

You have the power of your numbers, and if you use it, there is nothing you can't achieve. But you have to vote!

- Register to vote by going to vote.gov and following the directions.

- In some states you can preregister to vote at age 16 or 17, and then you are automatically registered to vote on your eighteenth birthday. To check the rules in your state, go to www.usa.gov/voter-registration-age-requirements.

- If you are at college out of state and wondering how you can vote, go to campusvoteproject.org/studentguides.

- Once you've registered to vote, support gun sense candidates in your area and nationally. Find out who they are at gunsensevoter.org.

- Support gun sense ballot measures and legislation in your area. Check with Students Demand Action (everytown. org/studentsdemand) in your area to get informed.

Even if you aren't old enough to vote yet, you can help get new voters registered and educate them about gun sense candidates and legislation. Student activist Julia Spoor spent the fall of 2018 getting young people registered to vote, even though she was only 16 at the time and couldn't yet vote herself (see her profile in chapter 2).

vocacy." Which means they are creating policies and writing bills
at could be voted into law. They are dedicated to countering the
n lobby.[7] To find out more and get involved, go to csgv.or.

DY HOOK PROMISE

national nonprofit organization founded and led by family mem-
s of students killed at Sandy Hook Elementary School in 2012,
dy Hook Promise has a mission to "build a national movement
parents, schools, and community organizations engaged and
owered to deliver gun safety programs and mobilize for the
age of sensible state and national policy." Members run mental
th and wellness programs that identify and help at-risk indi-
als. So far, 3.5 million parents, educators, community leaders,
students have completed Sandy Hook Promise trainings, and
million American's have signed their promise: "I promise to
I can to protect children from gun violence by encouraging
upporting solutions that create safer, healthier homes, schools
ommunities."[8] To find out more and get involved, go to
hookpromise.org.

NERS FOR RESPONSIBLE OWNERSHIP

a gun safety group for gun owners. The advocacy group sup-
Americans' right to own guns and urges gun owners to store
eapons safely—specifically, to store firearms and ammunition
and separate—and supports universal background checks.[9]
out more and get involved, go to responsibleownership.org.

Join a Gun Safety Group

Maybe you're not old enough to vote yet. Don't despair—there's
still a lot you can do! Most of the students profiled in this book—
students who have made huge contributions to the gun safety
movement—weren't old enough to vote when they first took action.

And you don't have to start from scratch or do anything by yourself. There are already great organizations out there ready to help
you. All you have to do is sign up, and they will tell you when and
where and how you can get involved. It can be as small as signing
your name to a petition or as big as starting a gun safety group at
your school. You can also donate. It takes money to counter the
NRA's deep pockets.

What you do is up to you!

STUDENTS DEMAND ACTION

Students Demand Action (SDA) was created in 2018, just after the
Marjory Stoneman Douglas High School shooting, by a group
of students who wanted a gun safety group of their own. Within
weeks, sixty-five thousand students had signed up. The group's goal
is to empower high school and college students to talk to their local
legislators and hold them accountable for gun issues, elect legislators
who will take action on gun safety, and work in their communities to advocate for gun safety. SDA is supported by Everytown
for Gun Safety (see the next section) but is run by the students
themselves—*they* make the decisions.[2] To find a chapter near you
and get involved, text STUDENTS to 64433 or go to everytown
.org/studentsdemand.

EVERYTOWN FOR GUN SAFETY

This is the biggest gun safety group in America with more than five
million members and counting. Founded in 2014 by former New

York mayor Michael Bloomberg, Everytown was created to oppose the NRA and its influence in Washington, DC. Everytown's mission is to "end gun violence and build safer communities." The group advocates for commonsense gun laws, including more background checks for gun owners, laws to keep guns away from domestic abusers, and tougher gun-trafficking laws. It also has a political action committee that supports and opposes various congressional candidates, depending on their gun safety record.[3] To find out more and get involved, go to everytown.org.

MOMS DEMAND ACTION FOR GUN SENSE IN AMERICA

Moms Demand Action (MDA) is part of Everytown. The two groups work together, with Everytown focusing on DC and national change and MDA focusing on local and state action. MDA was created in 2012, after the Sandy Hook massacre, by stay-at-home mom Shannon Watts (check out her foreword to this book!).

The group quickly became a leader in the gun sense n now has chapters in all fifty states. MDA is nonpar the Second Amendment, and has thousands of volu gun owners. MDA advocates for commonsense gun already improved gun laws at the local, state, and To find out more and get involved, go to momsder

BRADY CAMPAIGN TO PREVENT GUN VIOLENCE

Founded in 1974, this is one of the oldest gun vic groups in the country. It was renamed in 2001 to the White House press secretary who was shot du tion attempt on President Ronald Reagan. The has three main goals: universal background chec on "bad apple" gun dealers who sell guns to crir ing families on the dangers of guns in the home and unintentional shootings).[5] To find out mor go to bradycampaign.org.

GIFFORDS COURAGE TO FIGHT GUN VIOLENCE

This is a nonprofit political action committe Giffords and her husband after the 2012 S. Giffords, a former US congresswoman from tim of a mass shooting in 2011. The group elections to help get gun sense candidates unseat candidates who are opposed to gun have also helped pass more than two hund: forty-five states and Washington, DC.[6] T involved, go to giffords.org.

COALITION TO STOP GUN VIOLENCE

Founded in 1974, this nonprofit group " lence through data-driven policy dev

Start Your Own Gun Safety Group

Every student activist profiled in this book began their journey by taking one small step: they started a group at their school. Are you ready to take your beliefs to the next level? Why not start a gun safety group at *your* middle school, high school, or college?

Students all over America are doing just that. Some are starting their own groups, while others are starting a Students Demand Action (SDA) group. Starting an SDA group is simple. Just follow these quick and easy steps:

1. Go to everytown.org/start-sda-group/.

2. Fill out the online application.

3. You will need a group leader (you) and a group advisor, who can be a teacher, librarian, parent, or Moms Demand Action volunteer.

4. You can have as many roles/members as you want: coleaders, social media leader, DJ for events, etc.

5. Once you send in your application, SDA will mail you a starter kit.

6. Once you get your starter kit, identify a place to meet and how often you will get together.

7. Start meeting and taking action at your school.[10]

A Final Word

Changing the world most often starts with small steps. Register, vote, join a group—these are small steps that will add up to big change in our country.

STUDENTS TAKING A STAND

LANE MURDOCK, AGE 16, ORGANIZER OF THE NATIONAL SCHOOL WALKOUT

On April 20, 2018, the nineteenth anniversary of the Columbine shooting, hundreds of thousands of teenagers across America walked out in the middle of the school day. They gathered together in gyms and town squares to chant and yell, to protest weak gun laws, to send emails to politicians, and to register to vote—in short, to get politically active.

Among the marchers that day was one high school student who never expected to be at the center of an enormous national protest. Sophomore Lane Murdock grew up in Connecticut, just twenty minutes from Newtown, where twenty children and six adults were murdered at Sandy Hook Elementary School in 2012. Like you, she grew up doing regular active shooter drills in school. "It's muscle memory for a lot of us. I can even recite [the drill script]."[1]

By high school, she felt numb to all of it—the shooter drills, the mass shootings on the news. What could she, a high school kid, possibly do to change things?

Sound familiar?

And then Parkland happened. In her high school, students' phones buzzed with the news, but no one really freaked out about it. "I didn't have a huge reaction,"[2] Lane remembers. That bothered her. She felt like she should have a huge reaction. She should have been way more upset. Why wasn't she?

Her principal got on the intercom to address the students; she talked about school safety and asked for a moment of silence for the Florida victims. At the end of her speech, she said that change was up to them, the students.

"That infuriated me," Lane says. Lane wondered why it should be up to high school students when most of them couldn't even vote yet. She questioned why teens should be responsible for fixing a situation they had no part in creating. "It was up to them to change this, and they haven't," Lane says about the adults in power. As she sat listening to her principal, Lane had this epiphany: "OK, if it's up to us, watch us."[3]

And then she got busy.

Lane started an online petition she titled the National High School Walk-Out for Anti Gun Violence. She addressed it to President Trump and the US Senate. In it, she called on her fellow students to wear orange and walk out of class on April 20. She chose the anniversary of the Columbine shooting for a reason: politicians and lawmakers had had nineteen years to work on gun legislation, nineteen years to make changes that would have kept Lane and her friends safer from gun violence. But they had done almost nothing, and almost nothing had changed in those nineteen years.[4]

Lane's petition asked students to "walk out of school, wear orange, and protest online and in your communities. Sign the petition if you pledge to do so. Nothing has changed since Columbine; let us start a movement that lets the government know the time for change is now."[5]

She hoped that kids at her high school would sign it and walk out with her. She was not prepared for what happened next. Overnight, the petition got more than 150,000 signatures. Within days, 2,500 schools and 255,000 supporters all across the country promised to join Lane's march and support gun reform.[6] In the days that followed, Lane spent most of her waking hours organizing the march. Supporters kept their side of the deal: the National School Walkout was an enormous success. Nearly a million kids across America walked out of their schools to take part in the protest—for many, it was their first taste of political action. Tens of thousands of students registered to vote and signed up for gun sense groups. More than 150 new groups formed across the country, and Everytown for Gun Safety, the biggest national gun sense group, had such a flood of interest they started a chapter for and led by young people: Students Demand Action (everytown.org/studentsdemand/).[7]

Of course, the battle isn't over. Lane is working harder than ever as a gun safety activist. She speaks all over the country, she leads more protests, she voices her opinions on social media—all to empower students to demand action on gun violence at the federal and state levels and to demand solutions like banning assault weapons, instating universal background checks, and taking guns away from people at risk of hurting themselves or others.

"It is not conservative or liberal," Lane explains. "It's about making sure children don't get harmed in school and we don't live in a country that has institutionalized fear. No child should have to learn how to hide from a shooter."[8]

Lane wants to end school shootings before another generation of children grows numb to it, like she was. Her advice to student activists:

"OUR GENERATION HAS MADE CHANGE. AND WE AREN'T STOPPING."[9]

◎ ◎ ◎

Learn more about what Lane is working on and get involved at nationalschoolwalkout.net or follow her at @lanemurdock2002.

CHAPTER 14

DO SOMETHING

Even though there is over 90 percent support for gun sense laws like improved background checks, it is challenging, if not impossible, to get our politicians to take action. Part of that is certainly NRA contributions, but most of it is political influence.

Heidi Heitkamp, Democratic senator from North Dakota, explained that when universal background checks were being considered in her state, phone calls to her office were seven to one against. For her, that was a sign that the voters who really care about the gun issue—the ones who will vote on the issue and tell their friends to vote on the issue—are people who oppose gun safety. "At the end of the day, you got to listen to your constituents," she said.

She voted against the background checks.[1]

The ugly truth is that even though gun sense advocates outnumber gun rights supporters, the gun sense side is not as loud. We have not been as organized or as focused as the NRA and its supporters. That's why we don't have the same political power.

And that is why we are where we are—with almost no action on gun safety.

That must change.

But how?

ENOUGH IS ENOUGH: THIRTY-THREE FRIENDS KILLED BY GUNS

Camiella Williams has lost not one . . . not two . . . not three friends to bullets. Camiella has lost a staggering thirty-three friends to gun violence in her hometown of Chicago. This started with the shooting of her second-grade teacher, and most recently, a 19-year-old she was mentoring was shot while dropping his little brother off at basketball practice.

All that gun death has taken a toll. "I went through rage, depression. I still can't sleep," she said.

Guns have been a part of Camiella's life for a long time. As a kid, she was in a gang and used her allowance money to buy her first gun, in sixth grade. Camiella's feelings about guns shifted dramatically after she had children of her own. She decided to do everything in her power to stop guns from killing more people in her community. Now she works for Live Free Chicago, a group dedicated to preventing shootings by calming neighborhood conflicts before they erupt into gun violence. "She's dedicated to saving people's lives," said Georgia Congresswoman Lucy McBath, whose own son was shot and killed in 2012.

Camiella suffers from PTSD (post-traumatic stress disorder) from all the gun violence and loss in her life, so she understands how shootings can damage a kid's psychological health. Live Free Chicago also raises money for counseling for kids who need it. "It's like you're in a tunnel with no way out," she explained. "So I let people know you talk about it, you deal with it, you try to prevent it. The goal is to get other people like me to fight." Camiella is doing just that, turning her tragedy into empowerment by bringing new activists into the gun safety movement.[2]

Ring Your Rep

Make some noise! Be a squeaky wheel, like the gun rights supporters. That means, call your leaders and representatives. Call them
often. Tell them how you feel about gun violence in your state and
in our country. Tell them what you want them to do about it. Tell
them it's not acceptable to do nothing.

IT ONLY TAKES
A MINUTE.

Calling your state representative, senator, or governor is a great
way to be squeaky. When you call, they will tally up the number of
calls on each side of a gun issue (or a bill that's being decided on),
and that helps them decide how to vote. Your call will show them
how many gun sense supporters are out there, motivated, and paying
attention. Get your friends to call too! The goal is to make the list
of gun sense supporters longer than the list of gun rights supporters.

When you call, you will get a recorded message or maybe a real
staffer. Leave a message about gun safety and how important it is to
you. Your phone call can make a difference!

HOW DO YOU CALL?

State Representatives and Senators: Type in your address
at this website to get your state legislators' names and phone
numbers: openstates.org.

US Representatives and Senators: Do the same at this
website to find your federal legislators' names and phone
numbers: callyourrep.co.

Governor: Get your governor's number here: usa.gov /state-governor.

More Leaders: Go to 5calls.org/issue/action-against-gun-violence to find more people to call and demand action from.

WHEN SHOULD YOU CALL?

When you're feeling angry, frustrated, or scared about the gun violence you see on the news. When there's a vote on an important gun sense bill. When you want to thank your representative for doing something good.

WHAT SHOULD YOU SAY?

Talking to unfamiliar adults can be stressful, even for grown-ups! Reading from a script really helps. Fill in the blanks in the following script with the particulars you are calling about, and bingo! You have the perfect message to leave for your leaders. Also remember:

Keep it short. Staffers are just logging calls for or against. They don't need to know much about why you are calling. You don't have to explain yourself.

Be polite. Can you imagine how much it would suck to take angry calls all day long? The person answering the phone is human. They are trying to help you make your voice heard. Remember, you catch more bees with honey, so be kind and polite—even if you're mad as hell.

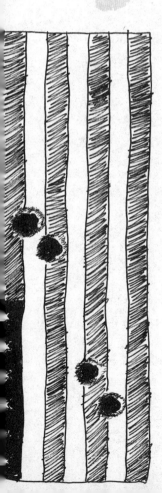

USE A SCRIPT

Hi, MY NAME IS
[YOUR NAME]

AND I'M CALLING FROM
[CITY AND ZIP CODE].

I DON'T NEED A RESPONSE.

I AM CALLING ABOUT
[iSSUE/BILL/LAW].

I WANT TO ENCOURAGE
[POLITICIAN'S NAME]

TO
[SUPPORT/OPPOSE]

THIS
[iSSUE/BILL/LAW].

THANK YOU![3]

Go to a Town Hall Meeting

Congressional town hall meetings give constituents (that includes you!) a chance to make our voices heard. They give lawmakers a chance to hear from their voters in person. This is an excellent time and place to tell your lawmakers how you feel about gun violence and what they should do about it.

FIND A MEETING NEAR YOU

- Find your legislator at openstates.org.

- Go to townhallproject.com or your legislator's website, Facebook page, or Twitter feed to find the date, location, and time.

- Events are often scheduled at the last minute, so check often or sign up for alerts.

BE PREPARED

- Register (if required) for the town hall meeting.

- Invite your friends—the more voices on your side, the better.

- Visit your legislator's website to read their latest press releases about their stands and action on gun safety.

- Write down one to two short questions to ask at the meeting. Tell them how you feel about gun violence and how it impacts your life directly and ask what they plan to do about it.

- Practice asking your question until you can do it in twenty-five seconds or less.

WHAT TO DO AT THE MEETING

- Arrive early and sign in. Ask if you need to sign up to ask a question.

- If possible, before the meeting starts, introduce yourself to your legislator and their staff. Shake their hands.

- Sit in the front of the room, so they can see you easily and won't miss you when your hand is raised to ask your question.

- When it's your turn to ask your question, start by telling them your name, your age, and where you live. Most people at town hall meetings are old. It will be unique and impactful that you are a young person taking political action.[4]

SAMPLE QUESTIONS

- What is your position on gun safety?

- How are you keeping young people like me safe from gun violence in our state?

- How will you vote on the next gun law? (Find out what that gun bill is before you go!)

March and Protest

Do you feel like taking to the streets and screaming your lungs out? Good for you! Here are some ways you can join with other students in the gun safety movement and show the world how you feel, together. Before you head out for your protest, don't forget to . . .

Get excused. It's your right as an American to protest and exercise free speech. If your school doesn't support the cause by letting students out to protest, ask your parents to call in and excuse your absence. Let them know how important it is to you to be at the protest and show them you're serious by finding out what work you'll miss and making it up.

Spread the word. It's a lot more fun to march and protest with friends. And the whole idea is to show the world how many gun sense supporters there are. More is better, so spread the word. Use that social media.

Make a sign. Get together with your friends the night before or even the day of and have a sign-making party. No one says political action can't be fun, right?

MARCH

Each year, there are protests on the anniversaries of mass shootings. If there were mass shootings in your state, there will be protests on those anniversaries, and there will be protests for nationally known shootings as well (see the following list). These are good times to band together with other gun sense supporters to show politicians our numbers. Check your local paper the week before to find out details on what's happening in your area and where and when to meet up.

IMPORTANT PROTEST DATES

February 14: Parkland anniversary

March 24: March for Our Lives

April 20: Columbine anniversary

June 1: Gun Violence Awareness Day

June 2: Wear Orange for Gun Safety Day

June 12: Pulse nightclub anniversary

October 1: Las Vegas anniversary

WALK OUT

The dictionary defines a walkout as "a sudden angry departure, especially as a protest or strike."[5] It literally means getting up and walking out of your school at a set time to protest gun violence. Especially for students too young to vote, walkouts have been a powerful form of protest for decades. Student walkouts led to change for black people during the civil rights movement. March for Our Lives is a national walkout.

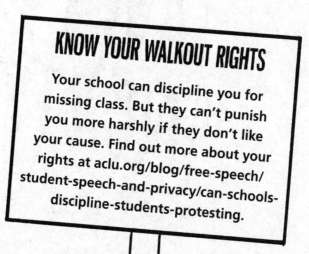

KNOW YOUR WALKOUT RIGHTS

Your school can discipline you for missing class. But they can't punish you more harshly if they don't like your cause. Find out more about your rights at aclu.org/blog/free-speech/ student-speech-and-privacy/can-schools-discipline-students-protesting.

DIE-IN

Another powerful way to protest gun violence is to organize a die-in. A die-in is a protest where people lie down as if they are dead. Die-ins were a big form of protest during the AIDS crisis of the 1980s. On the one-year anniversary of the Pulse nightclub massacre, high schooler Marcel McClinton helped lead a die-in on the lawn outside Congress. Protesters read the names of the victims, then lay down for twelve minutes, or 720 seconds—the number of mass shooting victims since the Pulse massacre.[6] There were lots of die-ins in Florida, where the Parkland and Pulse massacres happened, including one in front of Trump's Mar-A-Lago resort.[7]

Where should you stage a die-in?

Why not drop down in front of your local NRA offices, gun stores, and your state capitol, in front of the offices of politicians who accept donations from the NRA?

Vote with Your Wallet: Boycott

You can protest and put pressure on politicians to take action for commonsense gun reform, but we can also put pressure on companies to stop supporting the NRA and their deadly agenda. You can encourage brands you use and love to take a stand for gun safety. Some companies already have, and they deserve our support (because you know NRA members are putting pressure on them).

GUN SENSE COMPANIES TO SUPPORT

Dick's Sporting Goods led the charge for gun sense after they discovered one of the guns purchased by the 2018 Parkland shooter was from their store. The company immediately stopped selling assault-style weapons and raised the minimum age for buying guns to 21. "Thoughts and prayers are not enough," they said in a press release. "We have to help solve the problem that's in front of us. Gun violence is an epidemic that's taking the lives of too many people, including the brightest hope for the future of America— our kids."[8] Gun rights activists immediately called for supporters to boycott Dick's, and NRA-backed lawsuits quickly followed.

These companies followed Dick's lead and took action in their stores:

Walmart: The country's largest retailer had already stopped selling assault weapons back in 2015, but they raised their minimum age.

Kroger: This chain owns nearly 2,800 stores in thirty-five states, including Ralphs, Dillons, Smith's, King Soopers, City Market, Fry's, QFC, and Fred Meyer. In 2018 they raised their minimum age for firearm purchase to 21 in their stores that sell guns.[9]

REI: This outdoor company doesn't sell guns in its stores, but it does sell products made by other companies that do sell guns. REI pressured those companies by placing a hold on brands like Giro, Bell, and CamelBak (add to your list of companies to boycott), whose parent company also owns gun companies. Their statement read: "REI does not sell guns. We believe that it is the job of companies that manufacture and sell guns and ammunition to work toward commonsense solutions that prevent the type of violence that happened in Florida last month."[10]

Here's a short list of big national companies that cut ties to the NRA by ending discounts for their members (this list gets longer every day):

Delta and United airlines

Best Western and Wyndham hotels

Enterprise, Alamo, National, Hertz, Avis, and Budget car rental companies

Allied and North American Van Lines

First National and Republic Banks

MetLife Insurance[11]

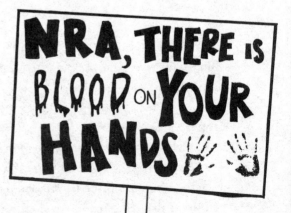

COMPANIES TO BOYCOTT

There are companies out there benefitting from their ties to the NRA and other gun groups. You can boycott these companies; stop buying their products. You can also write letters and emails to their customer service departments or even to their company presidents! Tell them how you feel about them making money while kids are getting shot. Learn more about which companies to boycott and how to hit the NRA financially at #boycottNRA.

BOYCOTTS WORK!

When the world boycotted South Africa from roughly 1965 to 1993 because of its racist apartheid policies, the financial pressure helped create political revolution there.[12] If boycotts can radically change the political and social structure of a whole country, surely it can make a difference in fixing America's gun violence epidemic.

A Final Word

Now that you've learned the facts about gun violence in America and the solutions, you're ready to do more. Like the other young activists in this book, I hope you will take some of these actions to make your voice heard and to help create change in your community and across America.

INSIDER TIPS FROM A GUN SENSE LEADER

JENNIFER WILLIAMSON, OREGON STATE REPRESENTATIVE AND HOUSE MAJORITY LEADER

Representative Jennifer Williamson (Democrat) has been proposing and passing gun sense legislation ever since she joined the Oregon House of Representatives back in 2013. She has the inside scoop for students and gun safety activists on how to jump into the political game and get things done. Marching is great, but it only gets you so far. There are more impactful things you, a young person, can do. Even if you're not yet old enough to vote.

Representative Williamsons should know—she started her political career when she was a freshman in college, by taking action on a cause she cared about.

Insider Tip #1: Just Do It!

Representative Williamson knows you can't sit back and wait for someone else to fix your problems—odds are they won't. It's a lesson she learned at a young age. She grew up on a farm in rural Oregon and was the first in her family to go away to college. But freshman year she discovered tuition would be going up and her federal Pell Grant would be cut. She worried she wouldn't be able to stay. Representative Williamson didn't wait around for the grown-ups to fix it—she headed to the US Capitol in Washington, DC. She explains:

> "A group of us sat down with US Senator Mark Hatfield (Republican from Oregon), chair of the Appropriations Committee, and I showed him my financial aid letter, which he had never seen before. We walked him through it: 'Here's how much it costs to go to college, here's how much it costs to live in a dorm, here's what your financial aid is supposed to cover.' He had never seen what cuts in those line items on the budget would do to students."[1]

The students were so persuasive, Senator Hatfield went back to DC and canceled the cuts. And when Representative Williamson graduated from college, he hired her to work with him on education issues.

"I SAW A PROBLEM THAT WAS IMPACTING ME, FOUND OUT THE PERSON WHO MIGHT BE ABLE TO FIX IT, AND SAT DOWN WITH THEM AND TOLD THEM MY STORY."

Insider Tip #2: Start Small

Representative Williamson's passion for gun safety started in a personal way. In 1998, there was a school shooting near her—four people were killed and twenty-five wounded. The parents of a friend were close with the shooter's family. Representative Williamson says, "The impact on that community and on a family I knew very well is where my passion about this issue started. When I decided to run for office, universal background checks were something I knew I could fight for." She helped get universal background checks passed after winning her election.

> ## "THIS STUFF IS HARD AND OFTEN VERY INCREMENTAL. EVERY STEP FORWARD IS AN IMPORTANT STEP."

Insider Tip #3: Stick with It

Before Representative Williamson got elected, there hadn't been any movement on state gun laws for fifteen years. She started by working on universal background checks, and each year she has worked to add one more gun sense law to Oregon's books. Here are the laws she's helped pass so far:

- Started school safety tip line (House Bill 4075) in 2016 as a way for students to anonymously report school safety threats to law enforcement

- Increased funding for background checks in 2016, so state police have the resources to adequately and promptly conduct background checks for gun sales

- Created Extreme Risk Protection Order (SB 719) in 2017, allowing families and law enforcement to get a court order to temporarily remove guns from a person who is deemed a danger themselves or others

- Closed boyfriend and stalker loopholes (HB 4145) in 2018 to keep abusive dating partners and people convicted of or under a stalking order from buying guns.[2]

"THESE ARE LONG-TERM ISSUES. STAY ENGAGED, LOOK AT YOUR LONG-TERM PLANS, AND WORK WITH POLICY MAKERS."

Insider Tip #4: Reach Across the Aisle

Representative Williamson knows that working with people who have different perspectives, who don't share all of your beliefs, is the only way to make progress in America. That is democracy. She believes it's time to broaden outreach in the gun safety movement:

It's time to reach out not just to politicians, but to community members in communities that might not always agree with us. People often say there's an urban-rural divide on guns. I disagree with that. I think we agree on the vast majority of things that will keep our communities safer. Engaging people who we may disagree with, having a conversation, is so much more productive than telling somebody they're wrong. Finding common ground is a good a place to start. For young people to talk to each other across these artificial barriers that adults have created is really powerful.

Insider Tip #5: You Have Power—Use It

Young people have much to offer our leaders. You see problems from a different perspective than adults and are impacted in different ways. You come up with unique solutions that can be turned into bills and then into laws. Too many politicians ignore young people because they don't think they vote as much as older constituents. Representative Williamson explains, "The number of times I've heard elected officials say, 'Young people don't vote, so why do we care what they think?' That just infuriated me."

Don't let those politicians ignore you. Vote, speak out, and get active.

After the 2018 Parkland shooting, students jumped into the fight, and it changed things. Representative Williamson explains, "Parkland felt like the first time students came out and said, 'No, let us tell you what needs to happen.' Students took control of the debate. It made all the difference." Now students need to take it further by showing up at the polls, showing up at their state capitols, and continuing to work on this issue.

"YOUNG PEOPLE KNOW WHAT KIND OF FUTURE THEY WANT. **WE NEED THEIR VOICES** AT THE TABLE HELPING CRAFT THOSE SOLUTIONS. WE NEED YOUNG PEOPLE TO ENGAGE."

Insider Tip #6: Get Face Time with Your Reps

Representative Williamson has one final tip for getting the attention of your leaders: go to a town hall meeting. Elected officials hold town halls in order to meet face-to-face with constituents and hear what's on their minds. Going to one is a surprisingly powerful act. Most young people don't know about town halls—Representative Williamson says there is almost never anyone under the age of 50 there!

She advises you be prepared when you go (see chapter 14) and press your elected leader on their gun safety views in front of their constituents. "Ask, 'What do you think about this issue? What are you going to do to solve it? How are you going to vote on this bill?'"

Town halls don't take a lot of time or energy—they're about two hours long—but they mean a lot to people like Representative Williamson. She says, "As a legislator, that's one of the most impactful ways for my constituents to talk to me. You've got witnesses."

"DOING SOMETHING IN PERSON **ALWAYS** HAS A **BIGGER IMPACT** THAN EMAILING, SENDING A FORM LETTER, OR CALLING."

231

Insider Tip #7: Speak Your Truth

Representative Williamson set a great example when she told Senator Hatfield about how his Pell Grant cuts would impact her ability to go to college. Follow her lead and speak truth to power.

"TALK TO YOUR REPRESENTATIVE. TELL THEM YOUR STORY. TELL THEM HOW GUN VIOLENCE IMPACTS YOU ON A DAY-TO-DAY LEVEL. TELL THEM WHAT YOU WORRY ABOUT AND WHY YOU WORRY ABOUT IT."

◎ ◎ ◎

Learn more about what Representative Jennifer Williamson is working on at oregonlegislature.gov/williamson.

HOW A BILL GETS MADE INTO A LAW

Representative Williamson explains the process: "There are lots of people you have to convince and lots of steps where a bill can die. It takes a lot of time and effort to convince all those people that this is the right solution to the problem.

1. Somebody has an idea for how to solve a problem. It could be a **constituent**, it could be a **legislator,** or it could be a group of people who come in and say, 'This is the problem, and this is what we think the solution is.'

2. We write a **bill** with that solution in it.

3. We take the bill to a **committee**. We tell them, 'Here's the problem, and here's what we think the solution is.' We have to convince the majority of that committee that it's the right thing to do.

4. If it passes the committee, it goes to the **floor** of the **House**, and we have to convince the majority of the legislators in the House that this is the solution to the problem.

5. Then we do it all again in the **Senate**. If we can convince the majority of the senators that this is the solution to the problem, they'll pass the bill through committee and pass it on the floor of the Senate.

6. Then we have to convince the **governor** that this is the solution to the problem. If we can convince her, then the governor will sign the bill and it becomes law."

POLITICAL JARGON

Appropriations Committee: Also called the US House Committee on Appropriations, a group of lawmakers responsible for passing bills that determine how the US government spends money.[3]

Bill: A draft of a proposed law presented for discussion and consideration by a legislature.[4]

Constituent: A voting member of a community.[5]

Floor: The place where legislative members sit and make speeches. When a person is speaking there formally, they are said to "have the floor."[6]

State House Majority Leader: This is a state representative chosen by other representatives in the political party holding the largest number of seats in the State House. It varies by state, but usually the House Majority Leader schedules legislation for floor consideration, plans legislative agendas, and works to advance the goals of the majority party.[7]

Legislator: A person who writes and passes laws, especially someone who is a member of a legislature. Legislators are usually politicians and are often elected by the people of the state.[8]

State Senates and Houses of Representatives: These two elected groups belong to the State Legislature, which means they make the laws for each state. The number of state representatives and senators is based on population, each one representing a specific area/group of citizens, so each state has a different number. For example, the Oregon House of Representatives has sixty members, and the Oregon Senate has thirty members, each representing different districts across the state. State representatives serve a two-year term, while state senators serve a four-year term.[9]

235

Step 1: Start on common ground to build trust.

Friend: *Americans have a Constitutional right to own guns. No one should be able to take that away.*

You: *I agree that you have the right to own a gun. But I don't think either of us wants criminals to own them, right?*

discussion will be more productive when it starts from common ground. Find ideas you can both agree on and focus on Starting with ideas you agree on lays a foundation of trust. ber that you are hoping to work together with this person plish a common goal—you're not trying to quickly change

Establish the facts you share them respectfully.

you know that one hundred die from gunshots every day?

that over half of school guns from a family home?

that one in five guns are sold without eck because of gaps in federal law?

mmon ground, share your knowledge about gun it bothers you. Give statistics that are hard to powerful pieces of information can be better

238

CHAPTER 15

HOW TO TA[LK]
TO FAMILY [AND]
FRIENDS ABO[UT]
VIOLEN[CE]

As Representative Jennifer W[
most important ways we can [
tion is to reach out and talk [
But how exactly do we hav[e
who disagree with you ca[
talk about gun violence [
common goals instead o[

Here are some sugg[estions
the Brady Campaign [
with your friends an[

th[

Yo[
comm[
those. [
Remem[
to acco[
their min[

Step 2:
know a[

You: Did [
Americans [

Did you kno[
shooters use g[

Did you know [
a background ch[

Once you find co[
violence and why [
rebut. One or two [

than a deluge of information. Don't belittle the other person but pull them in with "did you know?" questions. These will encourage them to speak their thoughts. This book is full of information you can use, plus the Brady Campaign has a short fact sheet to help you (go to bradycampaign.org/armed-with-facts).

Step 3: Actively listen to the other person's perspective.

You: *What do you think we should do to keep guns away from felons?*

I'd love to hear your ideas on how we can save lives from gun violence.

How do you think we can make America safer from gun violence?

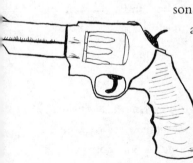

To have a truly productive conversation, the person you are talking to needs to feel respected and heard. You will build trust and compassion by showing that you care about their beliefs and want to hear what they have to say about guns. Use active listening by fully concentrating on what they are saying. Ask open-ended questions so they feel heard instead of dismissed.

Step 4: Don't be afraid to disagree.

Once you establish common ground and trust, and once your friend has voiced their opinions and feels heard, then you can have more of an active debate about the issue. Keep the conversation civil by remembering earlier tips: actively listen, stay open to their ideas, don't get defensive, and continue to share your opinions in a calm, rational manner. But remember—it's okay to disagree. In fact, it's likely to happen. But now is the time for you to share what you've learned throughout this book.

Step 5: Find common solutions based on your conversation.

You: *Can we agree that stopping dangerous people from getting guns is an important goal?*

Can we agree that requiring a background check for every gun sale is a good first step toward keeping guns out of dangerous hands?

Once you've done the hard work of finding common ground, building trust, and engaging in debate, it's time to close the deal. Hopefully, you found areas you agree on. And hopefully, you convinced your friend about the need to reduce gun violence.

A Final Note

Even if you don't think you found much common ground with the person you talked to, that's okay. Starting the conversation about gun violence is a critical first step. You can build on that conversation over time. Who knows? Maybe you will eventually recruit a new activist to the movement!

INSIDER TIPS FROM
A GUN SENSE LEADER

KATE BROWN, GOVERNOR OF OREGON[1]

Kate Brown has served the people of Oregon for more than twenty-five years, first in the state's House of Representatives and Senate from 1991 to 2009, then as secretary of state from 2009 to 2015, and finally as Oregon's governor since 2015. Kate is married to Dan Little, but she is also the first openly bisexual governor in the US.[2] She also is one of America's strongest gun sense leaders, courageous enough to stand up to the gun lobby and enact legislation that is making Oregonians safer from gun violence.

Her passion for reducing gun violence started before she entered politics, when she worked as a young lawyer. She explains, "My practice often focused on women or their children in the foster care system. Those cases occasionally involved domestic violence, and we know that the presence of a gun has a tremendous impact on the safety of everyone in the home." During her 2016 race for governor, Brown also revealed that in a relationship prior to her marriage, she was the victim of domestic abuse.[3]

However, it was the 2015 mass shooting at Umpqua Community College in Roseburg, Oregon, that really spurred Governor Brown to action. "In the hours and days that followed," she says, "I remember speaking with the families of the students and professor murdered that day, and with the members of a campus community forever changed by what occurred." With other gun sense state leaders in Oregon, such as Representative Jennifer Williamson and Senator Ginny Burdick, both Democrats, Governor Brown helped pass some important gun sense laws: requiring universal background checks, creating an Extreme Risk Protection Order (via a Red Flag Law), and closing the intimate partner loophole.

Passing those laws wasn't easy. "Despite the fact that many commonsense gun regulations are overwhelmingly popular, they are still somehow politically difficult to pass. There are powerful pro-gun lobbying groups who have, for years, organized to stop further legislation," Governor Brown explains. She believes there is a

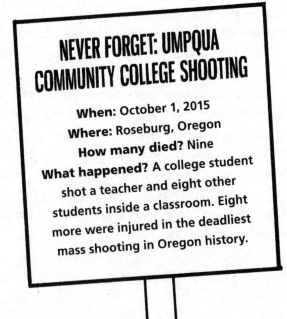

NEVER FORGET: UMPQUA COMMUNITY COLLEGE SHOOTING

When: October 1, 2015
Where: Roseburg, Oregon
How many died? Nine
What happened? A college student shot a teacher and eight other students inside a classroom. Eight more were injured in the deadliest mass shooting in Oregon history.

powerful force that can change that: "Young people being engaged and adding their voices to gun violence prevention measures is critical. There is power in numbers, and the numbers favor additional regulations."

Here are her thoughts on the most effective way to make change happen:

Insider Tip #1: Get to know your state legislators.

"Get to know your state representative and senator and where they stand on the issues. Does this person represent your values? If so, help them stay elected. If not, work on their opponent's campaign. Visit them at a town hall or in their offices [at your state capitol]. Have a clear ask and be prepared to defend your position."

Insider Tip #2: Speak up for bills you care about (in person).

"If there is a particular bill you support, you can submit written testimony or appear and testify in person for that bill. And stick with it—sometimes it takes several sessions for a concept to make it through the legislature."

Insider Tip #3: Join a group—there is strength in numbers.

"There are also lobbying groups, like Everytown for Gun Safety, who organize visits to state capitols and meetings with legislators (called Lobby Day). Joining an organized group is a great way to get started, because you will see how to best engage with legislators."

Insider Tip #4: Vote!

"Most importantly, when you're old enough: register to vote, make sure your friends are registered to vote, and then vote!!!!!"

Governor Brown's advice to young activists:

> "YOU HAVE A POWERFUL STORY TO TELL—YOU WANT TO LEARN IN A SAFE AND HEALTHY ENVIRONMENT, AND YOU CANNOT DO THAT WHEN YOU ARE WORRYING ABOUT BEING SHOT IN YOUR CLASSROOMS. WE MUST DO MORE FOR YOU, AND YOU MUST HOLD US—YOUR ELECTED OFFICIALS—ACCOUNTABLE."

◎ ◎ ◎

Learn more about what Governor Kate Brown is working on at www.actionplanfororegon.gov.

A FINAL NOTE

I know a lot of you out there are angry. It's okay to be angry. Heck, it's good to be angry. If I weren't angry, I never would have written this book.

But anger, fear, and frustration only get us so far. You can use those negative emotions to do positive things.

USE YOUR ANGER ABOUT GUN VIOLENCE TO GET INVOLVED.

USE YOUR FRUSTRATION WITH POLITICIANS TO TAKE ACTION.

USE YOUR FEAR OF SCHOOL SHOOTINGS TO GET OFF THE COUCH AND DO SOMETHING.

One of the most important things you can do is reach out to people who disagree with you: students, parents, grandparents, neighbors, coaches, and church leaders. Listen to their concerns and try to understand where they are coming from. Then help educate them with everything you now know about the gun violence issue. See chapter 15 for tips on how to do that.

Gun violence is a huge problem in our country. To fix it, we will need everyone's help, on both sides of the political aisle. We need to draw others into this fight with us instead of pushing them away.

WE NEED GUN OWNERS AND GUN VIOLENCE PREVENTION ACTIVISTS TO WORK TOGETHER.

WE NEED REPUBLICANS AND DEMOCRATS TO WORK TOGETHER.

WE NEED CITY KIDS AND RURAL KIDS TO WORK TOGETHER.

Don't let your anger, fear, and frustration burn you out. This battle for gun reform will not be quick and easy. If we want it to happen, then all of us need to be in it for the long haul. Young activist Nza-Ari Khepra explains, "Like other movements—women's rights, civil rights, LGBTQ+ rights—slow and steady wins the race. You may not see change immediately, but over time your activism will make a difference." (And see her profile in chapter 4.)[1]

DON'T GIVE UP. HAVE HOPE. THINGS WILL GET BETTER.

LEARN MORE, GO DEEPER: ADDITIONAL RESOURCES

As many young activists have pointed out, knowledge is power. The more you know about America's gun violence problem, the more convincing you will be when you discuss it with other students and adults, and the more effective you will be in making change. Here are some resources where you can learn more and go deeper.

Books

Here is a list of books I used to research *Enough Is Enough*, along with others that will add to your knowledge of the issue.

NONFICTION

These are mostly books for adults, but they have great information. And you are smart enough to read them.

> ***#NeverAgain: A New Generation Draws the Line*** by David Hogg and Lauren Hogg (Random House, 2018)
> Written by survivors of the Parkland massacre, this is their story and their statement of intent for the movement

they launched. Their generation is standing up to the inaction of our politicians and is determined to overcome all obstacles in their way. This is their guidebook to the #NeverAgain movement and student activism.

The Gun Debate: What Everyone Needs to Know by Philip J. Cook and Kristin A. Goss (Oxford University Press, 2014)
Written in Q&A format, the book explains the statistics and rhetoric surrounding America's gun debate. This book is helpful for getting a clear, fact-based account of the issues surrounding guns America.

Gunfight: The Battle Over the Right to Bear Arms in America by Adam Winkler (W. W. Norton & Co., 2013)
This book looks at the history of America's battle over gun control and the right to bear arms, since the ratification of the Second Amendment in 1791. It gives a detailed look into the emotional debate currently raging in our country.

Kids and Guns: The History, the Present, the Dangers, the Risk, and the Remedies by Ted Schwarz (Franklin Watts, 1999)
This book looks at the history of guns, questions around gun ownership, and the link between guns and violence that impacts young people all across America.

Over Our Dead Bodies: Port Arthur and Australia's Fight for Gun Control by Simon Chapman (Sydney University Press, 2013)
This book gives an account of Australia's historic action around gun violence prevention, after their deadliest mass shooting, when the government managed to unite the country and took action to dramatically reduce the country's gun violence.

The Second Amendment: A Biography by Michael Waldman
(Simon & Schuster, 2015)

> This book explains the most contentious and misinterpreted
> provision in the Bill of Rights—the Second Amendment. What
> does it mean? A look at the history reveals some unexpected
> answers.

Shot: 101 Survivors of Gun Violence in America by Kathy
Shorr (PowerHouse Books, 2017)

> In 101 photos, this book highlights survivors from across
> America (from all races and ethnicities) who have been shot and
> survived and have a story to tell. Most of the pictures were taken
> at the shooting locations.

FICTION

Reading fiction is a wonderful way to put ourselves in other people's
shoes. It's also a safe way to experience something scary and trau-
matic without actually being there. Reading fiction has been shown
to help us develop empathy—something the gun debate could really
use right now. Here's what the Saint Louis Public Library says about
the benefits of reading stories about gun violence:

> In a time when acts of gun violence are reported with
> such regularity, it is helpful for young people to see the
> emotional consequences of these tragic events. [Books]
> give readers a chance to understand the perspective
> of different characters dealing with the effects of
> gun violence. Perspective, ultimately, is needed in the
> aftermath of all tragedies.[1]

All American Boys by Jason Reynolds and Brendan Kiely (Atheneum Books for Young Readers, 2015)

Sixteen-year-old Quinn witnesses a police officer brutally beat classmate Rashad after he is accused of stealing. The officer is the older brother of Quinn's best friend. The story unfolds through Rashad's and Quinn's alternating voices.

And We Stay by Jenny Hubbard (Delacorte Press, 2014)

After her ex-boyfriend shoots himself, 17-year-old Emily is sent away to a boarding school. There she begins to express her feelings through poetry as she relives their love, deals with her guilt, and starts to heal.

Bang! by Sharon Flake (Hyperion, 2005)

Thirteen-year-old Mann has already had to deal with plenty of tragedy in his young life. His little brother was shot and each member of his family is dealing with the experience in a different way. Mann tells the story of his collapsing family and his own self-destructive actions as he faces the harsh realities of inner-city life.

The Day Tajon Got Shot by Teen Writers of Beacon House (Shout Mouse Press, 2017)

Written by ten teenage girls from Washington, DC, during the rise of the Black Lives Matter movement, their story is about 16-year-old Tajon. He's a good kid who works hard and has big dreams. He is determined to get out of the hood. Then, one day, Tajon gets shot. Each writer takes on the voice of a character in the story—Tajon, the police officer, a parent, a friend—to explore race, violence, and justice in America today.

Endgame by Nancy Garden (Harcourt, 2006)

This is the story of Gray Wilton, a 15-year-old who is bullied

at school by his peers and at home by his father. His response
is to go on a shooting rampage at his new high school. The
book explores the impacts of bullying and its connection to gun
violence.

Forgive Me, Leonard Peacock by Matthew Quick (Little,
Brown and Co., 2013)
This novel follows a suicidal teen through his last day, as he says
good-bye to the four most important people in his life.

Hate List by Jennifer Brown (Little, Brown and Co.,
2009)
Valerie's boyfriend, Nick, opened fire in their school cafeteria
five months ago, killing several classmates. Val was shot while
saving a classmate but is still blamed for the shooting because of
the Hate List she and Nick created together. Val must face the
tragedy and her part in it in order to atone and move forward
with her life.

The Hate U Give by Angie Thomas (Balzer + Bray, 2017)
After witnessing her friend Khalil get shot by a police officer,
Starr doesn't know what to do. If she tells what she saw, the
police and a local drug lord may come after her and her family.
But if she stays silent and lets Khalil become the bad guy in the
media, how can she live with herself? Starr learns about the cost
of staying silent and the power of speaking out.

How It Went Down by Kekla Magoon (Henry Holt and
Co., 2014)
When 16-year-old Tariq is shot to death, his community erupts
in outrage: Tariq was black and the shooter is white. After the
tragedy, everyone has a different version of how it went down.

Long Way Down by Jason Reynolds (Atheneum Books for Young Readers, 2017)

> Fifteen-year-old Will is out for revenge for the shooting murder of his brother, Shawn. But inside his apartment elevator, armed with his brother's gun, he is visited by seven ghosts who knew Shawn and explain to Will the truth about his brother and the deadly path he is on.

Tyler Johnson Was Here by Jay Coles (Little, Brown and Co., 2018)

> When Marvin's twin brother, Tyler, is shot and killed by a police officer, Marvin searches for answers and learns the true meaning of freedom.

Shooter by Walter Dean Myers (Amistad/HarperTempest, 2004)

> Told through interviews, reports, and journal entries, this is the story of three troubled teenagers that ends in a tragic school shooting.

The Stars Beneath Our Feet by David Barclay Moore (Alfred A. Knopf, 2017)

> After his older brother is killed in a gang-related shooting, Lolly tries to avoid being forced into a gang himself while constructing a beautiful, imaginative LEGO city at his community center.

This Is Where It Ends by Marieke Nijkamp (Sourcebooks Fire, 2016)

> After the principal finishes welcoming students to a new year, they discover they are locked in the auditorium as someone starts shooting. Four teen narrators, each with a different reason to fear the shooter, tell the story from alternating perspectives.

Underwater by Marisa Reichardt (Farrar, Straus and Giroux, 2016)

> After a mass shooting at her high school, Morgan has become agoraphobic. She can't go outside without having a panic attack. But when a new boy moves in next door, she starts to long for the life she is avoiding.

Unlocked by Ryan G. Van Cleave (Walker & Co, 2011)

> Andy is an outcast at his school. When he befriends another outcast, he discovers the boy may be planning a school shooting. A fascinating look at what it feels like to be the only one who can prevent a tragedy.

Violent Ends: A Novel in Seventeen Points of View by Shaun David Hutchinson et al. (Simon & Schuster, 2015)

> This uniquely structured book relates how one boy, who had never been in trouble before, turns into a monster capable of shooting his classmates. The story is told in the alternating voices of several victims, each written by a different YA writer. ·

When I Was the Greatest by Jason Reynolds (Atheneum Books for Young Readers, 2014)

> Ali and his sister, Jazz, stay out of trouble in their Bed-Stuy neighborhood known for guns and drugs. Until one night they go to the wrong party and one of them gets hurt.

Yummy: The Last Days of a Southside Shorty by G. Neri (Lee & Low Books, 2010)

> A graphic novel based on the true story of Robert "Yummy" Sandifer, an 11-year-old gang member in Chicago who shot a young girl and was then shot by his own gang members in 1994.

The story is told from the perspective of Roger, a friend trying to make sense of what happened.

Articles about Gun Violence

I read a ton of articles while researching this book. All of them contain fascinating info. Check the notes section at the end of the book if you want to dig into any of them. As a preview, here's a short list of the articles that I learned the most from (you can read them online by Googling the titles):

"America's Youth Under Fire: The Devastating Impact of Gun Violence on Young People" by Chelsea Parsons, Maggie Thompson, Eugenio Weigend Vargas, and Giovanni Rocco (Center for American Progress, May 4, 2018)

"After Parkland, a Push for More School Shooter Drills" by Alexia Fernandez Campbell (*Vox*, March 14, 2018)

"Rate of Mass Shootings Has Tripled Since 2011, Harvard Research Shows" by Amy Cohen, Deborah Azrael, and Matthew Miller (*Mother Jones*, October 15, 2014)

"Study: Many Suicidal Kids Have Access to Guns at Home" by Liz Szabo (*USA Today*, May 6, 2013)

"Black Kids Are 10 Times More Likely Than White Kids to Die from Guns, Study Says" by Emily Weyrauch (*Time*, June 19, 2017)

"Why Inner City Schools Don't Have Mass Shootings" by Joy Mohammed (*Wear Your Voice*, February 26, 2018)

"Report Shows Massive Increase in Anti-LGBTQ Violence Since Trump Took Office" by David Lohr (*Huffington Post*, January 22, 2018)

"The Demographics of Gun Ownership" by Kim Parker, Juliana Horowitz, Ruth Igielnik, Baxter Oliphant, and Anna Brown (Pew Research Center, June 22, 2017)

"Why Are White Men Stockpiling Guns?" by Jeremy Adam Smith (*Scientific American*, March 14, 2018)

"Banning Assault Rifles Would Be Constitutional" by Page Pate (CNN, March 2, 2018)

"Why Can't We Amend the Second Amendment?" by James Heffernan (*Huffington Post*, June 23, 2017)

"The NRA Wasn't Always Against Gun Restrictions" by Ron Elving (NPR, October 10, 2017)

"The Real Reason the NRA's Money Matters in Elections" by Charlotte Hill (*Vox*, March 24, 2018)

"How the Gun Industry Funnels Tens of Millions of Dollars to the NRA" by Walter Hickey (*Business Insider*, January 16, 2013)

"Why is the National Rifle Association So Powerful?" by Dominic Rushe (*The Guardian*, May 4, 2018)

"Why Can't the U.S. Treat Gun Violence as a Public-Health Problem?" by Sarah Zhang (*The Atlantic*, February 15, 2018)

"Four Reasons the NRA Should Fear the Parkland Student Survivors" by John Blake (CNN, February 22, 2018)

"How to Reduce Shootings" by Nicholas Kristof (*New York Times*, May 18, 2018)

"Gun Control That Works—Here Are Policies Lawmakers Should Pass" by Robert Gebelhoff (*Washington Post*, March 23, 2018)

"Are Massachusetts Gun Laws A Model for the Country?" by Natalie Delgadillo (Governing, March 27, 2018)

"Australia Enacted Strict Gun Control Laws After A Horrific Mass Shooting in 1996. It Worked" by Will Oremus (*Slate*, October 2, 2017)

"Australia, Japan and South Korea Rarely Have Mass Shootings" by Tara Francis Chan (*Business Insider*, February 22, 2018)

"What Can the U.S. Learn from Norway's Gun Laws?" by Daniel Ofman (PRI, June 16, 2016)

"Students Demand Action Gives Young People a Platform to End Gun Violence" by Heather Mason (Amy Poehler's Smart Girls, August 22, 2018)

"NRA Boycotts: A Running List of Companies Taking a Stand" by Tess Cagle (Daily Dot, March 2, 2018)

Articles about Student Activists

If you want to learn more about the young activists profiled, check out their social media. Here's a list of interesting articles about them, as well.

Hunter Yuille
"28 Young Advocates Seeking to Bring Change to Their Communities Selected for Inaugural Giffords Courage Fellowship" by Giffords Law Center to Prevent Gun Violence staff (Giffords press release, July 18, 2018)

Julia Spoor
"My Father's Suicide Made Me an Activist" by Jeff Truesdell (*People*, July 11, 2018)

Brandon Wolf
"Finding Purpose in the Wake of Tragedy" by Jenni Moore (*Portland* [OR] *Mercury*, May 16, 1018)

MAKE
AMERICA
SAFE
AGAIN

Nza-Ari Khepra
"I Couldn't Stay Silent After Hadiya Pendleton Was Shot and Killed" by Nza-Ari Khepra (*Bustle*, June 2, 2017)

Marcel McClinton
"Texas Teen Marcel McClinton Leads Students in Charge for Gun Reform," video interview (MSN *Now This News*, May 24, 2018)

Jazmine Wildcat
"Gun Control Activists Share Pain and Plans at the Teen Vogue Summit" by Lucy Diavolo (*Teen Vogue*, June 2, 2018)

Parkland Survivors
"How Parkland Teens Are Leading the Gun Control Conversation" by Charlotte Alter (*Time*, March 22, 2018). "David Hogg is Taking His Gap Year at the Barricades" by Lisa Miller (*New York Magazine*, August 19, 2018)

Colin Goddard
"Virginia Tech Shooting: Survivor on 10-Year Anniversary" by KC Baker (*People*, April 16, 2017)

Eli Counce and Penelope Spurr
"Lake Oswego High School Students Unveil 10-Point Gun Safety Plan" by Gary Stein (*Lake Oswego Review*, April 15, 2018)

Natalie Barden
"Natalie Barden Reflects on the Sandy Hook Shooting, the March for Our Lives, and Why She Still Fights for Gun-Violence Prevention" by Natalie Barden (*Teen Vogue*, August 15, 2018)

Lane Murdock
"Meet Lane Murdock, the 16-Year-Old Organizer of the National School Walkout" by Linley Sanders (*Teen Vogue*, April 20, 2018)

Websites and Social Media

You can learn a lot more about gun violence and solutions by visiting the websites of these top gun safety groups. Dig in to find answers to all your questions.

NATIONAL GROUPS

Students Demand Action
everytown.org/studentsdemand

Everytown for Gun Safety
everytown.org

Moms Demand Action for Gun Sense in America
momsdemandaction.org

Brady Campaign to Prevent Gun Violence
bradycampaign.org

Giffords Courage to Fight Gun Violence
giffords.org

Coalition to Stop Gun Violence
csgv.or

Sandy Hook Promise
sandyhookpromise.org

Gun Owners for Responsible Ownership
responsibleownership.org

ACTIVIST GROUPS AND SOCIAL MEDIA

Julia Spoor
everytown.org/studentsdemand
facebook.com/juliaspoor
Twitter @smartactivist

Brandon Wolf
thedruproject.org
facebook.com/bjoewolf
Twitter @bjoewolf

Nza-Ari Khepra
wearorange.org
facebook.com/nzaari.khepra
Twitter @NzaAriKhepra

Marcel McClinton
Twitter @MarcelMcClinton and @theorangegen

Paul Kemp
responsibleownership.org
facebook.com/GunOwnersForResponsibleOwnership

Jazmine Wildcat
Twitter @jazmine_wildcat

Parkland Survivors
facebook.com/NeverAgainMSD
Twitter @#NeverAgain, @davidhogg111, @cameron_kasky,
@al3xw1nd, @JaclynCorin, @Emma4Change

Colin Goddard
facebook.com/colin.goddard
Twitter @clgoddard

Eli Counce and Penelope Spurr
Twitter @s4cLO

Natalie Barden
facebook.com/NewtownActionAlliance
Twitter @NatalieBarden and @Junior_NAA

Lane Murdock
nationalschoolwalkout.net
facebook.com/lane.murdock
Twitter @lanemurdock2002 and @schoolwalkoutUS

Representative Jennifer Williamson
oregonlegislature.gov/williamson
facebook.com/jennifer.williamson
Twitter @Jennifer_for_OR

Governor Kate Brown
www.actionplanfororegon.gov
www.facebook.com/KateBrownforOR
Twitter @OregonGovBrown

Movies

The written word isn't the only way to learn. These movies chronicle the harrowing experiences of mass shooting survivors and give unique insights into America's gun violence epidemic.

101 Seconds, directed by Skye Fitzgerald (Gravitas Ventures, 2018)
Learn more at 101-seconds.com.
> Two Oregon families confront gun politics in America. Their experience, during and after the 2012 Clackamas Town Center shooting, inspires them to fight for gun safety, but they soon discover that changing minds and laws won't be easy.

Bowling for Columbine, directed by Michael Moore (United Artists, 2002)
Learn more at michaelmoore.com.
> This political documentary explores the 1999 massacre at Columbine High School and the policies that led to it. Filmmaker Michael Moore looks at America's glut of guns, increasing gun violence, and lack of gun regulations, while questioning companies and politicians on their roles in our country's gun violence epidemic.

The Hate U Give, directed by George Tillman Jr. (Fox 2000 Pictures, 2018)

Learn more at angiethomas.com.

Based on the bestselling YA novel (mentioned in the fiction resources earlier in this section), the movie tells the story of Starr, who witnesses the fatal shooting of Khalil, her childhood best friend, by a police officer. Starr must decide whether to keep the peace and keep quiet or speak out and become a leader.

Living for 32, directed by Kevin Breslin (FilmBuff, 2012)

Learn more at livingfor32.com.

This is the inspirational story of Colin Goddard (see his profile in chapter 10), a survivor of the massacre at Virginia Tech in 2007. Colin, a leader of the gun safety movement, shares his account of the terror he and his classmates endured during the shooting, and his courageous journey of hope after the tragedy.

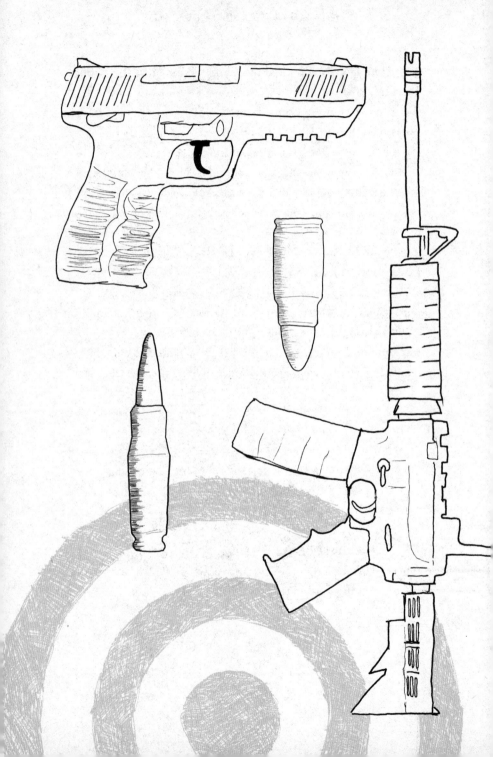

GUN GLOSSARY

People who own guns get peeved when gun sense advocates discuss gun issues using language that is incorrect. It shows a lack of knowledge about what they're arguing for, which makes the argument weaker. Here are some key gun terms to learn so you can use language to strengthen your case, not weaken it.

ammunition (ammo): Another word for bullets. Ammunition is measured in rounds, which is what's loaded into a gun. Ammunition comes in hundreds of sizes and must match the gun in order to be used.

AR-15: Stands for ArmaLite Rifle-15, a lightweight semiautomatic rifle that comes in a variety of models. Considered "modern sporting rifles" by some and "assault rifles" by others, AR-15 guns have been used in many high-profile mass shootings, including Sandy Hook, Aurora, San Bernardino, Las Vegas, and Parkland.

assault rifle: A technical term for a rapid-fire, magazine-fed automatic rifle designed for military use. It can fire in either semiautomatic or fully automatic modes. Examples include AK-47s and M16s.

assault weapon: A political term, not a technical one, that changes depending on who is using it. When the Federal Assault Weapons Ban passed in 1994, the US Department of Justice defined it as "semiautomatic firearms [rifles, pistols, and shotguns] with a large magazine of ammunition that were designed and configured for rapid fire and combat use."

automatic: A gun that continuously fires bullets as long as the trigger is pressed or held down and there is still ammunition in the magazine. More commonly known as a machine gun.

barrel: The tube through which the bullet is shot.

bolt action: A type of rifle that fires one round at a time. Once a round is fired, the user must manually pull back a metal mechanism

NEVER FORGET: SAN BERNARDINO SHOOTING

When: December 2, 2015
Where: San Bernardino, California
How many died? Fourteen
What happened? A married couple opened fire in the middle of a Christmas party at the Inland Regional Center in San Bernardino, killing fourteen people and injuring twenty-two more. A friend purchased the guns for the couple.

ctive fire weapons: Weapons that have safeties that switch
ween semiautomatic and three-round burst or automatic.

iautomatic: A self-loading firearm. It fires one bullet each
the trigger is pulled but also performs all necessary mechani-
eps to prepare another bullet to be fired. Once a magazine is
into a semiautomatic gun and the gun is cocked, a user could
he trigger over and over, firing bullets until the magazine is

n: A gun that fires groups of small pellets or very large slugs
of bullets. It's designed for shooting fast-moving targets, like
er, or rabbits, at close range.

: A slang term for a suppressor. This device is attached to
f a gun's barrel and reduces the sound of its discharge.

n purchase: When you have someone else purchase a
u and then they hand the gun over to you for a small fee.
but it's hard to stop in states where private party trans-
egulated. It's one of many loopholes in the background
m.

e mechanism that causes the gun to fire.

riod: The legally required time between purchasing
ceiving it. It can be anywhere from seven to twenty-
meant to give law enforcement time to perform a
heck and provide a "cooling off" period to help stop
of violence and suicides.

called the bolt to unload the empty shell and load another round into the chamber. Bolt action rifles fire much more slowly than assault rifles.

bullet: The projectile in a cartridge or round of ammunition.

Bump stock (or bump-fire stock): A bump stock lets a semiautomatic rifle fire without any reloading. Each time the gun recoils, it bounces back, which causes it to automatically pull the trigger again, which causes another recoil, and so on. Bump stocks are currently legal, even though they turn a legal semiautomatic weapon into an illegal automatic weapon.

burst mode: A firing mode that allows the shooter to fire a predetermined number of rounds, usually two or three, with a single pull of the trigger.

cartridge or round: Also called ammunition. A cartridge holds the bullet (the projectile), propellant (like gunpowder), and primer (which ignites the propellant) together in a metallic, paper, or plastic casing that fits within the firing chamber of the gun.

chamber: The part of the barrel or cylinder in which the cartridge is placed before firing. Rifles and pistols usually have a single chamber, while revolvers have multiple chambers.

clip: A unit of multiple ammunition rounds (usually stored on a metal strip) that are ready to be quickly loaded into a gun, as opposed to loading a single round at a time.

firearm: By federal definition, under the 1968 Gun Control Act, a firearm is a rifle, shotgun, or handgun using gunpowder as a propellant. Air guns, pellet and BB guns, and other devices that fire projectiles without combustion are not considered firearms.

flash suppressor: Lets hot air and gas escape from the barrel, creating a smaller flash as the round exits the barrel. It gives the user increased visibility while shooting and is a big indicator of an assault-style weapon.

Glock: A series of popular semiautomatic handguns designed and produced by Austrian company Glock Ges.m.b.H.

gun show: An event where gun dealers rent tables to display and sell guns. In most states (thirty-three out of fifty) sellers at gun shows are not required to do any background checks and do not need to record the sale or ask for ID, and waiting periods are not required. Approximately five thousand gun shows happen in the US every year. Gun shows typically attracts several thousand shoppers and more than one thousand guns are often sold over a weekend.

handgun: A category of gun that is designed to be handheld, in one or both hands. This includes pistols, machine pistols, and revolvers.

high-capacity magazine: To most people, that's any magazine that holds over ten rounds. Some high-capacity magazines can hold as many as one hundred rounds. Many semiautomatic rifles come standard with magazines holding between twenty and thirty rounds.

magazine: A container that holds ammunition to be fed into a gun's chamber. Magazines are usually detachable and refillable. With a semiautomatic or automatic weapon, a full magazine is inserted into the gun, the hammer is cocked, and rounds are automatically loaded into the gun's chamber from the magazine as it fires.

pistol: A type of handgun that fires bullets. It's a concealable gun that can easily be fired with or They can be single shot, semiautomatic, or fully form of a machine pistol.

pistol grip: A huge indicator of the difference for assault purposes and guns used for hunting an assault rifle improves stability on the rifle's

private party transfer: A secondhand pu someone pays cash for a gun from a priv asked, like at a gun show. Some states req such purchases, but most don't.

recoil: Often called a gun's "kick," it is t exerts when it's fired. The heavier the b the barrel, the more recoil there is.

revolver: A handgun or pistol with (usually holding six to eight rounds) the trigger. If you've ever seen a We

rifle: A gun with a long barrel th used for precision shooting. They bolt action, semiautomatic, and a

round: A complete unit of amn that has a casing, a primer, a pr

safety: A mechanism on mo being pulled, preventing th should be left on until a use

sel
bet

sem
time
cal st
loade
pull t
empty

shotgu
instead
birds, d

silencer
the end

strawma
gun for yo
It's illegal,
fers aren't
check syste

trigger: Th

waiting pe
a gun and re
five days. It'
background
impulsive acts

THANK-YOUS

This was not the easiest book I've ever written. Not by a long shot. Sitting down every day and facing my fear, frustration, and anger around guns in America; digging into the policy details, the survivor stories, and the obstacles still standing in the way of change—it was a hard place to go. I have a lot of people to thank for helping get me through the writing process in one piece.

My thank-yous start with Liz Rusch and the rest of my writing group, the Viva Scrivas (Amber, Addie, Nicole, Ruth, and Melissa). I don't think I would have written this book without you. I wasn't planning to—I just thought *someone* should. But when I told you the idea, you said, "*You* should write it . . . and now!" I dove in the next day and sold it a few months later. Without your encouragement and cheerleading, I would not have had the confidence to take the plunge. What would I do without you ladies? Thank you for making me feel like a "real" writer again (whatever that means)!

Thank you to Shannon Watts for writing the foreword. You were my inspiration for getting involved in the gun violence prevention movement, and you continue to be a guiding light for me and millions of others who are working to change our country and its laws. Thank you for starting Moms Demand Action and for the work you do every single day, in spite of death threats and daunting challenges, to make America safer for our kids. I am honored that you are a part of this book.

Thank you to Moms Demand Action and especially the wonderful volunteers in Oregon. Working with you is what inspired me to spread the word to the next generation and get more young people involved.

Thank you to the other adults I interviewed. Thank you, Paul Kemp, for sharing your incredibly painful survivor story and for the great work you do helping gun owners be safe. Thank you, Representative Jennifer Williamson, for sharing your inspiring personal story with me, for all those great insider political action tips, and for all that you do as a gun sense leader in Oregon. Thank you, Governor Kate Brown. I think you are the bomb, quite frankly, and I'm proud as heck that you let me include you in the book. I'm even prouder of all the fantastic work you do for Oregon, my home, each and every day. And for the difficult but important work you do as a gun sense leader to help make Oregonians safer from gun violence. Thanks to all of you—keep up the great work!

Thank you, Katie Hill, for creating the book's gorgeous artwork. Who else could make guns look so good? At just 15 years old, you are one of the most talented and professional artists I've worked with (and I've worked with a lot). I am thrilled we got to collaborate, and I'm excited to see what you do with your art in the future!

Thank you to Richard Cohn and Michele Ashtiani Cohn for immediately saying yes to this book (from a cruise ship!), for taking a chance on publishing a controversial topic, and for always being such wonderful friends and colleagues to me these many decades.

Thank you to Lindsay Easterbrooks-Brown for your tireless work getting this book done quickly and for making it *so much better*. And for putting up with my ineptitude with citations and endnotes! You are a perfectionist, and I'm grateful for that. Thank you to Kristin Thiel, my gifted copyeditor, for catching and fixing every little mistake and badly worded line. Thank you for making me sound like a better writer. God bless editors! Thank you to Sara Blum for creating all the cool graphics, which make those boring numbers a lot more interesting and easier to understand. Thank you to everyone else at Beyond Words who helped bring this book into the world and will help get it out to as many kids as possible— Emmalisa Sparrow Wood, Tara Lehmann, Corinne Kalasky, and Emily Einolander. I love my Beyond Words family!

Thank you to all folks at Simon & Schuster for saying yes and for doing such a stellar job of promoting and selling the book. I so appreciate all you do for my books.

As always, a huge thank-you to my friends for encouraging me and keeping my spirits up while I was writing this. All those drinks and movies and laughter got me through. Your friendship got me through. Thank you, Kristin Doherty, Kenan Smith, Lissa Kaufman, Kelly Burke-Doyle, and Beth Nelson. There are a lot more names I could list here (you know who you are). I am a lucky lady.

I am blessed with a pretty awesome family. Thank you to my parents—Kathy, Jeff, Jim, and Joy—for always supporting my dreams. For *still* helping me believe I can do it. Thank you to Jamie and Charlotte for being my sisters *and* my friends. Thank you to Jerry for always supporting my writing and for picking up the slack while I worked extra hours and was away at writing retreats. I couldn't have done it without you. And thank you to my kids, Ronan and Fiona, for being a constant reminder of why I was writing this book. This is not the country I want for you and your kids. Hopefully I'm doing my part to move things in the right direction. I love you both more than anything.

Thank you to my awesome cousin Karen DeWitz for taking my author photo. It's gorgeous, and that is all because of you.

My biggest thanks goes to the young people I interviewed and profiled in the book: Hunter Yuille, Julia Spoor, Brandon Wolf, Nza-Ari Khepra, Riley Mulberger, Marcel McClinton, Jazmine Wildcat, Colin Goddard, Eli Counce, Penelope Spurr, Cameron Kasky, Alex Wind, Jaclyn Corin, Emma Gonzalez, David Hogg,

Natalie Barden, and Lane Murdock. Talking with you was the highlight of writing the book. Your personal stories and the work you are doing totally inspired me and kept me going. Thank you for giving me hope for the future while I was dredging through the darkness. I am sure that you will make change happen—you already are! Soon you will be our country's leaders, and you will fix these problems. You are amazing human beings, and I'm incredibly proud to share your stories with other young people!

NOTES

All quotes in profiles that are not cited in this notes section are from personal interviews conducted by the author.

Introduction

1. CNN Staff, "Florida Student Emma Gonzalez to Lawmakers and Gun Advocates: 'We Call BS,'" CNN, February 17, 2018, https://www.cnn.com/2018/02/17/us/florida-student-emma-gonzalez-speech/index.html.

A Note to Gun Owners

1. Nicholas Kristof, "How to Reduce Shootings," *New York Times*, November 6, 2017, https://www.nytimes.com/interactive/2017/11/06/opinion/how-to-reduce-shootings.html.

Chapter 1

1. "Debunking Gun Myths at the Dinner Table," Moms Demand Action, accessed July 19, 2018, https://momsdemandaction.org/campaigns/debunking-gun-myths/#moregunshttps://www.thetrace.org/rounds/gun-deaths-increase-2017/.

2. "Debunking Gun Myths"

3. "Gun Violence Statistics," Giffords Law Center to Prevent Gun Violence, accessed February 10, 2019, https://lawcenter.giffords.org/category/gun-studies-statistics/gun-violence-statistics/.

4. Chelsea Bailey, "More Americans Killed by Guns Since 1968 than in All U.S. Wars—Combined," NBC News, October 4, 2017, https://www.nbcnews.com/storyline/las-vegas-shooting/more-americans-killed-guns-1968-all-u-s-wars-combined-n807156.

5. Springer. "Rapid Rise in Mass School Shootings in the United States, Study Shows," ScienceDaily, April 19, 2018. https://www.sciencedaily.com/releases/2018/04/180419131025.htm.

6. Sam Morris, "Mass Shootings in the US: There Have Been 1,624 in 1,870 Days," *The Guardian*, February 15, 2018, https://www.theguardian.com/us-news/ng-interactive/2017/oct/02/america-mass-shootings-gun-violence.

7. Morris, "Mass Shootings in the US."

8. "Mass Shootings in America," Stanford Libraries, accessed July 18, 2018, https://library.stanford.edu/projects/mass-shootings-america.

9. Christopher Ingraham, "There Are More Guns than People in the United States, According to a New Study of Global Firearm Ownership," *Washington Post*, June 19, 2018, https://www.washingtonpost.com/news /wonk/wp/2018/06/19/there-are-more-guns-than-people-in-the-united -states-according-to-a-new-study-of-global-firearm-ownership/?utm _term=.4752ec65f835.

10. Christopher Ingraham, "Just Three Percent of Adults Own Half of America's Guns," *Washington Post*, September 19, 2016, www .washingtonpost.com/news/wonk/wp/2016/09/19/just-three-percent-of -adults-own-half-of-americas-guns/?utm_term=.3412bed9a02c.

11. Jacqueline Howard, "Guns Kill Nearly 1,300 US Children Each Year, Study Says," CNN, June 19, 2017, https://www.cnn.com/2017/06/19 /health/child-gun-violence-study/index.html.

12. Chelsea Parsons, Maggie Thompson, Eugenio Weigend Vargas, and Giovanni Rocco, "America's Youth Under Fire: The Devastating Impact of Gun Violence on Young People," Center for American Progress, May 4, 2018, https://www.americanprogress.org/issues/guns-crime/reports /2018/05/04/450343/americas-youth-fire/.

13. Henry Grabar, "150,000 American Students Have Experienced A School Shooting," *Slate*, February 15, 2018, https://slate.com/news-and -politics/2018/02/150-000-american-students-have-experienced-a-school -shooting.html.

14. Parsons et al., "America's Youth Under Fire."

15. Parsons et al., "America's Youth Under Fire."

16. Parsons et al., "America's Youth Under Fire."

17. Parsons et al., "America's Youth Under Fire."

18. "The Counted: People Killed by Police in the US," *The Guardian*, accessed August 15, 2018, https://www.theguardian.com/us-news/ng -interactive/2015/jun/01/the-counted-police-killings-us-database.

19. "LGBT Youth," Centers for Disease Control and Prevention, accessed June 21, 2018, https://www.cdc.gov/lgbthealth/youth.htm.

20. "NCAVP Report on Hate Violence Against Lesbian, Gay, Bisexual, Transgender and HIV-Affected Communities Released Today," Anti-Violence Project, June 12, 2017, https://avp.org/ncavp-report -hate-violence-lesbian-gay-bisexual-transgender-queer-hiv-affected -communities-released-today/.

21. Jen Christensen, "LGBQ Teens Face Serious Suicide Risk, Research Finds," CNN, December 19, 2017, https://www.cnn.com/2017/12/19 /health/lgbq-teens-suicide-risk-study/index.html

22. "Disarm All Domestic Abusers," Center for American Progress, March 22, 2018, https://www.americanprogress.org/issues/guns-crime/reports /2018/03/22/448298/disarm-domestic-abusers/.

23. "Guns and Domestic Violence," Everytown for Gun Safety, accessed June 21, 2018, https://everytownresearch.org/guns-domestic-violence/.

24. "Guns and Violence Against Women," Everytown for Gun Safety, accessed June 21, 2018, https://everytownresearch.org/reports/guns-and-violence-against-women/.

25. "Gun Laws Vs. Gun Deaths: Does Legislation Matter in a Nation with Almost as Many Guns as People?" Safehome.org, accessed June 21, 2018, https://www.safehome.org/resources/gun-laws-and-deaths/.

26. Laura Santhnam, "There's a New Global Ranking of Gun Deaths. Here's Where the U.S. Stands," PBS, August 28, 2018, https://www.pbs.org/newshour/health/theres-a-new-global-ranking-of-gun-deaths-heres-where-the-u-s-stands.

27. AP, "Worldwide Gun Deaths Reach 250,000 Yearly; US Ranks High," CNBC, August 29, 2018, https://www.cnbc.com/2018/08/29/worldwide-gun-deaths-reach-250000-yearly-us-ranks-high.html.

28. "Gun Policy News," Gunpolicy.org, accessed June 21, 2018, https://www.gunpolicy.org/firearms/news/38853.

29. Tara Haelle, "Children Are Dying Because of Americans' Denial About Guns," *Forbes*, June 19, 2017, https://www.forbes.com/sites/tarahaelle/2017/06/19/american-denial-about-facts-on-guns-continues-to-kill-children/#79251754a9ad.

30. German Lopez, "America's Gun Problem, Explained," *Vox*, November 8, 2018, https://www.vox.com/2015/10/3/9444417/gun-violence-united-states-america.

31. Ingraham, "There Are More Guns than People in the United States."

32. Parsons et al., "America's Youth Under Fire."

33. Parsons et al., "America's Youth Under Fire."

34. Monkey Cage, "Here's Who Actually Attended the March for Our Lives," *Washington Post*, March 28, 2018, https://www.washingtonpost.com/news/monkey-cage/wp/2018/03/28/heres-who-actually-attended-the-march-for-our-lives-no-it-wasnt-mostly-young-people/?utm_term=.5dfe539b6638.

Hunter Yuille Profile

1. Hunter Yuille, in-person interview with author, May 21, 2018.

2. Fox 12 Staff, "Two Young Adults from Oregon Selected for Giffords Courage Fellowship," Fox12 Oregon, July 20, 2018, https://www.kptv.com/news/two-young-adults-from-oregon-selected-for-giffords-courage-fellowship/article_4b9ae8c9-4750-5e69-b6b5-8624e3e6125d.html.

Chapter 2

1. Alexia Fernandez Campbell, "After Parkland, A Push for More School Shooting Drills," *Vox*, March 14, 2018, https://www.vox.com/policy-and-politics/2018/2/16/17016382/school-shooting-drills-training.

2. Bryan Denson, "Teacher Terrified by Surprise 'Active Shooter' Drill in Eastern Oregon Schoolhouse Files Federal Lawsuit," *Oregonian* (Portland,

OR), April 21, 2015, http://www.oregonlive.com/pacific-northwest
-news/index.ssf/2015/04/teacher_terrified_by_surprise.html.

3. Kate Stringer, "Gallup Poll: Most Educators Don't Want to Be Armed with
   Guns," The74million.org, March 16, 2018, https://www.the74million.org
   /gallup-poll-most-educators-dont-want-to-be-armed-with-guns/.

4. Stringer, "Gallup Poll: Most Educators,"

5. Stringer, "Gallup Poll: Most Educators,"

6. Associated Press, "Idaho State University Teacher Accidentally Shoots Self
   in Class," CBS News, September 4, 2014, https://www.cbsnews.com
   /news/idaho-state-university-teacher-accidentally-shoots-self-in-class/.

7. Michele Richinick, "Utah Teacher Shoots Herself in the Leg While at
   School," MSNBC, September 12, 2014, http://www.msnbc.com/msnbc
   /utah-teacher-shoots-herself-the-leg-while-school.

8. Crimesider Staff, "Cops: Elementary Kids Find Loaded Gun Teacher
   Left in Pa. School Bathroom," CBS News, September 13, 2016, https://
   www.cbsnews.com/news/cops-teacher-left-gun-in-bathroom-elementary
   -kids-found-it/.

9. Rachel Estabrook, "Why a Colorado Lawmaker Who Survived Columbine
   Wants More Guns in Schools," Colorado Public Radio, March 1, 2018,
   http://www.cpr.org/news/story/why-a-colorado-lawmaker-who-survived
   -columbine-wants-more-guns-in-schools.

10. Amy Cohen, Deborah Azrael, and Matthew Miller, "Rate of Mass
    Shootings Has Tripled Since 2011, Harvard Research Shows," *Mother Jones*,
    October 15, 2014, https://www.motherjones.com/politics/2014/10/mass
    -shootings-increasing-harvard-research/.

11. CNN Staff, "Florida Student Emma Gonzalez to Lawmakers and
    Gun Advocates: 'We Call BS,'" CNN, February 17, 2018,
    https://www.cnn.com/2018/02/17/us/florida-student-emma-gonzalez
    -speech/index.html.

12. Sean Rossman, "Children Are Killing Themselves More and More with
    Guns," *USA Today*, June 19, 2017, https://www.usatoday.com/story/news
    /nation-now/2017/06/19/children-killing-themselves-more-and-more
    -guns/407068001/.

13. "Lethality of Suicide Methods," Harvard School of Public Health, accessed
    June 27, 2018, https://www.hsph.harvard.edu/means-matter/means-matter
    /case-fatality/.

14. "Teen Suicide and Guns," Healthychildren.org, accessed June 27, 2018,
    https://www.healthychildren.org/English/health-issues/conditions
    /emotional-problems/Pages/Teen-Suicide-and-Guns.aspx.

15. "Teen Suicide and Guns," Heathychildren.org.

16. "Safe Storage," Giffords Law Center to Prevent Gun Violence, accessed
    June 27, 2018, http://lawcenter.giffords.org/gun-laws/policy-areas
    /child-consumer-safety/safe-storage/.

17. Gaby Galvin, "Youth Suicide Rates Higher in States With More Guns," *U.S. News*, January 17, 2019, https://www.usnews.com/news/healthiest -communities/articles/2019-01-17/youth-suicide-rates-higher-in-states -with-more-gun-ownership.

18. "The Truth About Suicide & Guns," Brady Center to Prevent Gun Violence, accessed June 27, 2018, http://www.bradycampaign.org/sites /default/files/Brady-Guns-Suicide-Report-2016.pdf.

19. Vanessa Milne, Joshua Tepper, and Jeremy Petch, "The Suicide Gap: Why Men are More Likely to Kill Themselves," Healthy Debate, August 10, 2017, https://healthydebate.ca/2017/08/topic/male-suicide.

20. Corinne Riddell, Sam Harper, Magdalena Cerda, and Jay Kaufman, "Comparisons of Rates of Firearm and Nonfirearm Homicide and Suicide in Black and Non-Hispanic Men, by U.S. State," *Annals of Internal Medicine*, May 15, 2018, http://annals.org/aim/fullarticle/2679556/comparison -rates-firearm-nonfirearm-homicide-suicide-black-white-non-hispanic.

21. "Guns and Violence Against Women," Everytown for Gun Safety, accessed June 27, 2018, https://everytownresearch.org/reports/guns-and-violence -against-women/.

22. Guns and Domestic Violence," Everytown for Gun Safety, accessed June 21, 2018, https://everytownresearch.org/guns-domestic-violence/.

23. "Guns and Violence Against Women," Everytown for Gun Safety.

24. "Guns and Violence Against Women," Everytown for Gun Safety.

25. "Guns and Violence Against Women," Everytown for Gun Safety.

26. "Guns and Violence Against Women," Everytown for Gun Safety.

27. "Guns and Violence Against Women," Everytown for Gun Safety.

28. The grandparents in this case were charged with involuntary manslaughter, second-degree child abuse, and felony firearm. The grandfather was convicted of second-degree child abuse. "Grandparents of 5-Year-Old Girl Who Found Gun, Shot Herself Charged with Manslaughter," CBS Detroit, May 25, 2016, https://detroit.cbslocal.com/2016/05/25 /grandparents-of-5-year-old-girl-who-found-gun-shot-herself-charged -with-manslaughter/; Kat Stafford, "Grandparents Charged in Fatal Shooting of Detroit Girl, 5," *Detroit Free Press*, May 25, 2016, https:// www.freep.com/story/news/local/michigan/detroit/2016/05/25 /grandparents-charged-fatal-shooting-detroit-girl-5/84899562/.

29. Investigators in this case found in the house not only the shotgun that killed the 9-year-old but also a handgun under the mattress in the bedroom, an assault rifle in the closet, and one hundred rounds of ammunition in a grocery bag. The boy's mother was convicted of involuntary manslaughter and three counts of felony child abuse. Nick Penzenstadler, Ryan Foley, and Larry Fenn, "Added Agony: Justice Is Haphazard After Kids' Gun Deaths," *USA Today* and the Associated Press, May 25, 2017, https://www.usatoday.com/story/news/2017/05/24/justice -haphazard-when-kids-die-in-gun-accidents/101568654/.

30. In this case, the district attorney decided not to press charges against the father of the child or his girlfriend. Penzenstadler et al., "Added Agony."
31. "Safe Storage," Giffords Law Center to Prevent Gun Violence.
32. Kat Ainsworth, "More Americans Own Guns and Dogs than Cats," *The Truth About Guns*, September 30, 2018, https://www.thetruthaboutguns.com/2018/09/kat-ainsworth/more-americans-own-guns-and-dogs-than-cats/.
33. Nora Biette-Timmons, "Roughly 4.6 Million American Kids Live in Homes with Unlocked, Loaded Guns," The Trace, May 21, 2018, https://www.thetrace.org/rounds/study-american-children-unlocked-loaded-gun-storage/.
34. "Statistics on Youth Gun Violence & Gun Access," Giffords Law Center to Prevent Gun Violence, accessed June 27, 2018, https://lawcenter.giffords.org/youth-gun-violence-gun-access-statistics/.
35. "The Final Report and Finding of the Safe School Initiative," US Secret Service and US Department of Education, accessed September 10, 2018, https://www2.ed.gov/admins/lead/safety/preventingattacksreport.pdf.

Julia Spoor Profile

1. Julia Spoor, phone interview with author, October 8, 2018.
2. Jeff Truesdell, "My Father's Suicide Made Me an Activist," *People*, July 11, 2018, 51.

Chapter 3

1. In August 2018, the officer who shot and killed Jordan Edwards was convicted of murder and received a fifteen-year prison sentence. David Graham, "The Shooting of Jordan Edwards," *The Atlantic*, May 2, 2017, https://www.theatlantic.com/politics/archive/2017/05/the-shooting-of-jordan-edwards/525141; Faith Karimi and Emanuella Grinberg, "Texas Ex-Officer Is Sentenced to 15 Years for Killing an Unarmed Teen," CNN, August 30, 2018, https://www.cnn.com/2018/08/29/us/texas-jordan-edwards-death-sentencing-phase/index.html.
2. McInerney pled guilty to second-degree murder and was sentenced to twenty-one years in prison. Jim Dubreuil and Denise Martinez-Ramundo, "Boy Who Shot Classmate at Age 14 Will Be Retried as Adult," ABC News, October 5, 2011, https://abcnews.go.com/US/eighth-grade-shooting-larry-king-brandon-mcinerney-boys/story?id=14666577. Associated Press, "Brandon McInerney Sentenced to 21 Years, Lawyer Says He's Sorry for Killing Classmate," KPCC, December 19, 2011, https://www.scpr.org/news/2011/12/19/30409/brandon-mcinerney-sentenced-21-years-lawyer-says-h/.
3. Emily Weyrauch, "Black Kids Are 10 Times More Likely than White Kids to Die from Guns, Study Says," *Time*, June 19, 2017, http://time.com/4823524/gun-violence-black-children-study/.

4. Chelsea Parsons, Maggie Thompson, Eugenio Weigend Vargas, and Giovanni Rocco, "America's Youth Under Fire: The Devastating Impact of Gun Violence on Young People," Center for American Progress, May 4, 2018, https://www.americanprogress.org/issues/guns-crime/reports/2018/05/04/450343/americas-youth-fire/.

5. Structuralviolence.org, s.v. "structural violence," accessed August 4, 2018, http://www.structuralviolence.org/structural-violence/.

6. Chelsea Parsons, "America's Youth Under Fire."

7. "The Counted: People Killed by Police in the US," *The Guardian*, accessed August 15, 2018, https://www.theguardian.com/us-news/ng-interactive/2015/jun/01/the-counted-police-killings-us-database.

8. Lisa Miller, "David Hogg, After Parkland," *New York Times Magazine*, August 19, 2018, http://nymag.com/intelligencer/2018/08/david-hogg-is-taking-his-gap-year-at-the-barricades.html?gtm=bottom&gtm=bottom.

9. Nza-Ari Khepra, phone interview with author, October 12, 2018.

10. Lisa Marie Pane, "Mass School Shootings Mostly Happening in Small-Town America," *South Florida Sun Sentinel*, May 22, 2018, https://www.sun-sentinel.com/news/nationworld/fl-reg-mass-school-shootings-towns-20180522-story.html.

11. Pane, "Mass School Shootings."

12. Pane, "Mass School Shootings."

13. David Lohr, "Report Shows Massive Increase in Anti-LGBTQ Violence Since Trump Took Office," *Huffington Post*, January 22, 2018, https://www.huffingtonpost.com/entry/lgbtq-violence-https://moneyish.com/ish/anti-lgbtq-homicides-almost-doubled-in-2017/trump_us_5a625035e4b002283002897b.

14. "NCAVP Report on Hate Violence Against Lesbian, Gay, Bisexual, Transgender and HIV-Affected Communities Released Today," Anti-Violence Project, June 12, 2017, https://avp.org/ncavp-report-hate-violence-lesbian-gay-bisexual-transgender-queer-hiv-affected-communities-released-today/.

15. Lohr, "Report Shows Massive Increase in Anti-LGBTQ Violence."

16. Jen Christensen, "LGBQ Teens Face Serious Suicide Risk, Research Finds," CNN, December 19, 2017, https://www.cnn.com/2017/12/19/health/lgbq-teens-suicide-risk-study/index.html.

17. "Activists Stage 'Die-In' on Anniversary of Pulse Nightclub Massacre," NBC Los Angeles, June 12, 2018, https://www.nbclosangeles.com/news/local/Activists-Stage-Die-Anniversary-Pulse-Nightclub-Massacre-485302931.html.

18. James Michael Nichols, "Surviving the Pulse Massacre Propelled This Gay Man into Gun Reform Activism," *Huffington Post*, June 12, 2018, https://www.huffingtonpost.com/entry/brandon-wolf-pride-2018_us_5b1bf245e4b0bbb7a0dd5a2c.

19. Ayanna Alexander, "African-Americans Feel Left Out of the Gun Debate," *Politico*, April 23, 2018, https://www.politico.com/magazine/story/2018 /04/23/african-americans-feel-left-out-of-the-gun -debate-218068.

20. Alexander, "African-Americans Feel Left Out."

21. Creede Newton, "Gun Control's Racist Past and Present," *Al Jazeera*, October 6, 2017, https://www.aljazeera.com/indepth/features/2017/10 /gun-control-racist-present-171006135904199.html.

Brandon Wolf Profile

1. Jenni Moore, "Finding Purpose in the Wake of Tragedy," *Portland (OR) Mercury*, May 16, 2018, https://www.portlandmercury.com/feature /2018/05/16/19884953/finding-purpose-in-the-wake-of-tragedy.

2. Paul Crookston, "The Meaning of the Pulse Nightclub Attack," *National Review*, April 4, 2018, https://www.nationalreview.com/2018/04/pulse -shooting-lgbt-not-specifically-gargeted/.

3. Moore, "Finding Purpose in the Wake of Tragedy."

4. Moore, "Finding Purpose in the Wake of Tragedy."

5. Moore, "Finding Purpose in the Wake of Tragedy."

6. "About," The Dru Project, accessed August 12, 2018, http:// thedruproject.org/about.

7. "About," The Dru Project,

8. Moore, "Finding Purpose in the Wake of Tragedy."

9. Nichols, "Surviving the Pulse Massacre"

10. Moore, "Finding Purpose in the Wake of Tragedy."

11. Nichols, "Surviving the Pulse Massacre."

12. Josh Jackman, "Orlando Massacre Survivor Tears into Republican Politicians at Parkland Protest," PinkNews, February 22, 2018, https:// www.pinknews.co.uk/2018/02/22/orlando-massacre-survivor-tears-into -republican-politicians-at-parkland-protest/.

13. Moore, "Finding Purpose in the Wake of Tragedy."

Chapter 4

1. "Debunking Gun Myths at the Dinner Table," Moms Demand Action, accessed August 20, 2018, https://momsdemandaction.org/campaigns /debunking-gun-myths/#moreguns.

2. Dave Gilson, "10 Pro-Gun Myths, Shot Down," *Mother Jones*, January 31, 2013, https://www.motherjones.com/politics/2013/01/pro-gun-myths -fact-check/.

3. Gilson, "10 Pro-Gun Myths Shot Down."

4. Scot Peterson, resource officer at Marjory Stoneman Douglas High School during the shooting, resigned after the massacre. He was subsequently sued by the family of one of the victims for shirking his duties. The case is still

unfolding as this book goes to print. The governor of Florida suspended Broward County Sheriff Scott Israel for his inept response to the Parkland shooting. Eli Saslow, "It Was My Job and I Didn't Find Him: Stoneman Douglas Resource Office Is Haunted by Massacre," *Washington Post*, June 4, 2018, https://www.washingtonpost.com/national/it-was-my-job-and-i -didnt-find-him-stoneman-douglas-resource-officer-remains-haunted -by-massacre/2018/06/04/796f1c16-679d-11e8-9e38-24e693b38637_story .html?utm_term=.f43d18fc21e7; Amir Vera, "Florida Governor Suspends Sheriff Scott Israel Over Parkland Massacre Response," CNN, January 11, 2019, https://www.cnn.com/2019/01/11/us/florida-scott-israel-parkland -suspension/index.html.

5. Eugene Volokh, "Do Citizens (Not Police Officers) with Guns Ever Stop Mass Shootings?" *Washington Post*, October 3, 2015, https: //www.washingtonpost.com/news/volokh-conspiracy/wp/2015/10/03 /do-civilians-with-guns-ever-stop-mass-shootings/?utm_term= .16ea473442d0.

6. Gilson, "10 Pro-Gun Myths, Shot Down."

7. Daniel Arkin, "Here's What We Know About the Links Between Video Games and Violence," NBC News, March 2, 2018, https://www.nbcnews .com/news/us-news/here-s-what-we-know-about-links-between-video -games-n852776.

8. Arkin, "Here's What We Know About."

9. Gilson, "10 Pro-Gun Myths, Shot Down."

10. Gilson, "10 Pro-Gun Myths, Shot Down."

11. "Safe Storage," Giffords Law Center to Prevent Gun Violence, accessed June 27, 2018, http://lawcenter.giffords.org/gun-laws/policy-areas /child-consumer-safety/safe-storage/.

12. Gilson, "10 Pro-Gun Myths, Shot Down."

13. Gilson, "10 Pro-Gun Myths, Shot Down."

14. "Debunking Gun Myths at the Dinner Table," Moms Demand Action.

15. Shelby Bremer, "Majority of Guns Used in Chicago Crimes Come from Outside Illinois: Report," NBC Chicago, October 30, 2017, https:// www.nbcchicago.com/blogs/ward-room/chicago-gun-trace -report-2017-454016983.html.

16. Tage Rai, "The Myth That Mental Illness Causes Mass Shootings," *Behavioral Scientist*, October 13, 2017, http://behavioralscientist.org /myth-mental-illness-causes-mass-shootings/.

17. Patrick Ross, "Mental Health and Gun Violence," Healthcare in America, February 19, 2018, https://healthcareinamerica.us/mental-health-and-gun -violence-607dbb564fb6.

18. Natasha Lennard, "Half of People Shot by Police Are Mentally Ill, Investigation Finds," *Salon*, December 10, 2012, https://www.salon .com/2012/12/10/half_of_people_shot_by_police_are_mentally _ill_investigation_finds/.

Nza-Ari Khepra Profile

1. Andy Grimm and Jon Seidel, "Hadiya Pendleton Murder Trial: 'Seriously, I Think I Got Shot,'" *Chicago Sun-Times*, August 14, 2018, https://chicago.suntimes.com/news/hadiya-pendleton-held-chest-said-i-think-i-got-shot-before-dying/.

2. Nza-Ari Khepra, "I Couldn't Stay Silent After Hadiya Pendleton Was Shot and Killed," *Bustle*, June 2, 2017, https://www.bustle.com/p/i-couldnt-stay-silent-after-hadiya-pendleton-was-shot-killed-61672.

3. Jovona Taylor, "I Was in High School When a Shooting Turned Me into a Gun Violence Activist. Here's What I Want the Walk-Out Kids to Know," The Trace, March 14, 2018, https://www.thetrace.org/rounds/nza-ari-khepra-gun-violence-activist-student-walkout/.

4. "About," Project Orange Tree, accessed July 1, 2018, https://pottest.wordpress.com/about/.

5. Ashley Boucher, "Celebrities, Politicians Wear Orange for Gun Violence Awareness Day," *The Wrap*, June 1, 2018, https://www.thewrap.com/celebrities-politicians-wear-orange-for-gun-violence-awareness-day/.

6. Ashley Boucher, "Celebrities, Politicians Wear Orange."

7. Taylor, "I Was in High School When a Shooting."

Chapter 5

1. Kara Fox, "How US Gun Culture Compares with the World in Five Charts," CNN, March 9, 2018, https://www.cnn.com/2017/10/03/americas/us-gun-statistics/index.html.

2. Kim Parker, Juliana Horowitz, Ruth Igielnik, Baxter Oliphant, and Anna Brown, "The Demographics of Gun Ownership," Pew Research Center, June 22, 2017, http://www.pewsocialtrends.org/2017/06/22/the-demographics-of-gun-ownership/.

3. Parker, "The Demographics of Gun Ownership."

4. Parker, "The Demographics of Gun Ownership."

5. Christopher Ingraham, "Assault Rifles Are Becoming Mass Shooters' Weapon of Choice," *Washington Post*, June 12, 2016, https://www.washingtonpost.com/news/wonk/wp/2016/06/12/the-gun-used-in-the-orlando-shooting-is-becoming-mass-shooters-weapon-of-choice/?utm_term=.fe16d0a380cb.

6. "Birth of the AR-15," AR15.com, accessed December 18, 2018, https://www.ar15.com/guides/files/articles/history/birth.html?gid=192.

7. Justin Peters, "The NRA Claims the AR-15 Is Useful for Hunting and Home Defense. Not Exactly," *Slate*, June 12, 2016, https://slate.com/news-and-politics/2016/06/gun-control-ar-15-rifle-the-nra-claims-the-ar-15-rifle-is-for-hunting-and-home-defense-not-exactly.html.

8. Dina Fine Maron, "Data Confirm Semiautomatic Rifles Linked to More Deaths, Injuries," *Scientific American*, September 11,

2018, https://www.scientificamerican.com/article/data-confirm
-semiautomatic-rifles-linked-to-more-deaths-injuries/.

9. Monica Busch, "How Many AR-15s Are in America? The Reason We
Don't Know Is Intentional," *Bustle*, April 19, 2018, https://www.bustle
.com/p/how-many-ar-15s-are-in-america-the-reason-we-dont-know-is
-intentional-8804426.

10. Busch, "How Many AR-15s Are in America?"

11. Geoffrey Ingersoll, "18 Terms You Need to Know if You Want to be Part
of the Gun Control Debate," *Business Insider*, December 17, 2012, https://
www.businessinsider.com/heres-a-glossary-of-need-to-know-terms-for
-the-assault-weapons-ban-debate-2012-12.

12. "Federal Assault Weapons Ban Law and Legal Definition," US Legal,
accessed September 1, 2018, https://definitions.uslegal.com/f/federal
-assault-weapons-ban/https://www.congress.gov/bill/103rd-congress
/house-bill/3355/text.

13. Jeremy Adam Smith, "Why Are White Men Stockpiling Guns?" *Scientific
American*, March 14, 2018, https://blogs.scientificamerican.com
/observations/why-are-white-men-stockpiling-guns/.

14. Youyou Zhou, "Three Percent of the Population Own Half of the Civilian
Guns in the US," *Quartz*, October 6, 2017, https://qz.com/1095899
/gun-ownership-in-america-in-three-charts/.

15. Smith, "Why Are White Men Stockpiling Guns?"

16. Terry Goodrich, "White Male Gun Owners Who Have Felt Economic
Stress Are More Likely to Feel Morally and Emotionally Attached to Guns,
Baylor Student Finds," Baylor Media and Public Relations, November 27,
2017, https://www.baylor.edu/mediacommunications/news
.php?action=story&story=189113.

17. Goodrich, "White Male Gun Owners."

18. Goodrich, "White Male Gun Owners."

Riley Mulberger Profile

1. Riley Mulberger, phone interview with author, October 8, 2018.

Chapter 6

1. "Amendment II: Right to Bear Arms," Constitution Center, accessed
August 28, 2018, https://constitutioncenter.org/interactive-constitution
/amendments/amendment-ii.

2. Michael Waldman, "Constitutional Law Expert Dismantles Second
Amendment Myths," Facebook video, 0:48, MicMedia, March 19, 2018,
https://www.facebook.com/MicMedia/videos/1856543067701808/.

3. Page Pate, "Banning Assault Rifles Would Be Constitutional," CNN,
March 2, 2018, https://www.cnn.com/2018/03/02/opinions/banning
-assault-rifles-would-be-constitutional-pate/index.html.

4. *Merriam-Webster*, s.v. "militia," accessed August 8, 2018, https://www .merriam-webster.com/dictionary/militia.

5. Glenn Valis, "Tactics and Weapons of the Revolutionary War," from author's personal website, accessed August 8, 2018, http://www.doublegv .com/ggv/battles/tactics.html.

6. Ed Leefeldt, "Stephen Paddock Used a 'Bump Stock' to Make His Guns Even Deadlier," CBS News, October 4, 2017, https://www.cbsnews.com /news/bump-fire-stock-ar-15-stephen-paddock-guns-deadlier/.

7. James Heffernan, "Why Can't We Amend the Second Amendment?" *Huffington Post*, June 24, 2017, https://www.huffingtonpost.com/james -heffernan/lets-amend-the-second-ame_b_10599266.html.

8. Ron Elving, "What Would It Take to Repeal the 2nd Amendment?" NPR, February 27, 2018, https://www.npr.org/2018/02/27/589062018 /what-would-it-take-to-repeal-the-2nd-amedment.

9. Elving, "What Would It Take to Repeal the 2nd Amendment."

10. Heffernan, "Why Can't We Amend the Second Amendment?"

11. German Lopez, "New Zealand Parliament Votes 119-1 to Ban Assault Weapons," Vox, April 10, 2019, https://www.vox.com/2019/4/10 /18304415/new-zealand-gun-control-mosque-shootings-assault- weapons-ban.

Marcel McClinton Profile

1. Marcel McClinton, "Texas Teen Marcel McClinton Leads Students in Charge for Gun Reform," *Now This* video, 3:30, May 23, 2018, https:// nowthisnews.com/videos/politics/texas-teen-marcel-mcclinton -leads-students-in-charge-for-gun-reform.

2. McClinton, "Texas Teen Marcel McClinton Leads."

3. McClinton, "Texas Teen Marcel McClinton Leads."

4. McClinton, "Texas Teen Marcel McClinton Leads."

5. Jacob Carpenter, "Houston Teens Expecting Thousands for Student- Organized Gun Violence Protest," *Houston Chronicle*, March 17, 2018, https://www.chron.com/news/houston-texas/houston/article/Houston -teens-expecting-thousands-for-12759913.php.

6. Skyler Swisher, "Gun-Control Activists Hold Die-In Near Mar-A-Lago," *South Florida Sun Sentinel*, June 12, 2018, https://www.sun-sentinel.com /local/palm-beach/fl-reg-mar-a-lago-die-in-20180612-story.html.

7. Lucy Diavolo, "National Die-In Protester Marcel McClinton Shares How it Felt to Storm the U.S. Capitol," *Teen Vogue*, June 13, 2018, https://www .teenvogue.com/story/national-die-in-protester-marcel-mcclinton-storm -the-us-capitol-interview.

8. Orange Generation (@theorangegen), "This is the Orange Generation," Twitter, May 28, 2018, 1:01 p.m., https://twitter.com/theorangegen /status/1001191652118196225.

9. Marcel McClinton, "Texas Teen Marcel McClinton Leads."

10. Marcel McClinton (@MarcelMcClinton), "There's no excuse for you to not be involved. If you won't use your voice & if you won't vote you're part of the problem. Period," Twitter, July 22, 2018, 9:51 a.m., https://twitter .com/MarcelMcClinton/status/1021075299486904320.

Chapter 7

1. Jake Miller, "Firearm Injuries Drop During NRA Conventions, Research Shows," ScienceDaily, February 28, 2018, https://www.sciencedaily.com /releases/2018/02/180228174932.htm.

2. Ron Elving, "The NRA Wasn't Always Against Gun Restrictions," NPR, October 10, 2017, https://www.npr.org/2017/10/10/556578593/the-nra -wasnt-always-against-gun-restrictions.

3. Elving, "The NRA Wasn't Always Against Gun Restrictions."

4. Elving, "The NRA Wasn't Always Against Gun Restrictions."

5. Elving, "The NRA Wasn't Always Against Gun Restrictions."

6. Elving, "The NRA Wasn't Always Against Gun Restrictions."

7. Elving, "The NRA Wasn't Always Against Gun Restrictions."

8. "Membership," NRA, accessed August 15, 2018, https://membership.nra .org/FAQ.

9. Christopher Ingraham, "Nobody Knows How Many Members the NRA Has, But Its Tax Returns Offer Some Clues," *Washington Post*, February 26, 2018, https://www.washingtonpost.com/news/wonk/wp/2018/02/26 /nobody-knows-how-many-members-the-nra-has-but-its-tax-returns -offer-some-clues/?utm_term=.6745cd50b8ae.

10. "Who We Are," Everytown for Gun Safety, accessed August 20, 2018, https://everytown.org/who-we-are/.

11. Charlotte Hill, "The Real Reason the NRA's Money Matters in Elections," *Vox*, March 24, 2018, https://www.vox.com/the-big-idea /2018/2/27/17051560/money-nra-guns-contributions-donations -parkland-march.

12. Ben Popken, "America's Gun Business, by the Numbers," NBC News, December 3, 2015, https://www.nbcnews.com/storyline/san-bernardino -shooting/americas-gun-business-numbers-n437566.

13. Walt Hickey, "How the Gun Industry Funnels Tens of Millions of Dollars to the NRA," *Business Insider*, January 16, 2013, https://www .businessinsider.com/gun-industry-funds-nra-2013-1.

14. Hickey, "How the Gun Industry Funnels Tens of Millions."

15. Dominic Rushe, "Why Is the National Rifle Association So Powerful?" *The Guardian*, May 4, 2018, https://www.theguardian.com/us-news/2017/nov/17/nra-gun-lobby-gun-control-congress.

16. John Dunbar, "The 'Citizens United' Decision and Why It Matters," Center for Public Integrity, October 18, 2012, https://www.publicintegrity.org/2012/10/18/11527/citizens-united-decision-and-why-it-matters.

17. Gillian Walters, "How Much Did the NRA Donate to Trump? He's Been Loyal to the Organization Since His Candidacy," Romper, October 2, 2017, https://www.romper.com/p/how-much-did-the-nra-donate-to-trump-hes-been-loyal-to-the-organization-since-his-candidacy-2748576.

18. Rushe, "Why Is the National Rifle Association So Powerful?"

19. Robert Nott, "Committee Votes to Ban Guns From Joint Sessions at Capitol," *Santa Fe New Mexican*, January 11, 2019, http://www.santafenewmexican.com/news/legislature/committee-votes-to-ban-guns-from-joint-sessions-at-capitol/article_834c2719-95ca-50f0-bfd8-b204445ee56a.html.

20. Steve Terrell, "Senate Oks Ban on Openly Carrying Firearms in Capitol," *Santa Fe New Mexican*, March 4, 2017, http://www.santafenewmexican.com/news/legislature/senate-oks-ban-on-openly-carrying-firearms-in-capitol/article_b3dab795-025e-5c4e-9197-387866d95730.html.

21. Michele Richinick, "Legislators 'Hunted' with Threats from Pro-Gun Activists," MSNBC, September 13, 2013, http://www.msnbc.com/msnbc/legislators-hunted-threats-pro-gu.

22. Richinick, "Legislators 'Hunted.'"

23. Richinick, "Legislators 'Hunted.'"

24. Rushe, "Why Is the National Rifle Association So Powerful?"

25. Rushe, "Why Is the National Rifle Association So Powerful?"

Paul Kemp Profile

1. Paul Kemp, in-person interview with author, August 27, 2018.

2. Clackamas County Sheriff's Office, "Sheriff's Office Completes Investigation of Shootings of Forsyth, Yuille and Shevchenko," news release, May 1, 2013, https://www.clackamas.us/sheriff/pressreleases/2013-05-01-CCSOPR-CTCInvestigationSummary.html.

3. Clackamas County, "Sheriff's Office Completes Investigation."

4. "Safe Storage," Giffords Law Center to Prevent Gun Violence, accessed August 28, 2018, https://lawcenter.giffords.org/gun-laws/policy-areas/child-consumer-safety/safe-storage/

5. "Home," Gun Owners for Responsible Ownership, accessed August 27, 2018, https://www.responsibleownership.org

6. "Home," Gun Owners for Responsible Ownership.

Chapter 8

1. John Woolfolk, "Guns and Deaths in America: The Numbers," *Mercury News* (Bay Area, CA), February 28, 2018, https://www.mercurynews .com/2018/02/28/guns-and-deaths-in-america-the-numbers/.

2. Sarah Zhang, "Why Can't the U.S. Treat Gun Violence as a Public-Health Problem?" *The Atlantic*, February 15, 2018, https://www.theatlantic.com /health/archive/2018/02/gun-violence-public-health/553430/.

3. Christine Jamieson, "Gun Violence Research: History of the Federal Funding Freeze," American Psychological Association, February 2013, https://www.apa.org/science/about/psa/2013/02/gun-violence.aspx.

4. Zhang, "Why Can't the U.S. Treat Gun Violence as a Public-Health Problem?"

5. "Protection of Lawful Commerce in Arms Act (PLCAA)," Brady Campaign to Prevent Gun Violence, accessed September 1, 2018, http://www .bradycampaign.org the-protection-of-lawful-commerce-in-arms-act-plcaa.

6. Zara Whelan, "16 Things Banned in America That Aren't Guns," NorthWalesLive, February 15, 2018, https://www.dailypost.co.uk /whats-on/whats-on-news/weird-things-banned-america-us-14293789.

7. Matt Vasilogambros, "Since Sandy Hook, More NRA-Backed Gun Legislation Has Passed than Laws to Restrict Guns," *Huffington Post*, March 3, 2018, https://www.huffingtonpost.com/entry/hundreds-of-new-state -gun-laws-most-expand-access_us_5a995f07e4b06a04fecca7e6.

8. Vasilogambros, "Since Sandy Hood."

9. Vasilogambros, "Since Sandy Hood."

Jazmine Wildcat Profile

1. Jazmine Wildcat, phone interview with author, December 1, 2018.

2. Eliza Racine, "Native Americans Facing Highest Suicide Rates," Lakota People's Law Project, May 12, 2016, https://www.lakotalaw.org /news/2016-05-12/native-americans-facing-highest-suicide-rates.

3. "Domestic Violence Rampant Among Native Americans," Domesticshelters.org, March 13, 2017, https://www.domesticshelters.org /domestic-violence-articles-information/domestic-violence-rampant -among-native-americans.

4. Elise Hansen, "The Forgotten Minority in Police Shootings," CNN, November 13, 2017, https://www.cnn.com/2017/11/10/us/native-lives -matter/index.html.

5. "Annual Gun Law Scorecard: Wyoming," Giffords Law Center to Prevent Gun Violence, accessed December 10, 2018, https://lawcenter.giffords.org /scorecard/do/.

6. Alli Maloney, "Gun Violence Will Be Stopped by These 9 Young Activists," *Teen Vogue*, March 23, 2018, https://www.teenvogue.com /gallery/meet-gun-control-cover-stars.

Chapter 9

1. Bloomberg, "Most Gun Owners Support Stricter Laws—Even NRA Members," *Time*, March 13, 2018, http://time.com/5197807/stricter -gun-laws-nra/.

2. John Blake, "Four Reasons the NRA Should Fear the Parkland Student Survivors," CNN, February 22, 2018, https://www.cnn.com/2018/02/21 /us/parkland-shooting-youth-social-change/index.html.

3. Chelsea Parsons, Maggie Thompson, Eugenio Weigend Vargas, and Giovanni Rocco, "America's Youth Under Fire: The Devastating Impact of Gun Violence on Young People," Center for American Progress, May 4, 2018, https://www.americanprogress.org/issues/guns-crime/reports /2018/05/04/450343/americas-youth-fire/.

4. Elizabeth MacBride, "Gun Control Groups See Huge Surge as More than 500,000 Sign, Donate, Volunteer," *Forbes*, February 23, 2018, https:// www.forbes.com/sites/elizabethmacbride/2018/02/23/anti-gun-groups -see-huge-surge-as-more-than-500000-sign-donate-volunteer /#1ec571e639ff.

5. Giffords Courage to Fight Gun Violence, "National Law Enforcement Leaders Launch New 'Law Enforcement Coalition for Commonsense' to Urge Leaders to Opposed Federally Mandated Concealed Carry, Take Action to Prevent Gun Tragedies," press release, February 17, 2018, https:// giffords.org/2017/02/lawenforcement/.

6. Jessica Glenza and Lois Beckett, "Gun Control Still 'Not the Issue' for Law Enforcement Despite Police Attacks," *The Guardian*, July 19, 2016, https:// www.theguardian.com/us-news/2016/jul/19/gun-control-police-open -carry-law.

7. "Policy Agenda," National Law Enforcement Partnership to Prevent Gun Violence, accessed December 10, 2018, https://www.lepartnership.org /policy-agenda/.

8. Terry Gross, "A Trauma Surgeon Who Survived Gun Violence Is Taking on the NRA," NPR, November 28, 1028, https://www.npr.org/sections /health-shots/2018/11/28/671519701/this-trauma-surgeon-survived-gun -violence-now-hes-taking-on-the-nra.

9. Meagan Flynn, "Shot in the Neck at 17, This Is the Trauma Surgeon Now Leading Doctors Against Gun Violence and the NRA," *Washington Post*, November 14, 2018, https://www.washingtonpost.com/nation/2018 /11/14/shot-neck-this-is-trauma-surgeon-now-leading-doctors-against -gun-violence-nra/?utm_term=.e447421729a1.

10. Frances Stead Sellers, "'Being Silenced Is Not Acceptable': Doctors Express Outrage After NRA Tells Them 'To Stay in Their Lane,'" *Washington Post*, November 11, 2018, https://www.washingtonpost.com/national /being-silenced-is-not-acceptable-doctors-express-outrage-after-nra-tells -them-to-stay-in-their-lane/2018/11/11/5a8beca0-e5d5-11e8-b8dc -66cca409c180_story.html?utm_term=.22226da4d584.

11. Kate Smith, "'Stay in Your Lane': NRA Slams Doctors Over Guns, and Doctors Fire Back," CBS News, November 12, 2018, https://www.cbsnews.com/news/stay-in-your-lane-doctors-fire-back-at-the-nra-guns/.

12. Flynn, "Shot in the Neck at 17."

13. Sellers, "Being Silenced Is Not Acceptable."

14. Sellers, "Being Silenced Is Not Acceptable."

15. Sellers, "Being Silenced Is Not Acceptable."

16. Smith, "Stay in Your Lane."

17. Gross, "A Trauma Surgeon Who Survived Gun Violence."

18. Smith, "Stay in Your Lane."

19. Flynn, "Shot in the Neck at 17."

20. Sellers, "Being Silenced Is Not Acceptable."

Parkland Survivors Profile

1. Charlotte Alter, "The School Shooting Generation Has Had Enough," *Time*, March 22, 2018, http://time.com/longform/never-again-movement/.

2. Elaine Aradillas, "What to Know About Jaclyn Corin, Class President Who Became National Activist After School Shooting," *People*, March 1, 2018, https://people.com/crime/florida-school-shooting-survivor-activist-jaclyn-corin/.

3. Alter, "The School Shooting Generation Has Had Enough."

4. David Williams, "Parkland Shooting Survivor Emma Gonzalez Has More Twitter Followers than the NRA," CNN, February 27, 2018, https://www.cnn.com/2018/02/27/us/gonzalez-nra-twitter/index.html.

5. Virginia Heffernan, "The David Hogg 'Crisis Actor' Video Wasn't Bullying. It Was Propaganda," *LA Times*, February 22, 2018, http://www.latimes.com/opinion/op-ed/la-oe-heffernan-hogg-video-20180222-story.html.

6. Lisa Miller, "David Hogg, After Parkland," *New York Times Magazine*, August 19, 2018, http://nymag.com/intelligencer/2018/08/david-hogg-is-taking-his-gap-year-at-the-barricades.html?gtm=bottom&gtm=bottom.

7. Dana Liebelson and Nick Wing, "Behind Millions of Dollars Raised by Parkland Students, An Adult Board of Directors," *Huffington Post*, March 19, 2018, https://www.huffingtonpost.com/entry/march-for-our-lives-action-fund_us_5ab02dbbe4b0697dfe19a488.

8. Alter, "The School Shooting Generation Has Had Enough."

9. Miller, "David Hogg, After Parkland."

10. Miller, "David Hogg, After Parkland."

11. Alter, "The School Shooting Generation Has Had Enough."

12. Alter, "The School Shooting Generation Has Had Enough."

13. Alter, "The School Shooting Generation Has Had Enough."

14. Alter, "The School Shooting Generation Has Had Enough."

15. David Hogg, "David and Lauren Hogg Turned Their Pain into Progress," interview by Adrienne Westenfeld, *Esquire*, June 21, 2018, https://www .esquire.com/entertainment/books/a21750616/david-hogg-lauren-hogg -interview-never-again-book/.

16. Kara Voght, "The Troubling Connection Between Mass Shootings and Suicide," *Mother Jones*, March 26, 2019, https://www.motherjones.com /politics/2019/03/the-troubling-connection-between-mass-shooting -and-suicide/.

Chapter 10

1. Carina Storrs, "Connecticut's Strict Gun Law Linked to Large Homicide Drop," CNN, June 13, 2015, https://www.cnn.com/2015/06/12/us/gun -law-homicide-drop/index.html.

2. Quinnipiac University, "Quinnipiac University Poll," press release, February 20, 2018, https://poll.qu.edu/national /release-detail?ReleaseID=2521.

3. "Talking to Family & Friends About Gun Violence Prevention," Brady Campaign to Prevent Gun Violence, accessed February 10, 2019, http:// www.bradycampaign.org/talking-to-family-friends-about-gun -violence-prevention.

4. "Background Checks on All Gun Sales," Everytown for Gun Safety, accessed September 10, 2018, https://everytown.org/issue/background -checks/.

5. David Johnson, "Charleston Loophole Put 2,892 Guns in the Wrong Hands in 2015," *Time*, October 4, 2016, http://time.com/4512255 /charleston-loophole/.

6. Pamela Brown, Evan Perez, and Don Lemon, "FBI Says Dylann Roof Should Not Have Been Cleared to Purchase a Weapon," CNN, July 10, 2015, https://www.cnn.com/2015/07/10/politics/dylann-roof-fbi-gun -south-carolina/index.html.

7. "Close the Boyfriend Loophole," Everytown for Gun Safety, accessed September 10, 2018, https://everytownresearch.org/wp-content /uploads/2017/11/Boyfriend-Loophole-11.7.17.pdf.

8. "Brady Campaign Reports 3 Million Gun Sales Blocked by Background Checks on 23rd Anniversary of Brady Bill Signing," Brady Campaign to Prevent Gun Violence, accessed September 10, 2018, http://www .bradycampaign.org/press-room/brady-campaign-reports-3-million-gun -sales-blocked-by-background-checks-on-23rd.

9. "Safe Storage," Giffords Law Center to Prevent Gun Violence, accessed September 10, 2018, https://lawcenter.giffords.org/gun-laws/policy-areas /child-consumer-safety/safe-storage/.

10. "The Final Report and Finding of the Safe School Initiative," US Secret Service and US Department of Education, accessed September 10, 2018,

https://www2.ed.gov/admins/lead/safety/preventingattacksreport.pdf.

11. "Safe Storage," Giffords Law Center to Prevent Gun Violence.

12. "Safe Storage," Giffords Law Center to Prevent Gun Violence.

13. "Home," Gun Owners for Responsible Ownership, accessed September 12, 2018, https://www.responsibleownership.org.

14. Alex Yablon, "New Smart-Gun Company Says It's Making a Pistol Gun Owners Might Actually Want," *The Trace*, January 17, 2018, https://www.thetrace.org/rounds/smart-guns-lodestar-firearms-gareth-glaser/.

15. Robert Gebelhoff, "This Is How We Save Lives from Gun Violence," *Washington Post*, March 23, 2018, https://www.washingtonpost.com/graphics/2018/opinions/gun-control-that-works/?utm_term=.b12904344d5d.

16. "Extreme Risk Protection Orders," Giffords Law Center to Prevent Gun Violence, accessed September 12, 2018, https://lawcenter.giffords.org/gun-laws/policy-areas/who-can-have-a-gun/extreme-risk-protection-orders/.

17. Inside Edition Staff, "Nikolas Cruz's Caretaker Claims She Warned Authorities That Parkland Suspect Was 'Ticking Time Bomb,'" *Inside Edition*, March 20, 2018, https://www.yahoo.com/news/nikolas-cruz-apos-caretaker-claims-203433063.html.

18. "Extreme Risk Protection Orders," Giffords Law Center to Prevent Gun Violence.

19. "Extreme Risk Protection Orders," Giffords Law Center to Prevent Gun Violence.

20. "Extreme Risk Protection Orders," Giffords Law Center to Prevent Gun Violence.

21. "Extreme Risk Protection Orders," Giffords Law Center to Prevent Gun Violence.

22. "Extreme Risk Protection Orders," Giffords Law Center to Prevent Gun Violence.

23. Gebelhoff, "This is How We Save Lives from Gun Violence."

24. Maron, "Data Confirm Semiautomatic Rifles Linked to More Deaths, Injuries."

25. "Criminal Use of Assault Weapons and High-Capacity Semiautomatic Firearms," Center for Evidence-Based Crime Policy at George Mason University, June 2018, https://www.ncbi.nlm.nih.gov/pubmed/28971349.

26. Page Pate, "Banning Assault Rifles Would Be Constitutional," CNN, March 2, 2018, https://www.cnn.com/2018/03/02/opinions/banning-assault-rifles-would-be-constitutional-pate/index.html.

27. Pate, "Banning Assault Rifles Would Be Constitutional."

28. Dennis Silverman, "States That Ban Assault Weapons," UC Irvine *Energy Blog*, February 19, 2018, http://sites.uci.edu/energyobserver/2018/02/19/states-that-ban-assault-weapons/.

29. Brad Plumer, "Everything You Need to Know About the Assault Weapons Ban, in One Post," *Washington Post*, December 17, 2012, https://www .washingtonpost.com/news/wonk/wp/2012/12/17/everything-you-need -to-know-about-banning-assault-weapons-in-one-post/?utm_term=. 577a62c552ab.

30. "Key Federal Acts Regulating Firearms," Giffords Law Center to Prevent Gun Violence, accessed February 10, 2019, https://lawcenter.giffords.org /gun-laws/federal-law/other-laws/key-federal-acts-regulating-firearms/

31. Sarah Kliff, "Connecticut Made it Harder to Get Guns—and Suicides Fell Significantly," *Vox*, September 2, 2015, https://www.vox.com/2015/9/2 /9242147/gun-control-connecticut-suicides.

32. Daniel Webster, Cassandra Crifasi, and Jon Vernick, "Effects of Missouri's Repeal of Its Handgun Purchaser Licensing Law on Homicides," Johns Hopkins Bloomberg School of Public Health, December 17, 2013, https:// www.jhsph.edu/research/centers-and-institutes/johns-hopkins-center-for -gun-policy-and-research/_pdfs/effects-of-missouris-repeal-of-its -handgun-purchaser-licensing-law-on-homicides.pdf.

33. Jennifer Williamson, in-person interview with author, September 25, 2018.

34. "Large Capacity Magazines," Giffords Law Center to Prevent Gun Violence, accessed September 12, 2018, https://lawcenter.giffords.org /gun-laws/policy-areas/hardware-ammunition/large-capacity-magazines/.

35. CNN Library, "Zika Virus Infection Fast Facts," CNN, May 31, 2018, https://www.cnn.com/2016/07/18/health/zika-virus-infection-fast-facts /index.html.

36. "Past Summary Ledgers, 2016," Gun Violence Archive, accessed September 26, 2018, https://www.gunviolencearchive.org/past-tolls.

37. Sarah Zhang, "Why Can't the U.S. Treat Gun Violence as a Public-Health Problem?" *The Atlantic*, February 15, 2018, https://www.theatlantic.com /health/archive/2018/02/gun-violence-public-health/553430/.

38. "Gun Laws: Policy Areas," Giffords Law Center to Prevent Gun Violence, accessed September 26, 2018, www.lawcenter.giffords.org.

Colin Goddard Profile

1. KC Baker, "A Virginia Tech Shooting Survivor Remembers the College Massacre 10 Years Later," *People*, April 16, 2017, https://people.com/crime /virginia-tech-shooting-10-years-later/.

2. Colin Goddard, "Colin Goddard—End Gun Violence." Everytown for Gun Safety video, 1:58, December 25, 2015, https://www.youtube.com /watch?v=oW29QnGrUmc.

3. Baker, "A Virginia Tech Shooting Survivor Remembers the College Massacre."

4. Alexandra Wilson, "Virginia Tech Survivor Colin Goddard on the Future of the Gun Control Movement," *Forbes*, October 18, 2016, https://www .forbes.com/sites/alexandrawilson1/2016/10/18/virginia-tech-survivor

-colin-goddard-on-the-future-of-the-gun-control-movement
/#1c83a9cd6766.

Chapter 11

1. Luke Darby, "Connecticut Shows a Path Forward for Better Gun Laws," *GQ*, February 18, 2018, https://www.gq.com/story/connecticut-forward-gun-laws.

2. "Annual Gun Law Scorecard," Giffords Law Center to Prevent Gun Violence, accessed October 1, 2018, https://lawcenter.giffords.org/scorecard/.

3. "Firearm Mortality by State 2016," Centers for Disease Control, accessed October 1, 2018, https://www.cdc.gov/nchs/pressroom/sosmap/firearm_mortality/firearm.htm.

4. Natalie Delgadillo, "Are Massachusetts Gun Laws a Model for the Country?" *Governing*, March 27, 2018, http://www.governing.com/topics/public-justice-safety/gov-massachusetts-gun-laws.html.

5. Delgadillo, "Are Massachusetts Gun Laws a Model for the Country?"

6. Delgadillo, "Are Massachusetts Gun Laws a Model for the Country?"

Eli Counce and Penelope Spurr Profile

1. Eli Counce and Penelope Spurr, in-person interview with author, May 25, 2018.

2. "SB 501 The Students' Bill," Ceasefire Oregon, January 22, 2019, https://www.ceasefireoregon.org/bills/the-students-bill/.

3. "SB 501 The Students' Bill," Ceasefire Oregon.

Chapter 12

1. Will Oremus, "In 1996, Australia Enacted Strict Gun Laws. It Hasn't Had a Mass Shooting Since," *Slate*, October 2, 2017, http://www.slate.com/blogs/crime/2012/12/16/gun_control_after_connecticut_shooting_could_australia_s_laws_provide_a.html.

2. Oremus, "In 1996, Australia Enacted Strict Gun Laws."

3. Oremus, "In 1996, Australia Enacted Strict Gun Laws."

4. German Lopez, "Australia Is Often Held as a Model for Gun Control. That Doesn't Make It Immune to Mass Shootings," *Vox*, May 11, 2018, https://www.vox.com/policy-and-politics/2018/5/11/17345214/australia-mass-shooting-margaret-river-osmington.

5. Lopez, "Australia Is Often Held as a Model for Gun Control."

6. Lopez, "Australia Is Often Held as a Model for Gun Control."

7. "Fact Check: Australian Gun Stats," Snopes, accessed October 10, 2018, https://www.snopes.com/fact-check/australian-guns/.

8. Eugene Kiely, "Gun Control in Australia, Updated," Factcheck.org, accessed October 10, 2018, https://www.factcheck.org/2017/10/gun-control-australia-updated/.

9. Michael McGowan, "Margaret River Mass Shooting: Three Guns at Scene Belonged to Children's Grandfather," *The Guardian*, May 12, 2018, https://www.theguardian.com/australia-news/2018/may/12/margaret-river-deaths-three-guns-at-scene-belonged-to-childrens-grandfather.

10. Lopez, "Australia Is Often Held as a Model for Gun Control."

11. Tara Francis Chan, "Australia, Israel, Japan, and South Korea Rarely Have Mass Shootings—and the Reasons Are Clear," *Business Insider*, February 22, 2018, https://www.businessinsider.com/how-other-countries-avoid-mass-shootings-2018-2.

12. Chan, "Australia, Israel, Japan, and South Korea Rarely Have Mass Shootings."

13. Daniel Ofman, "What Can the US Learn from Norway's Gun Laws?" Public Radio International, June 16, 2016, https://www.pri.org/stories/2016-06-16/what-can-us-learn-norways-gun-laws.

14. Ofman, "What Can the US Learn from Norway's Gun Laws?"

15. Chris Weller, "American Police Kill More People in One Day than Norway Cops Have in 9 Years," *Business Insider*, July 30, 2015, https://www.businessinsider.com/american-police-kill-more-people-in-one-day-than-norway-cops-have-in-10-years-2015-7.

16. "Norway Population," Worldometers, accessed November 1, 2018, http://www.worldometers.info/world-population/norway-population/.

17. Wikipedia, s.v. "Chicago," last modified February 22, 2019, accessed November 1, 2018, https://en.wikipedia.org/wiki/Chicago.

18. Jennifer Richards, Angela Caputo, Todd Lighty, and Jason Meisner, "92 Deaths, 2,623 Bullets: Tracking Every Chicago Police Shooting Over 6 Years," *Chicago Tribune*, August 26, 2016, http://www.chicagotribune.com/news/watchdog/ct-chicago-police-shooting-database-met-20160826-story.html.

19. Chris Weller, "American Police Kill More People in One Day than Norway Cops Have in 9 Years," *Business Insider*, July 30, 2015, https://www.businessinsider.com/american-police-kill-more-people-in-one-day-than-norway-cops-have-in-10-years-2015-7.

20. Ofman, "What Can the US Learn from Norway's Gun Laws?"

21. Jim Michaels and Aamer Madhani, "Keeping Olympics Safe: South Korea Gun Laws Make a Mass Shooting Nearly Unfathomable," *USA Today*, February 18, 2018, https://www.usatoday.com/story/sports/winter-olympics-2018/2018/02/18/winter-olympics-south-korea-tough-gun-laws-mass-shooting/349138002/.

22. Michaels, "Keeping Olympics Safe."

23. Chan, "Australia, Israel, Japan, and South Korea Rarely Have Mass Shootings."

24. Chan, "Australia, Israel, Japan, and South Korea Rarely Have Mass Shootings."

Sandy Hook Survivors Profile

1. Natalie Barden, "Natalie Barden Reflects on the Sandy Hook Shooting, the March for Our Lives, and Why She Still Fights for Gun-Violence Prevention," *Teen Vogue*, August 15, 2018, https://www.teenvogue.com/story/natalie-barden-sandy-hook-march-for-our-lives-gun-violence-op-ed.

2. Barden, "Natalie Barden Reflects on the Sandy Hook Shooting."

3. Kristin Hussey, "Emboldened by Parkland, Newtown Students Find Their Voice," *New York Times*, August 26, 2018, https://www.nytimes.com/2018/08/26/nyregion/newtown-students-activism-parkland.html.

4. Barden, "Natalie Barden Reflects on the Sandy Hook Shooting."

5. Hussey, "Emboldened by Parkland, Newtown Students Find Their Voice."

6. Barden, "Natalie Barden Reflects on the Sandy Hook Shooting."

7. Hussey, "Emboldened by Parkland, Newtown Students Find Their Voice."

8. Hussey, "Emboldened by Parkland, Newtown Students Find Their Voice."

9. Barden, "Natalie Barden Reflects on the Sandy Hook Shooting."

Chapter 13

1. Richard Fry, "Millennials and Gen Xers Outvoted Boomers and Older Generations in 2016 Election," Pew Research Center, July 31, 2017, http://www.pewresearch.org/fact-tank/2017/07/31/millennials-and-gen-xers-outvoted-boomers-and-older-generations-in-2016-election/.

2. "Students Demand Action," Everytown for Gun Safety, accessed October 5, 2018, www.everytown.org/studentsdemand.

3. "Who We Are," Everytown for Gun Safety, accessed October 5, 2018, www.everytown.org.

4. "About Us," Moms Demand Action, accessed October 5, 2018, www.momsdemandaction.org.

5. "Who We Are," Brady Campaign to Prevent Gun Violence, accessed October 5, 2018, www.bradycampaign.org.

6. "Mission," Giffords Courage to Fight Gun Violence, accessed October 5, 2018, www.giffords.org.

7. "Our Mission," Coalition to Stop Gun Violence, accessed October 5, 2018, www.csgv.or.

8. "About Us," Sandy Hook Promise, accessed October 5, 2018, www .sandyhookpromise.org.

9. "Home," Gun Owners for Responsible Ownership, accessed October 5, 2018, www.responsibleownership.org.

10. "Start a Group," Students Demand Action, accessed October 5, 2018, www.everytown.org/start-sda-group/.

Lane Murdock Profile

1. Ray Sanchez, "This Is the 16-Year-Old Behind the National School Walkout," CNN, April 21, 2018, https://www.cnn.com/2018/04/19/us /national-school-walkout-organizer-lane-murdock/index.html.

2. Sanchez, "This Is the 16-Year-Old Behind the National School Walkout."

3. Sanchez, "This Is the 16-Year-Old Behind the National School Walkout."

4. Linley Sanders, "Meet Lane Murdock, the 16-Year-Old Organizer of the National School Walkout," *Teen Vogue*, April 20, 2018, https://www .teenvogue.com/story/meet-lane-murdock-16-year-old-organizer -national-school-walkout.

5. "Petition: National High School Walk-Out for Anti Gun Violence," Change.org, accessed October 15, 2018, https://www.change. org/p/u-s-senate-national-high-school-walk-out-for-anti-gun-violence.

6. Sanchez, "This Is the 16-Year-Old Behind the National School Walkout."

7. Sanchez, "This Is the 16-Year-Old Behind the National School Walkout."

8. Sanchez, "This Is the 16-Year-Old Behind the National School Walkout."

9. Lane Murdock (@lanemurdock2002) "Our generation has made change. And we aren't stopping," Twitter . May 19, 2018, 7:29 p.m., https://twitter. com/lanemurdock2002/status/998027844822425600.

Chapter 14

1. Manu Raju, "Heitkamp Defends Gun Vote," *Politico*, April 24, 2013, https://www.politico.com/story/2013/04/heidi-heitkamp-defends -gun-vote-090600.

2. Jeff Truesdell, "I Lost 33 Friends to Gun Violence," *People*, December 10, 2018, 69.

3. Standardhotels.com, "The Standard Telephone Co. Wants You to Ring Your Rep," press release, April 20, 2018, https://www.standardhotels.com /culture/Ring-Your-Rep-High-Line-Phone-Booth.

4. Amy Moreland, "How to Prepare for a Town Hall Meeting," *ThoughtCo*, August 14, 2017, https://www.thoughtco.com/how-to-prepare-for-a-town -hall-meeting-4147856.

5. *Oxford Dictionaries*, s.v. "walkout," accessed October 19, 2018, https://en.oxforddictionaries.com/definition/walkout.

6. Lucy Diavolo, "National Die-In Protester Marcel McClinton Shares How it Felt to Storm the U.S. Capitol," *Teen Vogue*, June 13, 2018, https://www.teenvogue.com/story/national-die-in-protester-marcel-mcclinton-storm-the-us-capitol-interview.

7. Skyler Swisher, "Gun-Control Activists Hold Die-In Near Mar-A-Lago," *South Florida Sun Sentinel*, June 12, 2018, https://www.sun-sentinel.com/local/palm-beach/fl-reg-mar-a-lago-die-in-20180612-story.html.

8. Chavie Lieber, Supporting Gun Control Is Great for Business, Racked, February 28, 2018, https://www.racked.com/2018/2/28/17062018/dicks-sporting-goods-gun-control.

9. Jack Moore, "These Are the Companies Ending Gun Sales to Buyers Under the Age of 21," *Newsweek*, March 2, 2018, https://www.newsweek.com/these-are-companies-ending-gun-sales-buyers-under-21-827475.

10. REI Co-Op, "REI Statement on Relationship with Vista Outdoor," press release, March 1, 2018, https://newsroom.rei.com/company-information/statements/rei-statement-on-relationship-with-vista-outdoor.htm.

11. Tess Cagle, "Every Company Cutting Ties with the NRA," Daily Dot, March 2, 2018, https://www.dailydot.com/irl/nra-boycotts-protests-list/.

12. Robert Longley, "The End of South African Apartheid," *ThoughtCo*, May 3, 2018, https://www.thoughtco.com/when-did-apartheid-end-43456.

Jennifer Williamson Profile

1. Jennifer Williamson, in-person interview with author, September 25, 2018.

2. Oregon House Democrats, "Oregon House Democrats Legislative Successes: Gun Violence Prevention," August 2018.

3. "House Committee on Appropriations," GovTrack, accessed September 27, 2018, https://www.govtrack.us/congress/committees/HSAP.

4. Wikipedia, s.v. "bill (law)," last modified February 4, 2019, accessed September 27, 2018, https://en.wikipedia.org/wiki/Bill_(law).

5. "Constituent," *Dictionary.com*, accessed September 27, 2018, https://www.dictionary.com/browse/constituent?s=t.

6. Wikipedia, s.v., "floor (legislative)," last modified May 24, 2018, accessed September 27, 2018, https://en.wikipedia.org/wiki/Floor_(legislative).

7. "House Majority Leader Law and Legal Definition," *US Legal*, https://definitions.uslegal.com/h/house-majority-leader/. https://definitions.uslegal.com/h/house-majority-leader/.

8. Wikipedia, s.v. "legislator," last modified September 21, 2018, accessed September 27, 2018, https://en.wikipedia.org/wiki/Legislator.

9. "Learn About the Senate," US Senate, accessed September 27, 2018, https://www.senate.gov/reference/Index/Learning_About_Senate.htm.

Chapter 15

1. "Talking to Family & Friends About Gun Violence Prevention," Brady Campaign to Prevent Gun Violence, accessed December 4, 2018, http://www.bradycampaign.org/talking-to-family-friends-about-gun-violence-prevention.

Governor Kate Brown Profile

1. Kate Brown, email interview with author, October 16, 2018.
2. Gordon Friedman, "Gov. Brown Recalls Anguish of Formerly Closeted Life," *Statesman Journal*, May 19, 2016, https://www.statesmanjournal.com/story/news/politics/2016/05/19/gov-brown-recalls-anguish-formerly-closeted-life/84599190/.
3. "Gov. Kate Brown Shares Domestic Abuse Experience on 'Straight Talk,'" KGW8, October 10, 2016, https://www.kgw.com/article/entertainment/television/programs/straight-talk/gov-kate-brown-shares-domestic-abuse-experience-on-straight-talk/283-333377192.

A Final Note

1. Nza-Ari Khepra, phone interview with author, October 12, 2018.

Resources

1. "13 Books for Teens That Address Gun Violence," Saint Louis Public Library, accessed October 15, 2018, www.slpl.bibliocommons.com/list/share/710025318/1146218277.